THE GLOBAL MANAGEMENT SERIES

Fundamentals of Marketing

Geraldine McKay, Paul Hopkinson and Lai Hong Ng

(G) Goodfellow Publishers Ltd

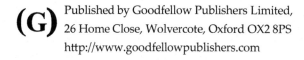 Published by Goodfellow Publishers Limited,
26 Home Close, Wolvercote, Oxford OX2 8PS
http://www.goodfellowpublishers.com

Published 2018
British Library Cataloguing in Publication Data: a catalogue record for this
title is available from the British Library.
Library of Congress Catalog Card Number: on file.

ISBN: 978-1-910158-97-5

This book is part of the Global Management series

ISSN: 2514-7862

 Design and typesetting by P.K. McBride, www.macbride.org.uk

Cover design by Cylinder

Printed by Baker & Taylor, www.baker-taylor.com

Contents

Dedications

To my wonderful husband, Kevin and my sons Joe and Jack,
with all my love
GM

Many thanks to my family members, colleagues and friends
for their support and guidance.
LH

For Nuong, John and Evie.
PH

List of contributors

Carrie Amani Annabi is an Assistant Professor in the School of Social Sciences, Heriot-Watt University, Dubai, United Arab Emirates. She has co-authored a number of refereed papers and book chapters on a range of topics, some of which focus on logistics and supply chain as well as teaching and management within International Branch Campuses. Prior to becoming an academic in Dubai, she had extensive industry experience working in a range of international roles in countries such as Cyprus, Finland, Singapore, Qatar and the United Kingdom.

Elaine Collinson is an Associate Professor in the Department of Management in the School of Management and Languages at Heriot-Watt University. She is Director of Postgraduate Studies within the school, Deputy Director of the Corporate Executive Development unit and George Davies Fellow. With over 25 years' experience in the Higher Education sector, she has held a series of roles, primarily in an academic and research capacity but also in developing transnational education and industry links across the globe. Elaine has had extensive experience in enhancing the student experience throughout her career. She has had a strong focus on inter-cultural learning and internationalisation within the classroom enabling students to assess their levels of international awareness and understanding. Working with international teams of academic colleagues across the globe to design and deliver a global experience for students is also great fun!

Gordon Jack is a Ph.D. student in the department of Business and Management at Heriot-Watt University, with his current research interests focussing on management in highly autonomous environments. His work analyses whether or not people can in fact be managed in a setting of quasi low-authority, including the judicial, medical and academic systems. Gordon received an MSc in Strategic Project Management from Heriot-Watt University in 2013 having gained a BSc (Hons) in Building Surveying from the same institution. His teaching commitments have included managing 1st year undergraduate Business Management and tutoring Business Entrepreneurship at 3rd year level, with publications including *Who'd Be a Dean* from the Association of Business Schools.

Geraldine McKay is an Associate Professor in Marketing and chartered marketer with a special interest in the impact of branding across stakeholder groups. Following a career in marketing, she became a university lecturer, developing and leading a number of postgraduate, undergraduate and professional programmes. She moved to New Zealand to manage an international education project and on returning to the UK she became the academic head for the globally delivered Heriot-Watt management programmes. She has previously contributed to the global management series and is currently registered for a PhD investigating transnational education and the teacher/student experience

Jack McKay After gaining a degree in Architectural Engineering at Cardiff University, Jack McKay went on to study a Masters in Design and Digital Media at the University of Edinburgh. He has since gone on to work as a front-end web developer for a digital marketing company, where he has worked across various projects. Jack's interests span a variety of different areas, including drawing and illustration, digital design, 3-D animation, graphic design and web design, as well as writing and performing comedy.

Paul J. Hopkinson is Associate Head of the School of Social Sciences and Assistant Professor of Marketing at Heriot Watt University Dubai. Paul has 19 year's work experience in Higher Education sector working for institutions in both the UK and Dubai specialising in teaching B2B marketing, CRM, Strategic and Digital Marketing. His research interests lie in the areas of relationship quality, commitment and trust in the context of channel member interactions (particularly in Financial Services) and the use of social media to facilitate and manage customer relationships. Prior to embarking on his academic career, Paul held marketing and commercial roles (Marketing Research, Product Management and Procurement) in the Aerospace and Telecommunications industries.

Lai Hong Ng is an Associate Professor in Marketing in the School of Management and Languages at Heriot-Watt University Malaysia. She has extensive experience in administration and teaching with a career that spans over 17 years across higher education institutions in Malaysia and UK. She teaches marketing and management courses to both undergraduate and post-graduate students. Her past research efforts have focused on services marketing, teaching and learning and student experience. Currently researching on developing learning spaces for educating Gen-Z in HEIs and the behaviour of interacting parties in service encounters – an interdisciplinary research borrowing literatures from social psychology.

Rodrigo Perez Vega is an Assistant Professor in the School of Marketing and Reputation at Henley Business School, University of Reading. His research interests are in digital marketing, social media, and consumer behaviour in online contexts. Rodrigo has published research in marketing and services journals such as *The Marketing Review* and *The Service Industries Journal*. He is also the social media editor at *The Service Industries Journal* and contributes periodically to practitioners' conferences and magazines on topics related to technology and marketing.

Graham Pogson has been a lecturer for twenty-five years, first in the field of Textile Technology with the Scottish College of Textiles and for the last fifteen years in Business Management subjects with the School of Social Sciences of Heriot-Watt University. He is a generalist having taught subjects from introductory economics and finance to strategic management, with marketing and organisational behaviour in between. Recent areas of interest have been in the field of employment relations within human resource management.

Kitty Shaw is an experienced marketing practitioner with 22 year's experience in the financial services sector, working in a variety of research, communications and planning roles, most recently in a senior role responsible for strategic marketing planning in a FTSE 100 company. Having originally completed an undergraduate degree in Politics at the University of Edinburgh, she took an MSc in Marketing Management from the University of Glamorgan and also holds post-graduate Diplomas from both the Market Research Society and Chartered Institute of Marketing. Her current research interest include the workplace marketing of pensions in the UK.

Kathryn Waite is an Assistant Professor in the School of Management and Languages at Heriot-Watt University. Her research interests relate to information provision and use within the online environment. She is interested in issues related to trust, engagement and empowerment. She is a member of the editorial advisory boards of the *Journal of Financial Services Marketing, Journal of Research in Interactive Marketing* and the *International Journal of Bank Marketing.* She teaches undergraduate and postgraduate courses in digital marketing.

Alastair Watson is Assistant Professor in Business Management at the University of Wollongong in Dubai (UOWD) and currently teaches Business Communications, Introduction to Management and Strategic Management on undergraduate and postgraduate level. Prior to joining UOWD he was Assistant Professor in Management and Teaching Assistant at Heriot-Watt University in both the Edinburgh and Dubai Campuses. He also spent a number of years as an active operating manager within branded restaurants and as well as hotels in the UK. Whilst completing his doctorate, he moved into training, quality and regional recruitment with a large branded restaurant operator in the UK.

Acknowledgments

This book was written for undergraduates requiring an accessible text that initiates and encourages interest in marketing as a concept, an integrated practice and as a possible career. Those involved in the writing of this text have a wealth of global experience in teaching, research and marketing practice and we sincerely thank them for contributing so generously. We are extremely grateful for the support and patience of colleagues at Goodfellow Publishers and the encouragement given by the series editors.

1 Marketing: Evolution, Idea and Action

Geraldine McKay and Lai Hong Ng

Marketing plays a significant role in creating successful organisations but its position within business and society, the methods it uses and its reputation continues to evolve. Fundamental to our understanding is the idea that marketing is both a way of thinking and a set of activities or functions. By taking a customer-centric view, needs are better understood and companies can actively use their available resources to continuously provide the best value goods and services for current and potential customers. The marketing concept proposes that long-term value for organisations will be achieved when customer and other stakeholder needs are satisfied. These needs will be satisfied as marketers engage a range of activities that constitute the marketing function.

This chapter introduces the fundamental concepts and functions of marketing. It discusses how the marketing exchange has evolved to meet the dynamic needs of customers and society. The emphasis of marketing has shifted from stimulating transactions towards developing relationships, with an understanding that the customer is essentially engaged in co-creating this joint venture. Marketing creates value through a coordinated and extended marketing mix that concentrates on service provision, no matter what the organisational context. The chapter concludes with an overview of the coverage in subsequent chapters.

Approaches to marketing

■ Marketing as exchange

The idea of marketing as exchange is well established. At the simplest level, customers exchange money for products or services and the business profits from this transaction. However all types of bodies and organisations use marketing, not just those who provide goods and services to customers in exchange for money. Public hospitals, for example provide healthcare for citizens in exchange for taxes, with an overall goal of improved individual and community health. Hair salons provide professional services in exchange for money. The salon's objective is profit but the customer's objective might be to feel more confident, look good or fit in with people that they associate with. The nature of the exchange can be quite complex. A charity, for example, provides support services for those in need but is funded through donations provided by those who will never use the services they offer. Those donors give money in exchange for a number of reasons – perhaps some just like the intrinsic 'warm glow' feeling (Andreoni, 1990) they achieve by 'doing good', whereas others may be motivated by the admiration gained from others.

■ Marketing as orientation

Organisational goals suggest the approach that needs to be taken and the focus or orientation of the business. Production, product and sales orientations were the main focus of business and dictated where effort should be made to realise objectives. Today, organisations understand the importance of customer-centric view (marketing orientation) and are gradually moving towards including the wellbeing of the society (societal marketing orientation). Figure 1.1 delineates the production, product, sales, marketing and societal marketing orientations which influence marketing in an organisation.

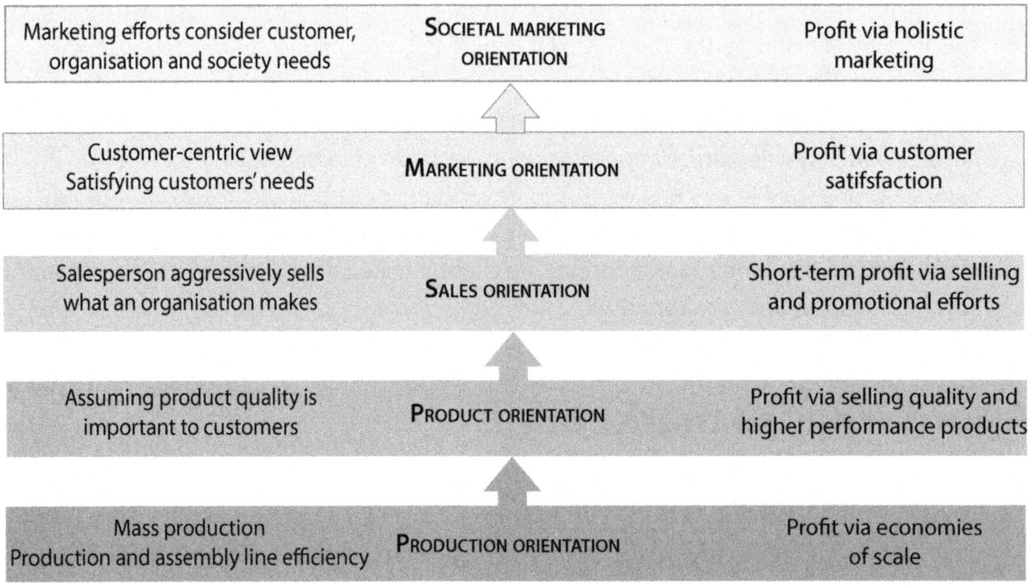

Marketing efforts consider customer, organisation and society needs	SOCIETAL MARKETING ORIENTATION	Profit via holistic marketing
Customer-centric view Satisfying customers' needs	MARKETING ORIENTATION	Profit via customer satifsaction
Salesperson aggressively sells what an organisation makes	SALES ORIENTATION	Short-term profit via sellling and promotional efforts
Assuming product quality is important to customers	PRODUCT ORIENTATION	Profit via selling quality and higher performance products
Mass production Production and assembly line efficiency	PRODUCTION ORIENTATION	Profit via economies of scale

Figure 1.1: Organisational orientation

The shift from a production to marketing and onto a societal marketing orientation is construed as a temporal change, linked to the economic and technological environment of a specific time. For example, production orientation was a reasonable approach when mass production became possible due to technological advances in automation. As products became more affordable, companies concentrated on producing efficiently and this is enough to ensure profitability. Once efficiency is achieved, the emphasis shifts to product quality, with an assumption that all customers desire and will seek out the 'better mousetrap'. Both production and product orientation require customers to have the same needs fulfilled with homogenous products, with very little market fragmentation.

The sales orientation, which was at its height post World WarTwo accepts that having a fantastic product is not enough and that customers need to be made aware of the product, its features and benefits, and that this requires aggressive advertising and sales practices to convince the customer they need the product.

Companies who adopt the marketing concept are deemed to be marketing oriented. This means that they:

- Place the customer at the centre of everything they do and know that satisfying customer needs is the key to success.
- Understand the competitive landscape and how their organisation fits in terms of capability vis a vis their competitors.
- Integrate all functions within the business to work together to achieve the goals of the organisation.

None of the above suggests that there is a marketing department or function, but rather puts customer needs first and recognises that long-term profitability can only be achieved by delivering customer satisfaction. As a marketing orientation is adopted, power and focus has moved from technical company excellence to individual consumer needs and more recently to society. This shift is recognised in the most recent American Marketing Association definition of marketing:

> *Marketing is the activity, set of institutions, and processes for creating, communicating, delivering, and exchanging offerings that have value for customers, clients, partners, and society at large.* (AMA, 2013)

It is useful to note the inclusion of other stakeholders in this definition. Although it seems that a marketing orientation is an inevitable evolution from the sales era, not all companies have fully embraced the marketing philosophy and very few place societal goals at their core. Nevertheless, many organisations do adopt many of the activities of marketing in order to achieve their goals, even those organisations whose primary purpose is not to make a profit.

■ Marketing as activity

Marketing theorists started to formally identify the essential activities of marketing in the last century. Borden (1964:7) suggested that marketers were 'mixers of ingredients' which could be mixed in different ways to create 'a profitable enterprise'. This list of twelve marketing activities became known as the marketing mix and was later distilled into four elements – product, pricing, promotion and place (McCarthy, 1960). Although an oversimplification of the actions and functions of a marketing department, the four Ps of the marketing mix are still used to encompass the fundamental activities of marketing.

Table 1.1: Borden's marketing mix policies

Product planning	Pricing	Branding	Channels of distribution
Personal selling	Advertising	Promotions	Packaging
Display	Servicing	Physical handling	Fact finding and analysis

The marketing mix facilitated the exchange between the organisation and its customer and "sought to 'bend' the customer to fit the product" (Harker and Egan, 2006). This suggests that marketing is used to achieve organisational outcomes by manipulating customers and implies that the functions of marketing are independent from and have no need to adopt the marketing concept. It supports the idea of marketing as a set of activities designed to initiate transactions and suggests a sales, rather than a marketing, orientation.

■ Marketing as relationship

Nowadays there is a much better understanding of marketing – one that takes into account both the role of the marketing mix, i.e. the functions of marketing, and also adopts a marketing orientation. It acknowledges that long-term customer satisfaction is central to achieving organisational goals. It accepts that satisfaction is accomplished by getting to know the customer and continuously providing and adapting the most suitable marketing mix to take account of changes in customer requirements, new product developments and other external influences. This shift from a transactional to a relationship-marketing model understands that consistently delivering value for mutual benefit is the key to marketing and organisational success.

Relationship marketing leads to improved profitability for the following reasons:

■ Understanding customer needs and creating a mix that closely matches requirements.

■ Improving trust.

- Increasing spend as the customer buys a greater range and trades up to more profitable products and services.
- It costs less to service existing customers than find new ones.
- Relationships act as a barrier to exit. Customers stay loyal in preference to spending time and effort establishing an alternative supplier relationship.
- The customer recommends to their friends.

Relationship marketing shifts the emphasis from mass market requirements and gaining market share to meeting individual customer needs and gaining a bigger share of their spend. It recognises that customers require different emphasis and attention. Within airlines, frequent business class flyers are classed as CIPs – commercially important passengers – and will be recognised as such by staff members. The relationship paradigm is well established and fuelled by the considerable amounts of data available and the technology to provide customised approaches. Standard segmentation methods were not able to reveal clusters of customers who demonstrate similar buying patterns but data mining techniques can do this. For example, individuals buying diapers for the first time also buy more beer at the supermarket and this shows that new parents have fewer occasions for socialising outside of the home. The opportunity for mass customisation or micro marketing allows the full offering (including message, price, distribution method and place, service, and sometimes the product) to be individually tailored to meet customer needs, based on information previously gained from similar groups of customers.

Loyalty cards- who benefits?

One often cited example of relationship marketing facilitated by technology is the British retailer Tesco. The consumer receives tailored messages and relevant offers, based on customer preference data obtained through the loyalty card. Consumers seem to like the perceived benefits of such schemes and there is the opportunity for such powerful data to be used for the social good, for example, using consumer behaviour information to promote healthy eating to those who currently overspend on less wise choices. Some commentators suggest that such knowledge provides too much power to commercial organisations and invades consumer privacy.

It costs Tesco £500million to run their Clubcard scheme, should they drop the scheme and reduce prices instead?

■ Marketing as profession

When every employee considers how they personally add value for the customer, the part-time marketer is born and the marketing department becomes obsolete (Gronroos, 1994). However, the professional marketer offers numerous skills that enable an organisation to meet corporate and marketing objectives efficiently and effectively. The skills include research, product and brand portfolios management, developing and implementing marketing plans, designing and running promotional campaigns, assisting sales force activity, pricing and forecasting demand. The marketer acts as:

■ Customer champions, representing customers in all decision making and reinforcing commitment to customer value

■ Brand guardians, protecting brand values when making decisions about the marketing mix.

Put simply, the marketing professional coordinates a number of ingredients to provide customer and other stakeholder value. As discussed earlier the functions or activities of marketing, typically referred to as the marketing mix (McCarthy, 1960) or the four Ps and includes:

■ **Product** – the offering, the benefits and value.

■ **Price** – how much the company charges or the cost to the customer, measured in monetary or non-monetary terms.

■ **Promotion** – communication and mutual understanding between the business and the consumer.

■ **Place** – where and how the product is accessed and customer convenience created.

For a services market three additional Ps are generally included (Booms and Bitner, 1982).

■ **Physical evidence** – the "look" of the business. As services are intangible, physical evidence such as the physical surrounding and promotional materials help the customer evaluate what is on offer.

■ **Process** – how the service is organised and delivered. This creates efficiency and effectiveness.

■ **Participants** or **People** – the boundary spanning service personnel dealing with the consumers and the customers themselves.

The marketing role is extremely broad and requires the skills of many specialists from advertising, marketing research, digital, data analysis, sales, consumer insight, forecasting, content creation, public relations as well as marketing management and strategy. Several bodies represent the profession; within the UK, these include the Chartered Institute of Marketing, the Market Research Society, Chartered Institute of Public Relations, Institute of Direct Marketing. In addition, numerous bodies represent organisations operating within the industry.

> Which professional bodies represent the marketer's interest in your country? What services do they offer their members? What qualifications are needed to become a member? Do they provide any information that might be useful to someone starting out in the profession?

Creating value for different markets

A fundamental question for every organisation and business is which market to serve. Answering this question determines the customers, the competitors and the factors that influence the macro environment whilst drawing the boundaries within which the business operates. Levitt (1960) suggested that companies were myopic (short-sighted) when defining their business in overly narrow product terms. Companies taking a broader view can offer a variety of products and services to solve multiple problems for a group of customers, rather than restricting their offering to just one item with potentially many substitutes. This wider view has encouraged companies such as IBM to move away from producing computers (where they could no longer compete on price) towards technology design and sales, software applications and business consultancy. Had the railways identified their business as transportation they would have seen that substitutes such as air travel and motoring were a threat. Ten per cent of Apple's revenue generates from digital content through the App store, iTunes and iCloud (Dredge, 2015; Apple, 2015) and this lessens reliance on selling physical items such as computers or iPhones.

Once an organisation has determined the markets to serve, they must decide how they can create value for that market. Fahy and Jobber (2012) identify four types of value:

- **Performance** value – the functional benefits achieved, i.e. what the product does. Competitors may copy tangible features relatively quickly but initial interest generated by unique features establishes the organisation's reputation as a problem solver. Patented pharmaceutical formulations cannot be copied for a specific period in time to recoup research and development costs.

- **Emotional** value – intangible benefits that emerge from consumer perceptions about how the product makes them feel. High end branded goods aim to create emotional value and this is difficult for a competitor to replicate.

■ **Price** value – low prices and saving money. Aldi in Europe, Australia, the US and China is an example of a company focusing on price. In Malaysia Giant stores position as providers of Everyday low prices (EDLP).

■ **Relationship** value – developed between a company and its customers and evident in personal services such as opticians and on business-to-business markets. Physical goods can add relationship value by setting up owners' clubs, online services and using research to discover more about customers.

Value creation is a two-way process and both the customer and the organisation must benefit. An organisation must fulfil its own objectives to continue creating customer value.

One of the developments arisen from relationship marketing is consideration of other stakeholders. Nurturing the relationship between the organisation and all stakeholders creates value for both parties. Within the banking industry, Payne et al. (2005) identified six stakeholder groups or markets requiring suitable relationships. Relationship planning requires stakeholder value propositions to be articulated for each group, following an internal and external audit of each of the six markets. The value proposition should state the mutual exchange of value, be transparent and fair and described in terms of perceived benefits. As with all relationship approaches, the objectives will be realised over time, not through a single transaction and will be co-created between the two parties.

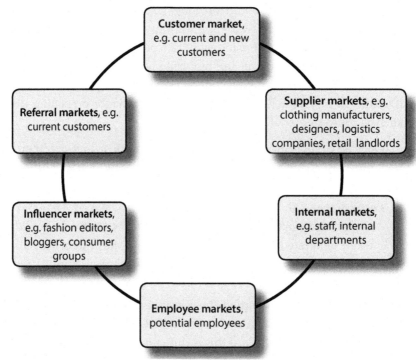

Figure 1.2: Six markets for fashion retailer (Adapted from Payne et al., 2005)

This model can be applied to other industries (Figure 1.2) but may not be complete. For example, it does not identify shareholders as a group but for many businesses, they will be one of the 'markets' that need to be targeted.

■ Creating value through service

In the last 10–15 years there has been a growing acknowledgement that marketing is fundamentally about creating value through service. That is not to say that physical products are unimportant, but products are primarily purchased to provide a service benefit that solves a problem. This moves away from the product, sales or production orientation and insists that creation of value is what marketing must do. Only the beneficiary of the service can determine if value has been created and therefore this view clearly places the customer (or other intended stakeholder) at centre stage.

Service is "the application of specialised competencies (knowledge and skills) through deeds, processes and performances for the benefit of another entity or the entity itself" (Vargo and Lusch, 2004:2). This is known as the **service dominant logic** with the proposition that:

■ Exchange fundamentally means applying specialised skills and knowledge to create value.

■ All economies are effectively based on service.

■ Customers are co-producers.

■ Goods are distribution mechanisms for service provision.

Vargo and Lusch (2016) have updated some of their premises but the fundamental idea has remained the same. There has been some criticism of the service dominant logic by academics (O'Shaughnessy and O'Shaughnessy, 2009) with debate about empirical evidence and whether there is, or should be a dominant approach (Brown, 2007; Prahalad and Ramaswamy, 2004). Nevertheless, the conceptual leaning towards service seems here to stay.

Marketing applications

Not all companies market physical goods or consumer services. Aimed at the consumer and/or the business-to-business market, products can be:

■ **Physical goods** such as cars, rice or shampoo

■ **Services** such as hairdressing or experiences such as holidays

■ **Ideas** such as management consultancy

- **Places** such as Scotland, Malaysia or Dubai
- **People** such a celebrities or politicians.

Most products include an element of service and most services offer some physical aspects.

Along with product features, the name and augmented package of services, the range of products or the product mix needs to be determined. A wide range enables the company to serve several market segments. However, supporting each product requires resources, and customers can find broad ranges confusing. Some corporations such as Unilever are trying to concentrate their marketing effort on core business and have reduced the number of products they sell, although they still manufacture over 400 brands bought by 2 billion customers each day (Unilever, 2015). Many businesses initially offer a single product but over time extend their portfolio to include a number of closely linked brand extensions or highly diversified products, covering the needs of many markets.

Consumer goods and services

Products and services aimed at consumers can be:

- **Fast moving consumer goods** – as suggested by the name, such products are frequently purchased and include food and household cleaning products.

- **Durables** – personal goods such as clothes, mobile phones and goods for households, e.g. refrigerators and furniture. As they are purchased less frequently, guarantees and aftersales service are extremely important.

- **Luxury goods** – High-end purchases that are infrequently purchased by most people, including designer goods. An example might be Mulberry handbags or Porsche cars, which are often seen as an investment.

- **Services** – The number and types of services targeted at consumers are vast. The increased number of families where both parents work outside the home has meant great potential for household services such as gardeners, childcare, cleaners, grocery delivery and takeaways.

Business-to-business marketing

With so many well-known consumer brands, it is easy to neglect the importance of the many essential activities performed to make favourite products and services available for consumers. Organisations must procure a range of services and products to ensure that they can operate and fulfil their purpose. Products and services sold between businesses are called business-to-business (B2B) products and might include capital equipment, raw materials, component parts and business services such as IT provision or accountancy. Personal selling is frequently used in business-to-business markets. Large sums may be involved and development of a personal relationship and trust is important.

■ Social marketing

Not all organisations claim profit as their primary objective and yet adopt the marketing concept and utilise the tools of marketing to achieve goals.

The British National Social Marketing Centre's (NSMC) official definition of social marketing as "the systematic application of marketing concepts and techniques to achieve specific behavioural goals relevant to a social good" (French and Blair-Stevens, 2006).

Governments and other organisations use marketing techniques to change behaviour and create awareness of public services. In the UK, central government spend nearly £600 million each year on marketing, which includes advertising spend, and in Dubai, the government is one of the top spenders on advertising. As with all organisations, social marketers are shifting to social media.

Charities also use marketing techniques to progress their cause. Consider a campaigning charity such as Greenpeace. Greenpeace needs to create awareness; change attitudes; change behaviour of companies and organisations undertaking practices that harm the planet; they need to recruit volunteers and gather donations to continue their work. This work includes lobbying various publics while undertaking interventions that stop activities like whaling and palm tree deforestation. For this, they will use the full marketing armoury to achieve their multiple objectives.

■ Other marketing applications

There are many other examples of marketing being used to advance ideas, political ideologies, lifestyles and personalities. Everyone is involved in some forms of 'self-marketing', whether this is to get a job, a promotion or a partner. It is out with the scope of this text to discuss the adaptations required when applying marketing techniques in all contexts but there are many opportunities for further reading.

Exercise: Using an appropriate website, such as Amazon, search for textbook titles that are tailored to cover speciality marketing contexts such as charities marketing, self-marketing, tourism and hospitality, health and social marketing and so on. What differences can you see in the contents?

Marketing fundamentals

This textbook introduces the fundamental principles of marketing to develop an understanding of the contribution of marketing to organisational success. It considers marketing to be a systematic process and each chapter provides insight to the various activities taken into account when developing marketing strategies. This section takes an overview of the process of marketing and signposts the relevant chapters that aim to develop knowledge and understanding of each step of the marketing journey.

■ Getting started: The organisational context

The organisational context strongly influences and shapes what can be achieved by the organisation and this, in turn, affects the marketing objectives and associated marketing activities required to achieve organisational goals. Chapter 2 will explore the marketing environment, both internal and external, and provide insight to the political, economic, technological and socio-cultural influences that affect all organisations, and their customers. Organisations engage in scanning to enable them to determine the opportunities and threats within the environment. They examine their competitive position, and consider their organisational philosophy, internal strengths and weakness in comparison to others in the market place. This environmental audit helps an organisation decide marketing strategy and set realistic marketing objectives.

■ Finding out: Marketing research

Organisations undertake marketing research in order to investigate the marketing environment, set relevant objectives, design a suitable marketing mix to create value for customers, and evaluate the outcomes of marketing. Chapter 3 provides insight into the systematic research process and considers the many tools available to support marketing decision-making.

■ Understanding consumers

The decision to buy a product or service may be influenced by several different people and before examining the marketing mix in detail, the concepts of customer and consumer need to be explored. The ultimate consumer or end user of the product may not be the buyer, but is usually influential in decision-making. Within a family, parents buy the family holiday or breakfast cereal but their choice is influenced through children's pester power. Within an organisation, the number of individuals with an influential role is even wider. Marketers must therefore understand the requirements of each and determine the most appropriate marketing mix for each 'customer' or member of the decision-making unit. Goods sold through third parties require marketing efforts targeted towards the retailer or wholesaler, who are the primary customers but not the ultimate consumer.

It can be seen that the idea of consumer and customer is often different, even if the terms are used interchangeably. Chapter 4, *Understanding the Consumer*, introduces the idea of the decision-making unit and the social and individual influences affecting consumer decision making. Not all customers are the same, and no single company can fulfil the needs of all consumers and the process of identifying groups of consumers with similar characteristics is segmentation and covered in Chapter 5. Once the organisation has identified a segment, based on a number of classification categories, it must position the offering to meet the needs of that targeted segment.

■ Managing products and services

Products are conceived, developed, named, launched and nurtured to ensure that continuous customer value is provided. Even so, products are not often successful forever and portray a lifecycle. Sales take off slowly, then accelerate and decline as the market matures and competition takes hold. Along with researching and launching new products, marketer must manage their existing portfolios and consider deletion when a product no longer creates sufficient value for the customer or the firm. Chapter 6 considers product as a broad concept, along with discussions of branding, managing products over time, including naming, and decisions on how many products to include in a portfolio.

Sweet-scented

Chanel No. 5, launched in 1925, has many loyal customers but this classic fragrance does not appeal to everyone. Visit the Chanel website to investigate the alternative fragrances and categories included in the brand portfolio.

Why do they offer so many products in each category? What differentiates each fragrance? Which segment is being targeted?

■ Managing price to create value

Setting prices can be challenging. Price signals the quality position and influences customer perception. From a business perspective, price is the only element of the mix that creates revenue and the price set must enable the achievement of organisational objectives. A company aiming for market share may set low prices to enable them to penetrate the market; others might wish to position themselves as innovators and set high prices to appeal to the early adopters. Price is often dynamic, changing throughout the life cycle of the product (McDaniel et al., 2013) and is an important tool for managing demand. Pricing strategies and tactics are covered in more detail in Chapter 7.

Ultimately, prices must be set somewhere between the upper or ceiling price (no customers) and the lowest possible price (no profit). The price set is influenced by customers, competitors and costs (Figure 1.3) and as stated above, the organisational focus and aims.

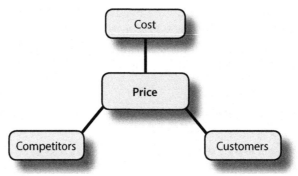

Figure 1.3: Influences on pricing

- **Cost** – Price is determined by calculating all costs with an additional amount for profit. This approach is more challenging than it sounds, as costs vary over time and allocation of the correct portion of fixed costs to a specific product is difficult. This method concentrates on creating value for the organisation rather than the customer.

- **Competitors** – The 'going rate' for the product category is ascertained and price set against this benchmark. Undercutting competitors may lead to a price war and a higher price requires additional value to be created.

- **Customers** – For marketers, the consumer is at the centre of all decisions and pricing is no exception.

Many businesses underprice their offering and fail to realise that price is just one element of the marketing mix. The marketing mix needs integration so that each element works together to help the consumer position the product, and very often promotion is the most discussed element of the mix

Managing promotion to communicate value

Communication is a dialogue that fosters mutual understanding between the company and its customers and other audiences. Much of what the consumer hears about the organisation is unplanned and stems from non-company sources, such as the press, employees and other customers. Some organisations find it difficult to maintain a good reputation amongst all stakeholder groups. Promotion can be expensive and money must be invested wisely to achieve clearly stated objectives. Typical promotional goals might include:

■ Raising awareness

■ Gaining preference and changing attitudes

■ Persuading consumers

■ Direct action such as clicking through to a website

■ Conversion to sale

Objectives extend beyond first purchase and should consider loyalty and relationship development, repeat purchase or encouraging recommendations.

Traditional communication tools include advertising, direct marketing, public relations, sales promotion and running experiences and events. Digital and social promotion is often considered as an additional promotional tool (and therefore included in Figure 1.4) but can be classed as a promotional channel or medium, just like TV or radio. This does not negate social and digital's importance and strength. Digital and social channels are employed across the communications mix and will continue to grow as consumers engage, share and contribute to content. Within the UK, digital channels take a greater share of advertising spend than traditional media. Facebook, which also own Instagram, posted advertising revenues of US$9.3 billion, delivering an audience of 2 billion users (Facebook, 2017), and video channels such as You Tube are increasingly popular. Nevertheless, traditional channels should not be ignored and it is interesting that Facebook spent more than £6m on traditional media in the UK in 2014; a massive increase on the £16,000 spent in the previous year (Cookson and Kuchler, 2015).

Figure 1.4: The communications mix

Chapter 8 discusses how each communications tool contributes to achieving promotional objectives. The tools are rarely used in isolation and must be integrated to complement each other, strengthen company messages and achieve required objectives for each target audience. Communications alone will not fully satisfy the consumer and customers must be able to access the product or service. This is why distribution or place is important.

Managing place: Convenience value

Distribution or place is about getting the product in the right place at the right time to create value for the customer. Decisions about the number and type of outlets that will meet organisational objectives and create customer convenience are a compromise between the amount of organisational control and direct contact with the end customers, and the coverage that might achieved. With direct and online sales methods, even relatively small organisations can trade with geographically distant customers, but transaction completion requires effective and efficient logistics management, including functions such as order processing, secure payment mechanisms, warehousing, transport, delivery and inventory control.

Those companies choosing to use a distribution network require the same logistical functions but their customer will be the next operator in the distribution chain who will need assurance that products stocked will realise profit and be supported with the manufacturer's promotional activity and that they will have access to sufficient inventory. They may insist on exclusivity, point of sale materials, training and additional incentives. Retailers, in particular, hold a great deal of power over manufacturers, and care of distributor relationships is a priority for businesses. Chapter 9 discusses the distribution function in detail, with a particular emphasis in the important of logistics.

The marketing plan and strategy

Marketing needs to be planned and coordinated to create maximum customer value. Before a plan is introduced, the marketing strategy (Chapter 10) needs to be determined and this requires detailed knowledge of the marketing environment (Chapter 2). Only then, can target markets be identified and specific, measurable, achievable, realistic and timely marketing objectives set. A marketing plan is then be devised to operationalise strategy by detailing and integrating the marketing actions required to achieve objectives within that timescale.

Marketing ethics and society

Marketing generally targets a specific group of customers and aims to create value by fulfilling individual needs, a positive outcome for both the consumer and the organisation. Earlier in this chapter, we introduced the idea of societal marketing as a business orientation and suggested that all organisations must take their corporate social responsibility very seriously, whilst still providing customer value. Unfortunately, some organisations fail to consider the societal impact of their marketing actions. They continue unethical practices until challenged by stakeholders such as pressure groups or shareholders, and profits tumble. Marketing as a concept has many critics. Current and future marketers must ensure that their practices are not designed to profit the firm without creating equivalent customer value. They have an ethical role to play in promoting socially responsible behaviour across the organisation and this is further discussed in Chapter 11.

The final chapter is dedicated to furthering interest in the contemporary issues that continue to influence the way that marketing is performed and understood, with coverage of contemporary technologies balanced against continuing interest in maintaining and improving the best of the past through upcycling.

Summary

For many successful organisations, marketing is central to business performance. Chapter 1 has introduced the fundamental marketing concepts and activities. To produce continued, mutually beneficial relationships and create real value the organisation must both act and think marketing. This book provides insight into the key theories and fundamental practices of marketing. It hopes to stimulate thought about the nature and application of socially responsible marketing in a contemporary, on- and off-line age, within a range of organisations, whilst encouraging a more critical debate on the contribution of marketing to consumer and society needs.

Further reading

Morgan, R.M. and Hunt, S. (1994), The commitment-trust theory of relationship marketing, *Journal of Marketing*, **58** (3), 20-38.

Sheth, J (2017) Revitalizing relationship marketing, *Journal of Services Marketing*, **31** (1), 6-10,

References

AMA (2013) Definition of marketing, American Marketing Association. Available https://www.ama.org/AboutAMA/Pages/Definition-of-Marketing.aspx [Accessed July 2017].

Andreoni, J. (1990). Impure altruism and donations to public goods: A theory of warm-glow giving. *Economic Journal*, **100**(401), 464–477.

Apple (2015). App Store Rings in 2015 with New Records and Apple Reports Record First Quarter Results. Apple Press Info. Available at: https://www.apple.com/uk/pr/library/ [Accessed January 2015].

Booms, B.H. and Bitner, M-J. (1982) Marketing strategies and organisational structures for service firms, in Donnelly, J. and George, W.R (Eds.) *Marketing of Services*, American Marketing Association, Chicago, IL.

Borden, N.H. (1964) The concept of the marketing mix. *Journal of Advertising Research*. **4**, 2-7.

Brown, S. (2007). Are we nearly there yet? On the retro-dominant logic of marketing. *Marketing Theory*, **7**, 291-300.

Cookson, R. and Kuchler, H. (2015). Facebook turns to old-fashioned methods for advertising campaign. Financial Times, 12 April 2015 [online]. Available at: http://www.cim.co.uk/files/tomorrowsword.pdf [Accessed April 15 2015]

Dredge, S. (2015). Apple reveals iPhone and iPad owners spent $10bn on apps in 2013. *The Guardian*, 7 January. Available at: http://www.theguardian.com/technology/2014/jan/07/apple-reveals-iphone-and-ipad-owners-spent-10bn-on-apps-in-2013 [Accessed April 2015].

Facebook. (2017). Stats. Available at: https://newsroom.fb.com/company-info/ [Accessed July 2017].

Fahy, J. and Jobber, D. (2012). *Foundations of Marketing*. London: McGraw Hill.

French, J. and Blair-Stevens, C. (2006). Social marketing national benchmark criteria. London: UK National Social Marketing Centre. http://www.snh.org.uk/pdfs/sgp/A328466.pdf. [Accessed July 2017].

Gronroos, C. (1994). From marketing mix to relationship marketing: towards a paradigm shift in marketing. *Asia-Australia Marketing Journal*, **2** (1), 9–29.

Harker, M.J. and Egan, J (2006). The Past, present and future of relationship marketing, *Journal of Marketing Management*, **22**(1-2), 215-242

Levitt, T (1960) Marketing myopia, *Harvard Business Review*, **38**, 24-47

McDaniel, C., Lamb, C.W. and Hair, J.F (2013). *Introduction to Marketing*. (12th International Edition). South Western: Cengage Learning.

McCarthy, E. J. (1960). *Basic Marketing, a Managerial Approach*. IL: Richard D. Irwin.

O'Shaughnessy, J. and O'Shaughnessy, N. (2009) The service dominant perspective: A backward step? *European Journal of Marketing*, **43**(5/6), 784-93,

Payne, A., Ballantyne. D. and Christopher, M. (2005). A stakeholder approach to relationship marketing strategy: The development and use of the "six markets" model", *European Journal of Marketing*, **39**(7/8), 855-871.

Prahalad, C.K and Ramaswamy, V. (2004). Co-creation experiences: the next practice in value creation. *Journal of Interactive Marketing*, **18**(3), 5-14.

Unilever. (2015). View our brands. Available at: http://www.unilever.co.uk/brands-in-action/view-brands.aspx [Accessed May 2015].

Vargo, S. L. and Lusch, R. F. (2004). Evolving to a new dominant logic for marketing. *Journal of Marketing*. **68** (Jan), 1–17.

Vargo, S.L and Lusch, R.F. (2016). Institutions and axioms: an extension and update of service-dominant logic. *Journal of the Academy Marketing Science*. **44**(5), 5–23.

2 The Marketing Environment

Elaine Collinson

The marketing environment is defined as those actors and forces external to the firm's marketing management function, which have the potential to affect the business' ability to successfully develop and maintain transactions with its customers. (Kotler, 1998). The factors affecting how well a company meets its customer needs are a combination of the external forces, which dictate the operating environment of the business and the internal organizational pressures, which determine the nature of responses to those forces.

Internal environmental forces tend to be of a more controllable nature than external forces. The external environment consists of a number of factors with degrees of influence at different stages in a product's life or a company's development.

Environmental analysis

All relevant external forces should be analysed as part of an ongoing planning process, in order to identify any changes in the operating environment, which could either represent a threat to the firm's current position or an opportunity to gain additional competitive advantage. This process is known as **environment scanning** or **analysis**.

External forces

The external forces, also known as the **macro environment**, are often outside the control of the firm:

Internal forces

The internal forces, or the **micro environment**, focus on the organization itself and how its characteristics and composition influence the ways it responds to the target market. It also considers how it is portrayed to the target market.

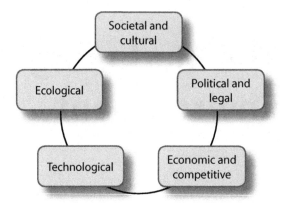

Figure 2.1: The macro environment

Figure 2.2: The micro environment

Both internal and external environments must be analysed in tandem, since they do not exist independently of each other. Many firms place a high importance on analysing the external environment without fully understanding the impact their own operating methods have on the way they respond to the external pressures

Marketing and customer focus

A marketing-oriented firm focuses on satisfying the needs of target customers as successfully and efficiently as possible. To achieve this goal, it is important to understand the environment within which customers live and the effect this has on their buying behaviour and their expectations. Equally, the business must attempt to calculate the extent to which the environment will impinge on its own ability to service customer needs.

■ Scanning the external environment

Environmental scanning of the marketing environment is crucial in order to have up to the minute information on the current position. Information gathered relating to the current state of play in the marketplace is assessed and interpreted through a process known as environmental analysis, a twofold process taking cognizance of both the external situation facing the business and a realistic understanding of the internal resources and skills. The impact of basing decisions on out of date or erroneous information can be loss of market share, customer dissatisfaction, damage to brand identity and potentially loss of faith in the business itself.

The societal environment

As people, we all live within a society with its norms and acceptable ethics relating to behaviour, business and beliefs. These beliefs form part of our cultural background, which over time develops into our shared culture and history. The societal environment is therefore the framework within which our personal cultural environment exists, influencing how we behave as consumers and our expectations of the companies that serve us.

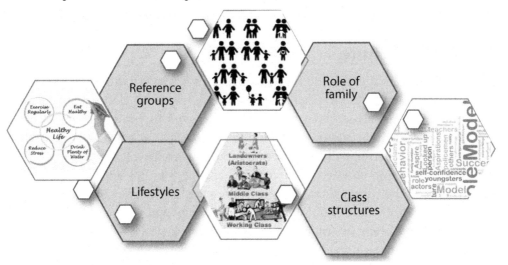

Figure 2.3: Societal and cultural environments

■ Role of the family

Families have developed in different ways in different societies. In some societies, for example, the 'traditional' family structure of the mother at home to bring up the children while the father supports the household is the norm. In the Western world, the role and composition of the family is changing and has seen the demise of the nuclear family. More women are in the workplace, one-parent families are numerous, as are new extended families with both parents in a second marriage and potentially a higher number of dependents between them. Offspring tend to leave home to follow job opportunities, which are often in a different location. The last 20 years has seen major changes in lifestyles with families being dispersed across the globe, international commuting becoming normal for many. Internationalisation has created an increased number of cross-cultural marriages, with people working in large multinationals often living and working in several countries over their working lives. Does this therefore mean the idea of family is changing or are we more eager to hold on to our traditional understanding of the family unit?

Understanding the family is of paramount importance since it is the primary reference point for most people and where our ideas of right and wrong, ethics and behaviour are first formed. The concept of the family life cycle looks at the different stages in a family, where we either influence or are influenced by others. Greater understanding of the influences within the family unit enables marketers to position their promotional messages to directly target the main decision maker or influencer. The way in which family is depicted within a specific market also requires to be aligned to its societal norms to ensure that the target customers identify with the scene.

■ Class structure

In each market, there will be class structures operating within that society. In the 21st century, there are still many countries across the globe where the difference between classes is extreme with high levels of poverty living alongside the super-rich. In others, the class differences may not be so apparent but still exist. Marketers initially developed a social class scale which attempted to group customers into socio-economic bands, ranging from the high earning professional to the basic manual worker, represented by a series of grading from A to E. With the advent of information technology and the increased sophistication of marketing information systems, marketing professionals can now target customers at the individual level, aligning bespoke products and services to meet their individual requirements.

Criteria such as income, education and lifestyle are used to ascertain a person's social class – the reference group to which people turn when making decisions, either seeking to conform to norms or behaving in an aspirational fashion. In creating an image for a product in the consumer's minds, marketers need to ensure that the product is offered through an outlet, which provides the appropriate impression to the consumer. Recent years have seen the development of the customer journey where the focus is not only on the transactional element of the purchase itself but across the whole buying experience. This includes key elements such as packaging, customer service, retail premises and their physical layout, use of emotional cues such as music and scent and the all-important after sales service which attempts to build a long-term relationship with the customer.

Consumer research evidence has found that there is a constellation of specific lifestyle factors, shared beliefs, attitudes, activities and behaviours that distinguish the members of one social class from those in other social classes. (Schiffman and Lazar, 1997). Marketers must attempt to measure the strength of the influence of the social class with reference to their product. Does it conform to pricing norms? Is the way in which its message is communicated aligned with the consumers' expectations? Is it available to the target market in the outlets they expect?

■ Reference groups

Reference groups influence an individual's beliefs, opinions, attitudes and behaviour. The primary category relates to friends, family and work colleagues and the secondary category of relates to groups such as political parties, sports clubs or local community groups. Such groups provide a frame of reference for individuals to gauge what is acceptable if they are to aspire to become a member of that group. For example, in the fashion sector high quality brands are often seen as a sign of status or belonging to a certain reference group and outlets selling these brands are perceived 'THE place to shop' for those aspiring to this socioeconomic group. The advent of the internet however means that aspirational consumers can access branded goods at reduced cost and the retail outlet is virtual. Notwithstanding this, brand conscious consumers still aspire to be seen in the 'right' outlets.

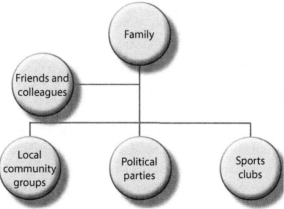

Figure 2.4: Reference group influencers

Understanding the strength of the influence is important in marketing. If there is a key influencer within a group who is setting a trend for consumers to follow, this may indicate future consumer needs. The advent of blogging and celebrity status in the last 20 years has had a particularly strong influence on younger consumers, with many following bloggers and vloggers, such as Zoella with over 11 million followers on YouTube (https://www.zoella.co.uk/).

■ Lifestyles

Lifestyle refers to how people choose to live, influenced by both culture and the social setting. Lifestyles are important since they highlight people's behavioural traits, aspirations and expectations of the products they buy. Chisnall (1985) describes lifestyles as:

> *"distinctive or characteristic ways of living adopted by certain communities or sections of a community, with regard to their general attitudes and behaviour towards the use of time, money and effort".*

Market segmentation attempts to identify characteristics associated with different lifestyles to understand a target market but situational, personal and psychological factors all play a part in determining consumer behaviour so it is not an exact science.

The cultural environment

■ Macro culture

Culture refers to a set of values, beliefs, rituals, customs, symbols and artefacts, acting as a person's framework within which the individual can interpret, evaluate and communicate with others. Palmer et al. (1999) define culture as having three important features:

- Comprises abstract (symbols, rituals and values) and material elements (literature, art, music and buildings)
- Is socially transmitted and learned
- Influences human behaviour.

Within the broader range of cultural influences, there are those, which are perceived as enduring 'core' beliefs and others, which may change over time. In many countries core beliefs relate to a person's right to an education and free speech, whereas attitudes towards divorce, one-parent families and same sex marriage have shifted in recent years. The role of marketing is to be clear on the core beliefs and their impact and identify changing beliefs in that target market.

In studying culture, marketers aim to create a product, which is both appealing and acceptable to the targeted consumers. This impacts on the way in which a message is conveyed, whom the message is directed at, the setting of an advertisement, the language used, colours and names of specific products, the use of humour in marketing communications, the supply chain and its traceability, along with green packaging and manufacturing processes. Cultural influences form the core of consumers' beliefs and values and a firm's values must align with those of the target market.

■ Micro culture

Within a country, there will be an 'umbrella' culture within which there are also subcultures, consisting of any groupings of consumers by race, religion, geographical location, language, age or any other factor, which may influence behaviour. In the UK for example, there are four large and very well defined subcultures: the Scots, Welsh, Irish and English, along with smaller ethnic minorities in various parts of the country. In the USA, there is a multicultural society but a strong micro culture of Hispano Americans with around 17% of the US population now classifying themselves as of Hispanic origin. (US Census, 2015).

Subcultures may have increased influence on buying behaviour since they consist of more identifiable groups and operate on a much more personal level. Sieger (2016) states that this changing demographic in the US is forcing brands to rethink their approach, since there is a clear link between ethnic background and products chosen. Within the US, the Hispanic population has $1.2 trillion buying power, with a projected growth of over 7%, with top product categories such as telephone services, hair care, fragrances, baby food and used cars (Selig Centre for Economic Growth, 2015)

Subcultures are also important as influencers. If a large migrant population establishes itself in a particular geographical area, this in time influences the local population, for example a growing population from East Asia may lead to increased awareness of Thai, Vietnamese or Chinese cuisine, resulting in hitherto exotic ingredients becoming commonplace.

Sieger (2016) suggests that companies adopt a Total Market Strategy ensuring that their message is relevant to all in the target market. At a lower level still, within the micro culture, marketers must also recognise certain fashions or trends with which people identify, such as the culture around a music style, goths or hacker culture.

Culture represents a personal part of an individual's character, one perceived by society to be morally acceptable. In developing both its marketing strategy and plan, influences on the consumer need to be fully understood.

Political and legal environment

In any given market, be it domestic or international, the prevailing political and legislative conditions will have an impact on society and its consumers. The degree of influence will vary, with economies such as China being highly regulated by government legislation, whilst others have less stringent rules affecting inward investment.

From the political standpoint, the overarching issue is that of stability. This has a direct effect on the value of the currency, international exchange rates and how profitable it is to do business in and with that country. Current uncertainty in the European Union and its future has had a direct impact on the value of the euro and on-going issues relating to the solvency of some member states, such as Greece, do not encourage international investors. June 2016 saw Britain vote against remaining in the European Union. The immediate effect of this vote has been a devaluation of the pound, uncertainty in stock markets across the globe and loss of share value in both the banking and property sectors. The longer-term implications of this vote have yet to be seen but from a marketing environment perspective, continuing uncertainty is never good for business.

There are numerous examples of fragile political environments impacting on firms who did not foresee a political change, e.g. Iran, Iraq, Nicaragua, Egypt, Thailand and Venezuela. It is crucial that firms understand the prevailing political situation and evaluate its potential impact.

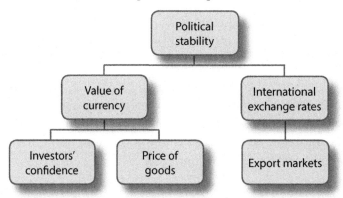

Figure 2.5: Understanding the political environment

This impact however is not always negative. Some governments may offer incentives encouraging inward investment from overseas or preferential deals for firms enabling technology transfer into a developing market's economy. In the 1980s and 1990s, China restricted entry to certain types of firm but actively encouraged investment for companies dealing in high technology products.

Although the political environment is outside the control of individual firms, political lobbying by groups of large firms to encourage laws and regulations favourable to their industry is long established. In addition to political lobbying on legislation, companies also aim to establish relationships with government officials.

Governments are also major customers, especially in industries such as defence, where some firms rely entirely on government contracts. The impact of government cutbacks in a given sector can have a catastrophic effect on an industry, so charting government policy and thinking is a crucial part of environmental scanning.

From the legal perspective, there are two key areas, which are of particular importance: competition legislation and consumer protection laws. Legislation relating to competition and monopolies may limit the extent of growth and influence a firm has – in the UK, firms can be referred to the Competition and Markets Authority, a non-ministerial body covering both UK and EU legislative practices, their key responsibilities covering:

- Mergers which could restrict competition.
- Market studies and investigations in markets where there may be competition and consumer problems.
- Investigating possible breaches of UK or EU prohibitions against anti-competitive agreements and abuses of dominant positions.
- Criminal proceedings against individuals who commit the cartel offence.
- Enforcing consumer protection legislation to tackle practices ensuring consumer choice.
- Co-operating with sector regulators, encouraging them to use their competition powers.
- Regulatory references and appeals.

Consumer protection legislation has grown from focusing on product content and delivery to protecting consumers against unscrupulous financial practices, ensuring clear labelling on products and defending consumers' rights for after-sales service and support. With ever-increasing volumes of on-line trade over the last two decades, additional legislation to protect consumers on-line has come into force, with a company's website requiring adherence to relevant legislation.

In addition to the legislation, any restrictions on pricing techniques and/or trade barriers in certain markets need to be considered. The interpretation of legislation is often difficult since it can be vaguely defined and previous court rulings on an issue tend to be a more accurate indicator of acceptable limits.

The legal environment also includes regulatory forces either via government or non-government agencies, with the former including ministries and Customs and Excise Agencies and the latter trade associations. Levels of enforcement and importance will vary dependent on the government and industry, but companies seeking to enter new markets must be aware of these regulatory bodies, with any restrictions imposed and degrees of influence determining market attractiveness.

Economic and competitive environment

All organisations operate within an overall economic climate, be it of prosperity, recession or depression. The prevailing economic climate will affect both consumers and firms. From a marketing perspective, if a specific market is in recession, promotional campaigns need to be focused on the value-for-money aspects of the product offering. Channel intermediaries may need to be offered longer credit terms and sustain losses in the short term. If the market is prosperous, conditions are very different and the way in which a product is brought to market will reflect this, e.g. a company can increase prices and/or introduce luxury brands in the expectation that consumers are affluent and demand for aspirational products is high.

Economic forces are outside the control of the company but environmental scanning should attempt to gauge the effects of the prevailing economic conditions and their impact on market success.

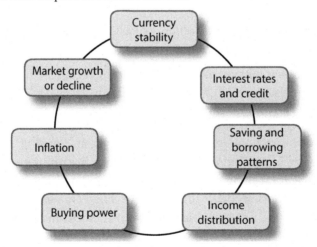

Figure 2.6: Key indicators of economics forces

Economic forecasting is difficult; many multinationals sustained losses in the early 1990s when the recession was longer and more intense than predicted, and recent scandals in the worldwide banking community resulted in firms finding it more difficult to access finances for expansion. Despite the uncertainties, firms need to assess the economic environment facing them and consider the potential impact for marketing decisions.

The competitive environment is directly linked to the economic environment within which all companies are operating. The wider competitive environment is determined by the number and strength of firms in a given sector, with historically four general types of competitive structure.

Figure 2.7: Potential competitive structures

In a **monopoly** situation, the company's product has no close substitutes and the company has complete control over the supply, enabling it to erect barriers to entry for new competitors. For example, Microsoft has exclusive ownership of a scarce resource, the Windows operating system, and is the only firm that can exploit it. Normally monopoly power exists when a firm controls more than 25% of a market, and mergers which create a monopoly situation, are often closely monitored to ensure competition laws are not breached. Where monopolies exist, the industry may be highly regulated to protect consumers from unfair trading practices or regulatory barriers may be introduced to prevent companies from establishing a monopoly position. Instances where monopolies exist are often temporary and relate to a patent, licence or government grant to deliver a service.

In an **oligopoly**, a small number of firms have control over a large proportion of the supply of a product. Again, barriers to entry can exist, with new entrants often requiring high financial outlay and technical/marketing skills. OPEC (Organization of Petroleum Exporting) is an example of an oligopoly, established in this case by governments rather than companies.

Monopolistic competition is where there are many potential competitors and firms strive to gain competitive advantage through differentiated marketing techniques. Product supply is easily available and spread over a large number of companies. Firms will try to differentiate their product offerings if not in functionality, then in after-sales service or customer loyalty programmes to create barriers to entry. Most businesses will find themselves competing in this type of environment.

A **perfectly competitive** environment has many suppliers, none of which can influence either the supply or price of a product. Products tend to be homogeneous, both customers and companies have full market knowledge and no barriers to entry exist.

Perfect competition represents one extreme with a monopoly situation at the other extreme; the majority of firms operate somewhere between the two.

Figure 2.8: Analysing the competitive environment

When analysing the competitive environment, it may be either extremely difficult or relatively straightforward for a firm to enter and succeed in a new market. Prior to this decision, firms need to be fully aware of the level, intensity and strength of competition.

Technological environment

The development of technology affects the technological environment both inside the company and in the wider market.

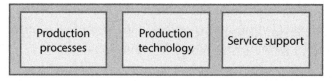

Figure 2.9: Components of the technological environment

To fully understand the market's technological requirements, firms undertake a technological assessment to ascertain how their product compares to both competitors' offerings and customer expectations. Failing to ascertain this can lead to either a product, which is too highly advanced for the target market's needs or is quickly made obsolete by advances by competition.

Internal computerised processes, smart databases and tracking systems all add to the value customers receive when choosing a particular product. Integrated supply chains where companies are sharing the same systems with their suppliers enables both firms and customers to track their orders, make changes to delivery times or places and receive a more customised service.

Advances in technology have not only had an impact on the supply chains however, since marketing information systems have enabled firms to undertake more accurate forecasting, and smartphones enable customers to have a one-to-one relationship with the business.

The impact of technological change has been immense and continues to grow, with major changes predicted by 2025. The mobile internet, automation of knowledge work, the internet of things, 3-D printing, renewables and other technologies will potentially affect all economies.

Firms which are technology ready can take advantage of cost savings and efficiencies across their processes, developing accurate customer databases and information, building virtual relationships with customers and managing efficient supply chains, all of which add to competitive advantage.

When operating in international markets however, firms need to be aware of the levels of technology infrastructure and development in the overseas market. Factors to consider include the local market's expectations regarding technology, current technology in international supply chains, compatibility of operating systems and the country-level infrastructure required to deliver product or service.

Initial market research needs to clearly identify the level of technology suitable for each market and assess the costs of any adjustments required to easily operate in the market. Simple issues such as not being able to accurately share information across an international supply chain can have a direct and damaging impact on both short and long-term reputation.

Ecological environment

The ecological environment includes areas such green marketing, management of the wider environment, waste management and recycling, ethical supply chains and all areas of business associated with conducting business in a way which does not harm the planet. The late 1990s saw the emergence of the term *ecological footprint*, whereby a firm could calculate the impact its activities were having on the planet (Wackernagel and Rees, 1998). This increased focus on protecting natural resources has resulted in consumers being more interested in product traceability, whether products were sourced locally and whether ingredients and the processes utilised to make them are ecologically safe. This has had a major influence on product packaging, with many businesses now clearly labelling how all elements of their packaging can be recycled.

The evolution of ecological awareness has resulted in a shift in consumer values, with product safety, production processes and the company's environmental credibility often outweighing the price paid. Companies who were aware of these changes early on and adapted their products and processes accordingly could use this feature as a unique selling point. However, others lost brand reputation and customer loyalty by making false claims on the levels of environment friendliness of their products, which subsequently were found untrue and damaging to the environment.

These shifts in consumer values are largely beyond the control of the firm since they are indicative of society-level changes relating to acceptable ways to produce and deliver products and services. Companies need to ensure they are fully cognisant of the strength of feeling on ecological issues in a given market. In Europe, Germany and the Scandinavian countries have been trailblazers in green marketing, with laws are in place to protect the environment. This level of law enforcement has taken longer in the USA and Latin America however. Recent years have seen global commitment to the environment through such agreements as the Kyoto Protocol in 1997, leading to the establishment of the United Nations Summit on Climate Change. In 2015, the 11th session of the Meeting of the Parties agreed the way forward in reducing harmful greenhouse gases. The conference negotiated the Paris Agreement, a global agreement on the reduction of climate change, the text of which represented a consensus of the representatives of the 196 parties. The agreement will become legally binding if joined by at least 55 countries which together represent at least 55% of global greenhouse emissions (Green Alliance, 2015).

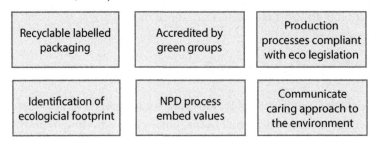

Figure 2.10: Communicating ecological credentials

In addition to communicating their ecological credentials, firms should develop processes that ensure quality and compliance across the supply chain, whilst developing close associations with organisations such as Friends of the Earth.

The internal environment

The external environment although often complicated and diverse is the situation in which all companies are operating. Each company will, however, deal with these external pressures differently and this is determined by their internal environment depicted below.

Figure 2.11: The internal environment

■ Organisational structure

An organisational structure may be flexible or rigid, centralised or decentralised, with decisions made by top-level management or by more independent middle and lower level teams. This internal structure will determine the way in which information is disseminated and decisions made and implemented. Where a firm's personnel are located in different geographical areas, people may not perceive their colleagues as being readily accessible; in other cases, organisational hierarchies and reporting flows may restrict communications.

Firms should be aware of how their structure affects internal communications to ensure a good flow of relevant information between departments. Ideally each department should be aware of the needs of other business units within the organisation and be working as a cohesive team as opposed to isolated operations. Distinct competitive advantage can be gained by firms whose intranet and internal technology processes enable them to make quick and accurate decisions ahead of competition.

Insight: Internal change – Optos

Optos Ltd. is a small business operating in Scotland, manufacturing high-end retinal imaging laser technology to support practitioners diagnosing and treating ocular pathology. The company was successful in its niche market but recognised that internal functions could be improved to make them more efficient and enhance their productivity. Through a period of re-organisation they introduced a programme of change, empowering the workforce in their decision-making processes, ensuring efficient warehousing of stock, improved labelling of goods and more collaborative management. The result over a 3-year period was an increase in profitability of 29% and a reduction in waste of both commodities and staff hours. This programme of change was solely focused on Optos' internal environment, but following this, they found themselves in a much more competitive situation when looking to the external context.

■   Management philosophy

Management philosophy determines a company's view of itself. A firm may have either a customer-, market- or production-driven philosophy. This philosophy sets the tone of an organisation's culture. The culture has a direct impact on the level of bureaucracy in the firm; it may encourage people to be proactive and take initiatives or it may adopt a dictatorial style, where every decision must be approved by senior managers. A rigid culture often leads to poor flexibility and an inability to respond quickly to market needs, and in this environment, creative individuals are likely to feel thwarted.

The philosophy or culture will also affect how the firm responds to opportunities and threats. A firm whose management are prepared to take risks will adopt very different strategies to one whose management philosophy is very defensive and aimed at maintaining the status quo.

Firms need to be aware of their culture and its impact on the way they do business. It is not an easy process to change a business' culture, however management research studies show that agile, proactive firms are more likely to survive and succeed long term than their centrally organised and reactive counterparts.

Individual characteristics

The characteristics of those in both the marketing function and the decision-making team will also influence how the business reacts to external changes. Some people may be more open to risk-taking, more entrepreneurial in style, others more risk averse and cautious. Any given company is made up of several individuals working within a particular management style. The size of the firm has an important bearing here since in SMEs with a small management team, tensions can easily arise if there is lack of agreement on how best to develop the business and address market opportunities. Collinson and Shaw (2001) explore this impact further by looking at the entrepreneurial scenario facing the small firm, which is characterised by the perceived level of risk, the available resources and the individual's need for skills, knowledge, experience and personal independence.

■ Market position

As part of the micro environmental analysis, firms will assess their current market position, analysing the following factors:

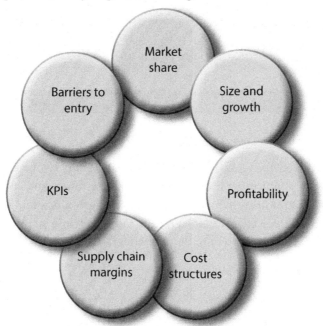

Figure 2.12: Market position

This analysis is undertaken for current markets but also in potential new markets. This type of analysis will enable improved accurate decision-making in marketing strategy and the approach will be aligned to strengths.

Operating relationships

In the micro environment, a company has more direct contact with other players than in the macro environment. Key relationships include those with suppliers, channel intermediaries and key publics.

Supplier relationships

A business has a close and long-term relationship with its suppliers, who provide the firm with everything from raw materials for production purposes, IT equipment, component parts to after-sales service support. Recent years have seen many large retailers adopt an integrated approach to their supply chain, from being involved in the new product development processes of firms supplying them, to sharing integrated IT systems to support the chain. Any breakdown in supply will have a direct and immediate effect on a firm's ability to both meet its own customers' orders and maintain its brand reputation.

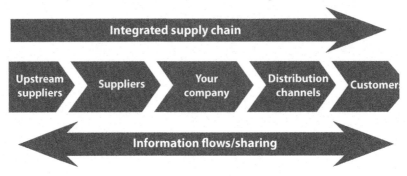

Figure 2.13: Channel intermediaries

These firms facilitate the exchange relationship by promoting, selling or transporting the firm's product to the final consumer, and include advertising agencies, distributors, wholesalers, retailers and couriers. Growth in on-line purchases has placed greater significance on the role played by couriers and transport partners in ensuring timely delivery to customers.

Black Friday in retail

In 2014 the UK experienced its first 'Black Friday' event – prior to then this phenomenon had only happened in the US. This is where a high proportion of retailers offer their goods at discounted prices the first Friday of December. In the UK in 2014, this resulted in riots in stores, websites crashing due to high levels of traffic, the transport infrastructure unable to cope, with firms expected to deliver in one day a normal week's worth of business. In 2015, many retailers opted out whilst others extended the sale period to cover a week and distribution centres took on more short-term staff to cover the spike in sales.

■ Publics

A public is any group that has an interest in the company or may affect the company's ability to serve its target market.

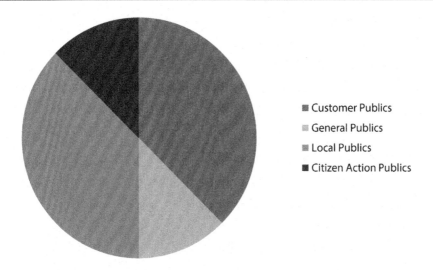

Figure 2.14: The publics

All of these groups are affected by the company's operation to some degree. Firms should therefore be aware of the expectations of each. Some will have greater influence than others and local publics, although not customers, can seriously affect the firm's reputation if they are having a negative impact on the local community.

Customer markets

Within the wider term of market, firms are often operating in a series of customer markets. These include:

- **Consumers** – buying for personal or household use.

- **Industrial buyers** – firms buying goods for use in production processes or as components of their own products.

- **Resellers** – products are bought to sell on at a profit, e.g. antique dealers.

- **Governments** – agencies buying products and services for use in public services.

- **International** – include potentially all the above markets.

Different markets will display different types of buying behaviour with the industrial buyer being very different to the individual consumer, the complexity of the contract will vary, the nature of the transaction and the number of people involved in the buying decision. The nature of the relationship the firm has with its markets will also differ, with many business-to-business purchases being undertaken within the framework of an integrated supply chain.

■   ## Competitors

As mentioned earlier, the competitive environment is seen as part of the external environment. However, since competitors are operating under the same market conditions, relationships are usually close and competitors' actions have a direct impact on the firm, they are therefore considered an intrinsic part of the firm's microenvironment. Competing firms in a given market will examine each other's actions before taking any major decisions and strategy is often strongly influenced by what competitors are doing.

Conclusion

Understanding both the internal and external environments that affect a company's operating efficiency supports the decision-making process. All elements of the marketing environment are of importance at different stages of development and a good environmental scanning process, which furnishes the organisation with up-to-date, relevant marketing information, creates a strong competitive advantage.

A firm must strive to understand the largely uncontrollable external environment, whilst being fully cognisant of its internal strengths and weaknesses. Competitive differential advantage can often be created by improving the internal processes and customer service elements of a product, even when the external environment is highly competitive and difficult to predict.

Further reading

Palmer, A. and Hartley, B. (2008) – *The Business Environment*, 6th Ed.
A comprehensive introduction to today's business environment, both within the internal organisation and in the wider environment.

Baker, M.J. (1996) *Marketing – An Introductory Text*, 6th ed. London, Palgrave MacMillan.

Collinson, E. (2002) Marketing Environment, in *International Encyclopaedia of Business and Management*, 2nd ed. Thomson Learning.

Kotler P. and Armstrong G. (2015) *Principles of Marketing*, 6th Ed., Pearson.

References

Chisnall, P. (1985) *Marketing: A Behavioural Analysis*, 2nd ed. New York: McGraw Hill.

Collinson, E. and Shaw, E. (2001) Entrepreneurial marketing – a historical perspective on development and practice, *Management Decision*, **39**(9), 761-766.

Green Alliance (2015) http://www.green-alliance.org.uk/paris2015.php. [Accessed June 2017].

Kotler, P. (1998) *Marketing Management, Analysis, Planning, Implementation and Control*, 9th ed. Engelwood Cliffs, NJ: Prentice Hall.

Palmer, A., Worthington, I., Hartley, B. and Mulholland, M. (1999) *The Business and Marketing Environment*, 7th Ed., New York Mc-Graw Hill.

Schiffman, L.G. and Lazar, L.K. (1997) *Consumer Behaviour*, Prentice Hall College Division

Selig Centre for Economic Growth (2015) Asians, Hispanics driving U.S. economy forward, according to UGA study - Multicultural Economy report reveals trends in U.S. spending, September 24, 2015, University of Georgia. http://news.uga.edu/releases/article/2015-multicultural-economy-report

Sieger, M. (2016) Finding and influencing Latino consumers, Digital and social media, http://fleishmanhillard.com/2015/11/true/finding-and-influencing-latino-consumers/ [Accessed June 2017].

US Census (2015) -US Census Bureau (2015): Hispanic Roots, US Department of Commerce and Statistics Administration,. https://www.census.gov/content/dam/Census/newsroom/facts-for-features/2015/cb15-ff18_graphic.jpg

Wackernagel, M. and Rees, W. (1998) *Our Ecological Footprint – Reducing Human Impact on the Earth*, New Society Publishers.

3 Marketing Research

Geraldine McKay

Marketing research promotes understanding of customers, identifies current and future needs and how to best serve them. A recent report by PwC (2016) stated that evidence based research leads to more confident decision making, reduces costs and increases efficiency. Although there is a tendency to think of marketing research in terms of questionnaires or surveys, those undertaking research use a wide variety of tools for gathering and analysing marketing information.

Marketing research: nature and scope

Sometimes a distinction is made between the terms *market* and *marketing research*. Marketing research is the broader term and encompasses market research into the micro and macro environments (including competitor research) and research to help understand customer needs and choose an appropriate marketing mix. Knowledge of current and forecasted environmental trends (political, legal, economic, social, cultural and technological) affecting company performance is obtained through broad environmental scanning counterbalanced by the tightly focused requirement to analyse the internal intricacies of marketing activities (such as a change of price or package size) and their impact on customers. The scope of marketing research is therefore both broad and deeply focused and utilises a number of techniques.

Traditional techniques used by researchers are increasingly disrupted by emerging techniques such as innovative, wearable technology, behavioural economics and neuroscience. Big data from social media and web traffic analysis has increased (PwC, 2016) but qualitative methods are also popular. Online surveys using mobiles are gaining popularity in comparison to traditional face-to-face or telephone methods. Such changes require marketers with the following qualities and skills (PwC, 2012):

- Business knowledge and commercial literacy

■ Strong in data analysis and interpretation

■ Good communication and storytelling skills

■ Flexibility and the agility to be an early innovator.

Research offers insight into which marketing mix creates the most customer value as indicated in Table 3.1.

Table 3.1: Researching the marketing mix.

Product/Service: Concept testing, product testing, naming and packaging	**Pricing**: Perceived value
What do you like/ dislike about this product/ competitor product(s)?	How much do you currently pay?
What additional benefits/services would provide value?	Would you pay extra for additional benefits?
How do you use the product?	What value do you place in the product/ service?
How should this product be packaged?	Would a price rise/drop affect the amount you buy?
Promotion: Promotional mix, media, message and meaning research	**Place**: Supply chain, channel and customer search research
What media do you use?	Where would you research and buy the product/service?
How often do you read a magazine?	How long would you wait/travel to obtain the product?
Which creative approach is most effective?	What type of retailer should stock the product?
How did you discover and navigate the website?	
What does this advert say about the brand?	

Marketing research provides evidence to promote better understanding of customers and improve commercial success. However, noncommercial organisations also use research to provide insight into multiple stakeholders (employees, funders, distributors, neighbours, policy makers, interest groups and suppliers). Governments and charities also undertake social and behavioural research. Thus, marketing research has broad scope and application.

Marketing research uses a diverse range of tools, techniques and skills to provide a more complete understanding of customers and other stakeholders and the factors that influence them. It aims to deliver evidence-informed decision making to create the value sought by the target audience. Companies may undertake unsystematic and poorly construed research to 'prove' that their decisions are sound, but research should be planned, systematic and with bias minimised. Research informs decision-making but should not replace or delay marketing decisions. Where the cost of doing research outweighs the benefits, it may be reasonable to act without formalised research. This depends on the research objectives, the resources available and the potential outcomes or risks arising from uniformed decisions.

Although it is tempting to immediately collect data, many other stages are essential before data gathering can commence. A systematic approach (Figure 3.1) requires that the marketing problem is clearly defined so that research objectives, or research questions can be set. Marketing problems can be broad (e.g. sales have been falling) or narrow, and research objectives may be defined in terms of a marketing tactic (e.g. most appropriate advertising for a new product) or more broadly (e.g. why are sales falling). Once objectives are agreed a decision can be made about who completes the research (in-house or external agencies for some or all the research), and the research design can be determined.

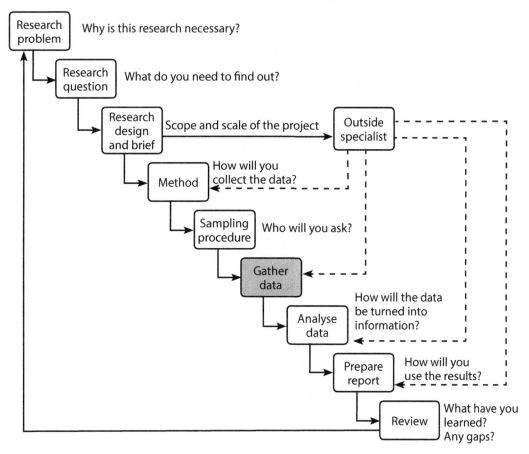

Figure 3.1: The systematic research process. Source: McKay and Phillips, 2015; adapted from Stone and Desmond, 2010.

Research brief

The research brief is a written document that summarises what is known, defines the problem and specifies the research questions. It indicates how the research will be used and by whom. It is essential because it clarifies objectives and gives direction to those commissioned to carry out the research. The brief (Figure 3.2) should be concise (often around two pages) but provide sufficient information to allow a realistic proposal. Where outside agencies are being commissioned to undertake the research, commercially sensitive information may be withheld until contracts have been signed.

Figure 3.2: Research brief

Table 3.2 compares the benefits of carrying out the research in-house or using external specialists. A combination approach might require that secondary research is completed in-house with external specialists engaged to undertake primary research.

Table 3.2: Benefits of external agency and in-house research

External research agency	In house research
Objectivity	Opportunity to get first-hand knowledge of the market
Specialist skills	Confidentiality
May elicit more candid answers	Can be cheaper
Project is likely to be completed	Questionnaire design and implementation software is available
Externally produced results seen as more credible	In house researchers have better understanding of context

The commissioned team will respond to the brief and the research design, methods, budget and timescales approved.

Research design

Exploratory research uncovers background information with the aim to raise further questions, but not to fully answer them or make final decisions. Descriptive research provides a fuller picture and might involve a systematic review of current information about the micro environment such as:

- A list of competitors sourced from web and printed directories
- Competitor offerings
- Demographics and lifestyle data about customers.

Causal research tries to establish a connection between marketing activities such as the effect of a sales promotion on short and long-term sales or the impact of an advertising message on customer perception of a brand.

Research undertaken on a longitudinal or continuous basis monitors trends, and predicts change. Media research, such as the National Readership Survey continually monitors readership (print and on-line) through a survey administered to a representative sample of respondents. Cross-sectional research gathers data on an ad hoc basis provides a snapshot of the current state of the market. Repeating an ad hoc study may reveal trends, but usually after changes have happened. Ad hoc research is less resource intensive and appropriate when testing a new marketing tactic.

Table 3.3: Research design types

Design	Examples of question
Exploratory	What technological changes will affect our marketing in the next 3 years?
Descriptive	Which customer segment is most loyal? Which customers spend most online
Causal	How much does a price change affect demand? Which website content is more engaging?

Research can be qualitative or quantitative, depending on whether detail and depth or quantifiable 'facts' are required.

Table 3.4: Qualitative and quantitative research

	Quantitative data	Qualitative data
Type of data	Objective: Measurement, numbers, facts	Subjective: Words, impressions, thoughts and feelings. Open to interpretation
What questions does it help answer?	Descriptive: Who, what, when and how many/much?	Diagnostic: Why? How?
Type of study	Causal and descriptive Spotting trends Segment comparison Correlating data Causation Describing behaviour e.g. media use.	Exploratory and evaluative- adds to understanding Clarifies issues for investigation Creative ideas for advertising and product development Explains behaviour patterns Sensitive or personal studies
Typical Research tools	Questionnaires, observation, tests and experimentation	Focus groups, depth interviews, projective techniques, observation
Results	Generalisable if sample large and representative	Not generalisable but insight provided
Sample size	Large	Small

Both primary and secondary research may be included in the research design. Secondary research uses 'second hand' information already published for another reason. Secondary sources may fully answer the research question but are usually part of exploratory research and a precursor to primary research. Most research projects use a combination of both primary and secondary approaches.

■ Secondary research

Secondary research or desk research is sometimes available from internal company sources or alternatively may be sourced externally. Table 3.5 provides examples of both internal and external secondary data.

Table 3.5: Sources of secondary information

Internal	External
Sales, accounting and inventory records	Government statistics
Profit and Loss statements	Trade association reports.
Reports from salesforce or distributors	Journals, trade magazines and newspapers
Marketing information systems	Competitor annual reports
Digital data such as google analytics	Websites and specialist blogs
Customer complaints	Industry-wide research published by commercial research companies such as Mintel, Euromonitor and Keynote

There are numerous sources of freely available external research. The University library or an online search can be a useful starting point. Many sources seem to be relevant but need filtering for clarity, reliability and accuracy using the following ADORE questions:

- **Authors** – Who wrote this? Was it peer reviewed? Does the writer (or their sponsor) have an agenda that affects accuracy? For example, reports commissioned by the sugar industry may play down the negative consequences of consumption whilst concentrating on economic benefits of their sector.

- **Date** – Data age. In fast-moving markets, even relatively recent information may be irrelevant. Competitor and environmental changes affects the relevance of published data. Many books are dated on publication.

- **Opinion or Fact**? Is data based on objective evidence or has detail been omitted to present a point of view?

- **Rigour** – How was the evidence obtained? Was the sample representative and sufficiently large? Was research systematically undertaken and without bias?

- **Extent** –What is the work's scope? How relevant is the data? Does it cover the appropriate sector or region? Is coverage broad or specific?

It can be difficult to know the source, authors, provenance and date of some internet sources.

■ Primary research

Although secondary research may give a complete picture, it is usually just a starting point. Bespoke, primary research (also known as field research) provides up-to-date, relevant data and is designed to solve specific research questions, using multiple tools.

Research methods

The choice of research tool depends on objectives and resources available. Companies use a myriad of methods (Creusen, Hultink & Eling, 2012) but questionnaires are still the most popular.

■ Questionnaires

Creating a questionnaire is challenging and even professional companies sometimes get it wrong. Taking care over the question order and flow, along with the wording ensures internal validity, i.e. the questionnaire is clearly asking what is required to provide valid results.

Question order and flow

Opening questions should be broad and followed by more specific questions to logically smooth flow. This helps respondents focus and is known as the **funnel technique**.

- Categorical or classification questions such as age, income and gender are intrusive and asked at the end of the survey, when respondents are at ease. However, if a particular type of respondent is sought, classification questions are posed up front to avoid wasting respondent and interview time.

- **Skip** statements, such as "Go to question x", guide the respondent to essential and relevant question depending on their previous responses.

Question type

Open questions allow the respondent to answer in their own words and provide richer detail, whereas **closed questions** provide pre-defined categories. Closed questions take less time to answer and easier to analyse but restrict respondent choice. Providing an 'other' category allows the listing of additional responses.

Scaling questions use a five or seven-point scale to elicit strength of feeling. **Likert scales** allow the respondent to show their level of agreement with a statement and **semantic differential scales** ask respondents to match their beliefs with statements provided. Ranking scales permit the placing of factors in order of importance. For a more detailed review of question types see Taheri et al. (2014).

Exercise: Comparing scales

Likert scales

Q. Choosing my university programme was very difficult

A. Strongly disagree ○ ○ ○ ○ ○ Strongly agree

Semantic differential scale

Q. Choosing my university programme was:

A. Very easy ○ ○ ○ ○ ○ Very difficult

Consider these scales: Will these two scales produce the same data?

Questionnaires should be concise so that they take less than 10 minutes to complete although technical surveys may take much longer as respondents should be interested in the subject matter.

Question wording

Questionnaire wording requires great care, and qualitative research can help to develop questions and categories for inclusion. Surveys administered in person allow rephrasing of misunderstood questions but this is not possible with self-completion questionnaires, including those distributed online.

- Keep language simple and avoid jargon.

- Define all terms to avoid misinterpretation, e.g. regular publication readership is defined as "seen or read" on at least x days in the previous week.

- Consider current attitudes and recent behavior only. Ask about behaviour over the previous week or month, as annual spending estimates are usually incorrect.

- Questions must be essential. It is tempting to pose additional questions but overlong surveys induce fatigue. Use skip questions where appropriate to accelerate completion.

- Avoid questions that lead the respondent to answer in a particular way.

- Ensure that instructions are clear – indicate where a respondent can choose more than one category.

- Keep questions relevant and interesting.

- Rotate answers to avoid question order bias.

- Use a "prefer not to say "category for personal questions such as age or income

- Ensure that categories are unique and do not overlap.

To overcome these pitfalls the questionnaire should be piloted between 5-10 respondents and refined where necessary.

■ In-depth interviews

In-depth interviews are semi-structured or unstructured and administered face-to-face, by phone or on-line. An interview guide ensures that conversations are on track whilst allowing free-flowing responses. In-depth interviews provide rich, detailed information but from a small number of people. Transcription is a lengthy process but necessary to ensure validity. Such techniques are common in business-to-business environments where discussion is technically detailed.

■ Focus groups

Focus groups discover opinions or gain initial feedback to marketing ideas such as reactions to advertising or brainstorming for new product ideas. Typical features of focus group discussions are:

- 5-8 participants to encourage balanced interaction in a relaxed environment.

- Participants are recruited to ensure a variety of responses but are not too dissimilar so they are able to discuss ideas freely.

- A skilled moderator to ensure that no individual dominates the conversation (Henderson, 1992).

- An interview guide is prepared, but the conversation is fluid to encourage group members to contribute new ideas.

- Groups run on-line, via Skype or through bulletin boards allow flexible, 'synchronous' or 'asynchronous' discussion across time zones and locations.

- Results not representative due to small numbers.

As with most qualitative research, data from group discussions may not be generalised. Focus groups provide swift, initial reactions and may highlight emerging concepts to be included in later research using other methods.

■ Observation

Observation helps discover customer behaviour during authentic situations such as shopping, navigating websites or using products.

- Observation may be qualitative or quantitative. Google analytics and EFTPOS (electronic funds transfer at point of sale) information provided by retailers is observed quantitative behaviour data and extremely insightful.

- Observation may be undertaken virtually or in the physical environment.

- Participant observation takes place when the observer accompanies the respondent during activity. In covert observation, the subject is unaware that they are under observation. This raises data protection and ethical questions.

- Mystery shopper exercises. Here the researcher acts as an ordinary customer and reports on service quality, process, and retail layouts.

■ Ethnographic research

Ethnography requires researchers to immerse themselves into the lives of the respondents to discover behaviour within natural settings, activities and family routines. It is a form of participant observation but is occasionally covert. It is regularly undertaken in conjunction with in-depth and semi-structured interviews and often recorded (videography).

- Outcomes from ethnography include slice of life advertising based around typical families.

- Consumers can be encouraged to build their own ethnography by recording and generating their own data to show how they live

- Is useful in unearthing detail that a consumer may not report with other methods.

- **Netnography** includes observation and evaluation of on-line activity such as participation in blogs and social media.

Projective techniques

Projective techniques use unstructured stimuli, objects or situations to elicit an individual's world perception. Table 3.6 provides some examples.

Table 3.6: Projective techniques

Technique	Example	
Sentence completion	When I am searching for a holiday on line I feel………………..	
Word association	What words come to mind when thinking about taking a long-haul flight?	
Cartoon/ picture completion		What is happening in this picture?
Fantasy situations	Describe your perfect holiday if money and time was no object.	
Drawing	Draw a picture showing how you feel when returning from holiday.	

Quantitative methods are scientific and highly valued but qualitative research is increasingly popular for its ability to delve more deeply and elicit findings that do not arise from quantitative methods.

In pursuit of customer understanding, research is using ever-more sophisticated techniques such as neuroscience, biometrics and digital observation methods (web analytics). In reality, many projects use more than one method.

Experimentation

Experimental methods have much to offer a market researcher but they are under-utilised in practice, except within the on-line environment where every activity is a potential experiment, providing data for learning about consumer behaviour. Research under controlled experimental conditions establishes causation between variables and investigates whether a dependent variable (such as customer demand) is affected by a change in an independent variable (such as price, advertising message or colour of packaging). A true experiment requires test units and treatments to be randomly assigned to the experimental groups and this ensures that observed changes are caused by manipulations to independent variable(s). Extraneous elements are constant so that they do not affect the experiment. Marketing experiments in artificial, laboratory type environments run as rigged up shops (where extraneous factors are negligible) monitor consumer reactions to price or shelf position. Alternatively, a field experiment takes place in a real-world environment such as a shopping mall, where the consumer is subject to a host of other influences that are uncontrollable by the researcher.

Table 3.7: Comparing laboratory and field experiments. Adapted from Zikmund, 2015

Laboratory experiments	Field experiment
Artificial environment	Naturalistic, real-life setting
Limited interference from extraneous environment	Many extraneous variables
High control	Lower control
Short term	Longer term possible
Respondent aware that they are part of an experiment	Respondent may not be aware that they are part of an experiment
Higher internal validity	Higher external validity

Laboratory experiments have higher internal validity as researchers can be reasonably sure that outcomes are due to manipulations made in the experiment. They may not have external validity, as changes observed in an artificial environment may not be replicated in the field. In part, this is because participants act differently when they know they are taking part in an experiment and extraneous elements (such as changes in competitor activity) are absent.

The A/B split test is commonly used in marketing, particularly for testing advertising treatments or pricing exercises. It is the basis for on-line experimentation. The researcher randomly assigns participants into one of two (or more groups) and each group will be exposed to a different treatment. The researcher compares results to determine the most effective treatment. Consider these split test experiments for an airline:

- **Pricing** – Group A and B offered a different price for the same journey.
- **Pricing** – Group A offered price for whole journey with all the extras included; Group B sees same total price but with individual elements priced separately.
- **Message** – Group A exposed to message with price prominent; Group B message emphasises journey comfort.
- **Convenience** – Group A offered online booking; Group B must telephone.

■ Test marketing

A pop-up shop is a test market on a small scale, but a full test market requires a product launch supported with a fully integrated marketing communication campaign and retail listings.

Various cities, regions, countries or digital spaces that are deemed a microcosm of wider society are used in full test markets. New Zealand is a test market for the UK; Phoenix, Arizona is a well-used test market for US businesses, and media companies like Sky offer the opportunity to digitally reach a sample of customers reflecting the client's target market. Primary research supplements sales data obtained during the test market. It is essential to ensure that tests run long enough to give customers a chance to rebuy, otherwise product acceptance figures are distorted by those trying as a one-off novelty. Test marketing is expensive and risks competitors using spoiling tactics to affect results, but the benefits of testing a full marketing package in a natural, external environment are clear.

For a detailed discussion of experimentation and test marketing, refer to Babin & Zikmund (2015).

Ikea: Concept test

Ikea are testing a smaller store concept that bridges the gap between on-line and in-store shopping, and have chosen the market town of Norwich in the East of England to test the 'planning studio' concept. Customers will be able to order and collect goods ordered on-line and get expert advice on home furnishing. A limited range of take home today stock will be available, along with a café.

If this test of the satellite concept is successful, the idea is likely to be rolled out to other centres without easy access to a full Ikea store (Ikea, 2015).

■ Emerging methods

Interviews require consumers able to express responses accurately using words or other means. Answers are then subject to interpretation by the researcher. Consumers cannot always consciously express their feelings and may rationalise responses to reflect social norms. Emerging methods attempt to monitor changes in brain and bodily responses to various stimuli such as advertising or other experiences.

Neuroscience

Neuroscience techniques establish how the brain processes information and two emerging methods include:

■ **Electroencephalography (EEG).** This a non-invasive method and relatively inexpensive to employ. A worn device monitors the electrical activity of the brain surface whilst participating in an activity such as searching on-line, watching advertising, or choosing ingredients for a meal. Immediate monitored reactions are attributed to the stimulus, with some devices showing which part of the brain is activated.

■ **Functional Magnetic Resonance Imaging (fMRI).** This machine measures blood flows and provides an in-depth view of the brain. It is expensive and invasive, and the participant is enclosed, immobile in a tunnel-like machine. It can provide information on long-term memory formation, consumer trust and emotional responses to marketing stimuli, but it is not suitable for field experiments and has limited use.

Reports show that such methods are in use, but they are still inaccessible to smaller businesses. Samsung (Neff, 2016) have used neuroscience to devise advertisements that would appeal to rival Apple's customers.

Facial and eye tracking

Although eye tracking is not an entirely new technique, recently available technology has made it far more accessible. Eye cameras and specialist eye-tracking equipment on a fixed or mobile device observes consumer eye movements in natural surroundings. Wearable devices are now sufficiently portable to observe normal, daily behavior in real time, monitoring attraction, arousal and brand purchase in both digital and retail environments. Software has analysed small changes in facial expression on thousands of people and applies this knowledge to consumers engaged in different experiences, with automatic analysis of results.

Galvanic reponses

Unobtrusive technology monitors heart rate, stress, engagement and excitement. Slightly more sophisticated than a wearable Fitbit or similar device, galvanic measurements, monitored constantly, show embodied reactions throughout the consumer decision-making process.

Mars have tested facial responses and eye tracking on 110 advertisements to predict sales and the results were 78% accurate, compared to 58% for traditional survey based testing (Neff, 2016).

Carlsberg: Measuring customer response

Carlsberg, a European beverage company used ethnography and accompanied 250 people to bars and observed buying behaviour. Specially made eyeglasses monitored eye movement and instantly fed back results indicating the impact of point-of-sale design on buying. (Barda, 2015). What other ways can biometric methods such as eye tracking and galvanic responses can be used for research?

3

None of the above methods replace traditional approaches. They augment findings and delve more deeply into the minds and reactions of customers but are only accurate and useful if enough of the right people are included in the research. The following section considers the selection of research participants.

Selecting participants

Any sample should include opinions that represent as many of the chosen population as possible. Sampling aims to provide 'good enough' data in a cost-effective manner. Many sampling methods can typically be useful.

Example: Pollsters get it wrong

In 2015, the political pollsters wrongly predicted the result of the UK general election. This was not the first time that polls were inaccurate and the Market Research Society and the British Polling Council concluded that the methods used to recruit participants led to an unrepresentative sample and that the statistical adjustments made were not sufficient to counter the imbalance (Sturgis et al, 2016).

■   Probability sampling

This is the most accurate form of sampling because everyone in the chosen population has an equal chance or probability of selection.

Random sampling

Random sampling requires a full list (sampling frame) of the target population such as all adults, homemakers, current customers.. The list could be in the form of a map, or a database of individual or business names or zip codes. The choice is made systematically (so every nth name on the list is chosen) or truly randomised (simple random sampling), which is equivalent to drawing names from a hat but is now computer generated.

Stratified random sampling

The population is stratified or grouped according to criteria that potentially affect responses. For example, the database is sorted into groups of customers who exhibit different buying behavior (e.g. loyal versus non-loyal customers) and a random but equal sample taken from each of the strata.

Probability sampling requires the selected person to take part in the research even if this requires repeated contact attempts or travelling long distances.

■   Non-probability sampling

For small research projects with no current sampling frame and tight resources non-probability methods are used. This is a typical approach for commercial market research.

Convenience sampling

Easily accessible respondents are chosen (e.g. whilst shopping in a mall). Although convenient, this method is neither random nor objective (Denscombe, 2003). **Snowball sampling** gathers respondents through friend's recommendations via social network and is a popular method of convenience sampling (Baltar and Brunet, 2012).

Quota sampling

To improve representativeness, it helps to establish a sample quota to include certain groups and replicate the proportion found in the total population, along criteria such as gender, socio-economic status, full or part time working.

What are the limitations of using your own social media to recruit samples for your research?

■   How big should a sample be?

A survey should attempt to capture all shades of opinion. If every customer has similar views, then a sample of one is all that is required. A census (everyone in the target population) gives maximum confidence, but is not efficient. Suggestions that a notional 100 respondents is big enough does not consider any comparisons between groups when the total number is split (e.g. male versus female opinions) and the initial sample is reduced to 50 within each subgroup. Splitting further, by age, reduces the subgroup sample and inferences become unreliable. Free survey software regularly limits the numbers of questionnaires that can be distributed. To summarise, sample size depends on population variability, the budget and time available. Generally bigger is better.

For qualitative research, the number of participants is comparatively low. this research seeks depth, rather than breadth of opinion. Nevertheless, careful recruitment of participants is essential so that the research captures the views of influential target audiences.

Data collection

Data collection can take place in person, with an interviewer present or remotely through a self-completion questionnaire. Each approach to data collection has its own benefits and pitfalls and these are summarised in Table 3.7.

Table 7: Data collection methods compared. Adapted from Bryman (2008)

	Face-to-face	Telephone/video chat	Online/mobile	Postal
Speed of response	Immediate	Immediate but call backs may be necessary	Medium - allow 1 week	Lengthy - allow 3 weeks
Relative cost	high	medium	low	medium
Qualified respondents	yes	yes	no	no
Response rate	best			worse
Reach	low	low	medium	medium
Suitable questions	open and closed	open and closed	some inter-activity can be programmed	mainly closed
Visual and aural stimuli	yes	Visual - video chat; Aural - telephone and video chat	yes	static visual
Probing possible	yes	yes	some possible	no
Interviewer bias	yes	yes	no	no
Non-response bias	least likely			most likely

Personal, face-to-face interviews give higher response rates, permit the qualification of respondents (i.e. the respondent is genuine) and allow prompting, explanation and response clarification. Personal interviews are most likely to be subject to both interviewer bias (where the researcher's manner inhibits or influences the respondent) and social desirability bias, where socially acceptable responses are given to please the interviewer. It is easier for a respondent to answer questions of a more sensitive nature via remote means. Note these additional points:

- E-mail methods share characteristics of both postal and on-line methods.

- Reminders and callbacks where needed to ensure a robust sample.

- Responses written or digitally recorded (video or just sound), subject to participant permission.

- On-line and mobile surveys layouts to be checked for suitability for every device.

Survey fatigue is a problem and it is important to engage participants so that they genuinely want to take part and provide carefully thought-out answers. Incentives can help but may distort the sample to include reward seekers, rather than those with genuine interest. To get sufficient response it may be necessary to undertake a multi-mode (perhaps on-line and some face-to-face) and multi-method piece of research (using some qualitative and quantitative methods) to provide full understanding.

Turning data into information

Data by itself is not information. Once systematically analysed, error-free and presented in a format understood by its intended audience, data becomes information.

■ Quantitative data analysis

1 Check every response. Exclude incomplete questionnaires or retrace respondents.

2 Code each respondent, question and answer category for analysis using relevant software such as SPSS.

3 Enter data and double check data entry.

4 Discard missing cases.

5 Undertake descriptive analysis considering frequency counts, ratios and means for each question.

6 Compare results between groups. Highlight relationships using relevant statistic techniques.

A variety of graphical tools (e.g. pie and bar charts, histograms and graphs) alongside narrative explanation enlivens reporting but researchers should only present relevant data. The analysis should highlight:

- Limitations of method, question design.
- Statistical significance of the results.
- Representativeness of the sample.
- If results can be generalised.
- If there is confidence that results are reproducible.
- Typical pitfalls when reporting quantitative data include
- Assuming cause and effect. Correlation between two sets of data does not always mean that one causes the other.
- Small sample sizes (particularly in subgroups).
- Failure to look at the result distribution and impact of outliers on the mean.

■ Qualitative data analysis

Qualitative data takes time to transcribe and analyse, even using specialist software such as NVivo. Qualitative research produces narrative (transcripts of interviews or reports of an observation), photographic and pictorial evidence. Data is reviewed several times until similarities, differences and themes emerge and evidence is sorted into thematic examples. Typically, video clips and sample quotes illustrate main points and enrich findings, but without exclusion of context. Objectivity is more achievable when data is analysed by an experienced qualitative researcher and when additional people are invited to independently review the evidence.

The research report

The report or presentation should reduce the volume of data into information, true to findings and understandable to the audience. Every piece of information should pass the 'so what?' and 'now what?' tests, so that only significant and relevant data is highlighted and less relevant detail moved to an appendix. For both quantitative and qualitative research, it is important that the research is not subject to confirmation bias when highlighted evidence concentrates on findings that confirm existing beliefs. More complex and detailed statistical techniques such as regression analysis or significance testing do not usually appear in the main report but are provided separately in the appendices.

Following completion, a debrief, comprising of a written report, presentation, or combination, is given to the marketing teams and senior executives who use the findings to finalise decisions or commission further research as required.

Figure 3.4: Typical research report

☐ Title page

☐ Contents

☐ Executive Summary

☐ Research background and objectives

☐ Methodology

   ■ Research design

   ■ Sample choice

   ■ Analysis

☐ Findings

☐ Recommendations

☐ Appendices

Being ethical

All primary research relies on the goodwill of respondents and is designed to be engaging, so that a good number and range of respondents take part and the research avoids non-response bias. The collection of data involving human respondents undoubtedly raises ethical issues. Research is intrusive and the researcher must:

■ Be honest about the purpose and uses of research.

■ Protect anonymity of participants and confidentially of their views.

■ Make it clear that taking part is optional and that opt-out is possible.

■ Be truthful when reporting methods, results and project limitations.

■ Be sensitive to cultural needs.

■ Do not use research as an excuse to make sales. This unethical behaviour is known as **sugging** or **frugging** (in the case of fundraising).

Organisations commissioning and carrying out research also have a responsibility to keep researchers safe. New methods raise ethical questions, particularly about privacy (Ochoa and Savin, 2015; Nunan and Di Domenico, 2013). The potential of on-line observation is clear, but ethical and legal frameworks have not kept pace. Smartphones, tablets and other connected technologies generate large volumes of personal information and fears that personal data will be used to compromise privacy reduces the willingness to participate, ultimately leading poorer decision making.

Ultimately, ethical research is evidence-based and performed in a systematic, transparent way that restricts bias and clearly states limitations. Only this will produce good evidence to inform decision-making and lead to marketing strategies that truly create highest customer value.

Further reading

Kozinets, R.V. (2002). The field behind the screen: using netnography for marketing research in online communities, *Journal of Marketing Research*, **39** (Feb), 61-72.

How to undertake netnography.

Van Hal. G, Van Roosbroeck. S, Vriesacker. B, et al. (2012) Flemish adolescents' perceptions of cigarette plain packaging: a qualitative study with focus group discussions. BMJ Open; 2: e001424. http://bmjopen.bmj.com/

Focus groups being used to research packaging.

Neff, J. (2016). Neuromarketing exits 'hype cycle,' begins to shape TV commercials. *Advertising Age*, April 19. http://adage.com/article/cmo-strategy/neuromarketing-exits-hype-cycle-begins-shape-tv-ads/303582/

Discussion of how neuroscience is becoming more mainstream

Treacy, B. (2015). Big data-science fact or fantasy, The Marketer. Available at http://www.themarketer.co.uk/analysis/in-depth/big-data-science-fact-or-fantasy/

Big data usage and potential.

References

AMA (2004). Definition of Marketing Research. https://www.ama.org/AboutAMA/Pages/Definition-of-Marketing.aspx

Babin, B.J. and Zikmund, W. G (2015). *Exploring Marketing Research*. Cengage. USA

Baltar, F and Brunet, J. (2012). Social research 2.0: virtual snowball sampling method using Facebook, *Internet Research*, **22**. (1), 57 – 74

Barda, T. (2011). Carlsberg. *The Marketer*, CIM. 23 March 2011.

Bryman, A. (2008). *Social Research Methods*, Oxford, OUP

Creusen, M.E.H.; Hultink, E-J. & Eling, K. (2012). Choice of consumer research methods in the front end of new product development, *International Journal of Market Research*. **55** (1), 81-104.

Denscombe, M. (2003). *The Good Research Guide: For Small-Scale Social Research Projects*, (2nd ed.). London: Open University Press.

ESOMAR (2001). How to Commission research. Available at https://www.esomar.org/uploads/public/knowledge-and-standards/codes-and-guidelines/ESOMAR_Code-and-Guidelines_HowToCommissionResearch.pdf [Accessed March 2015].

Henderson, N. (1992). Trained moderators boost the value of qualitative research, *Marketing Research.* (June), 4 (2), 20-23

ICC/ESOMAR (2015) International Code on Market and Social Research. https://www.esomar.org/uploads/public/knowledge-and-standards/codes-and-guidelines/ICCESOMAR_Code_English_.pdf

Ikea (2015) IKEA to test a new retail format to get closer to UK customers. Press release 24 June 2015. http://www.ikea.com/gb/en/about_ikea/newsitem/order-collection-points

Neff, J. (2016). Neuromarketing exits 'hype cycle,' begins to shape TV commercials. *Advertising Age* (April). http://adage.com/article/cmo-strategy/neuromarketing-exits-hype-cycle-begins-shape-tv-ads/303582/

Nunan, D. and Di Domenico, M.L. (2013). Market research and the ethics of big data. *International Journal of Market Research.* **55**(4), 2-13.

Ochoa, C. and Savin, F. (2015). The Tracker, the technology that will change market research. https://rwconnect.esomar.org/the-tracker-the-technology-that-will-change-market-research/ [Accessed March 2015]

PwC (2016). Business of Evidence 2016. As assessment of the size and impact of the UK research and evidence market, commissioned by the Market Research Society. http://www.p wc.co.uk/assets/pdf/business-of-evidence-report.pdf

Stone, M. and Desmond, J. (2010). *Marketing Fundamentals*, Edinburgh: Heriot-Watt Management Programme.

Sturgis, P. Baker, N. Callegaro, M. Fisher, S. Green, J. Jennings, W. Kuha, J. Lauderdale, B. and Smith, P. (2016). Report of the Inquiry into the 2015 British general election opinion polls, London: Market Research Society and British Polling Council.

Taheri, B., Lu, L., and Valantasis (2014) Gathering quantitative data, in K. O'Gorman, K & R. MacIntosh, R. (eds) *Research Methods for Business Management,* Oxford: Goodfellows Publishers Ltd.

4 Understanding the Consumer

Rodrigo Perez-Vega

Marketing efforts are designed with targeted consumers in mind, therefore understanding the mechanisms behind their behaviours as well as the different sub-processes involved in the decision making process is crucial for marketers. The way consumers take decisions affects all elements of the marketing mix, from the type of product, the pricing and how it is assessed, depending on the level of involvement or the decision making process involved. It is unlikely that the same effort is spent when choosing a fizzy drink as a choice of university. Similar considerations affect where to place a product. For example, impulse buying products (e.g. chewing gum, crisps, etc.) are located close to the cashier at the supermarket, and highly technical products are sold through outlets where appropriate advice is available. All marketing decisions are informed by our understanding of consumer behaviour and this chapter aims to cover some of the important models that help explain these behaviours.

The ABC model of attitudes

Developing opinions and forming dislikes and likes about everything around us are part of daily life. Opinions known as attitudes affect the way we live and the choices that we make. Attitudes can be defined as "a summary evaluation of an object or thought" (Vogel and Wanke, 2016:2). Attitudes can be positive or negative, or even uncertain. For example, it is not uncommon to have mixed feelings about what to order at a favourite restaurant, and this involves a series of attitudes towards different choices. Every attitude has three components, represented in the ABC model of attitudes developed by Allport (1935) and Table 4.1 exemplifies these three components for organic products:

Table 4.1: The ABC model of attitudes

Affective	Emotional reaction towards a target object (e.g. Feeling good about doing good to your body and to the environment by buying organic food)
Behavioural	Behavioural reaction towards a target object (e.g. Choosing organic products over non-organic ones).
Cognitive	Thoughts towards a target object (e.g. Analysing the benefits of buying organic products by reading the label and other information available online).

Every attitude has all three components; however, any particular attitude can be based on one of the components more than another. This means that each component could potentially answer the question: where does an attitude come from?

Attitudes are a central construct of well-established models that aim to explain behaviour, such as the theory of reasoned action or the theory of planned behaviour (Ajzen, 1991; Ajzen and Fishbein, 1980). These models have been extensively used to understand and predict behaviours in marketing and broader fields such as health, psychology, and economy. Broadly speaking, the theory of planned behaviour posits that behaviour is determined by intentions which are determined by attitudes (what we think about the action), subjective norm (what others think about a given action) and perceived behavioural control (how much we feel we are capable of performing the given action). For example, if my attitude towards Bentley cars is positive and everyone around has a Bentley (subjective norm) but I do not have the money needed to actually buy one (perceived behavioural control), my intentions to buy are diminished and purchase is unlikely in the near future. Alternatively, if my positive attitudes towards organic food are shared and I have the extra money needed to buy it and it is accessible to me, then the intention to buy is high. So attitude may affect behaviour but not necessarily predict it.

Can you think of other factors that influence consumer behaviour? Are there any limitations with the theory of planned behaviour by reflecting on how your own personal experience (e.g. choosing university buying a car or buying shampoo?

Decision-making: Choosing, using and disposing

The decision-making process describes the consumer going through several stages when purchasing a product. The process starts when the consumer identifies a problem and perceives that purchase of a good or service is a solution. They identify the available alternatives and evaluate them. The choice is made and the purchase will go ahead. Post-purchase, the consumer evaluates the decision. This process is often portrayed as a simple, linear process, with each stage following the previous. Figure 4.1 shows the process as circular, recognising that consumers gain experience during purchase and this influences future decision-making. Where the decision outcome is successful, the consumer is more likely to rebuy without going through the full process. Marketers can influence the consumer at each stage of decision making, initially by ensuring that the consumer is aware of the product and its benefits, and then providing stimuli for action. In addition they can encourage current customers to discuss positive experiences on blogs and review sites

Consumers continuously evaluate purchase choices and many experience uncertainty throughout each stage of the decision-making process. Uncertainty tends to be stronger when buying for the first time and the purchase is perceived to be risky. Uncertainty after purchase is known as *post-purchase dissonance*. In order to lessen dissonance the consumer may take a variety of actions.

Table 4.2: Overcoming dissonance

Action	Through
Return the purchase	Money back request (multiple reasons)
Elicit positive support from peers	Asking: What do you think about my new ....?
Justify the decision	Saying: I only bought it because it was so...cheap It was the only one available (In my size...) It had the best (feature)
Information search	Searching: Reviews Checking : guarantees and accompanying labels and literature Paying attention: Advertising, owners

Decision making does not end on purchase and consumers must also decide what to do with products for which they no longer want or have a use – keep, recycle or dispose? Options available for recycling have grown, with many opportunities to give away, swap or resell. So the consumer problem changes but the process of decision-making continues.

> What role can marketers play to influence each stage of the consumer decision making process and help them move quickly to purchase? Does marketing have any role to play post purchase?

Decision making is conceived as a rational, cognitive process, where thought and judgment precede choice. However, not all decisions are made rationally and the following section shows that consumer engagement and involvement levels affect decision making hierarchy.

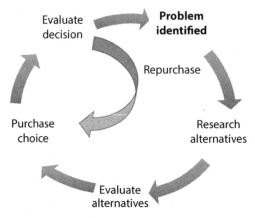

Figure 4.1: The systematic decision-making process

Consumer involvement and engagement

Two key factors that influence the application of consumer behaviour models are the levels of involvement and engagement that a consumer has towards a product. Products such as chewing gum are commonly used as examples of low involvement products and therefore prone to impulse buying behaviour. However, if we take into account a special condition (for example, allergy to an ingredient) the product can become high involvement. Conversely, a highly engaged consumer for fair trade products may engage in activities that typically go beyond purchasing behaviour for this type of products (Van Doorn et al., 2010), such as educating other consumers, participating in demonstrations in favour of fair trade and actively sharing related content on social media channels. Thus, the level of involvement and engagement can be moderating factors affecting the behavioural, affective and cognitive consumer outcomes.

■ Involvement

The level of involvement that consumers show towards a certain object (e.g. a product or brand) will affect perception and attitudes towards that object and the decision-making process. Involvement is defined as "a person's perceived relevance of the object based on their inherent needs, values and interests" (Zaichkowsky, 1985). Understanding the antecedent and consequences of involvement, as well as the different levels of involvement will help marketers design strategies to affect certain behaviours from consumers.

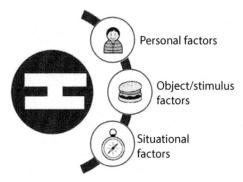

Figure 4.2: Antecedents of involvement

Three main factors drive involvement: personal, object or stimulus and situational factors (Figure 4.2). Personal factors can be expressed as the needs, interests and values that a person holds towards a particular object. For example, someone who is diabetic may need to consume sugar-free products and the level of involvement for food products is high. In terms of object or stimulus factors, this relates to the characteristics of the object of focus. For example, a product competes in a market with little differentiation (e.g. salt), then levels of involvement are low, regardless of branding efforts taken. Interestingly, we can see that even salt brands have made an effort to differentiate themselves by offering added value characteristics.

Visit an online grocery website and search for salt products. Try to identify how manufacturers are trying to differentiate themselves and therefore trigger higher levels of involvement from consumers of their products.

Finally, another antecedent of involvement relates to the situational factors that affect how consumers get involved with certain products. For example, if you are inviting someone you really care about for dinner, then the products that you buy are likely to be different from those in your normal shopping basket. It is because the situation is special and therefore higher levels of involvement will be triggered than when buying daily grocery items.

Levels of involvement

Involvement levels vary according to antecedents, and this in turn affects information processing for decision-making. This can range from inertia, where there is a complete lack of interest for a given object. The consumer is in this state when making decisions out of habit or when not motivated by evaluating alternatives.

At the other end of the spectrum there is a high level of involvement to products and people that the consumer really cares about.

There are some general influences that affect the level of individual involvement (Stone & Gronhaug, 1993). Goods purchased for the first time, higher priced goods and those that pose greater perceived performance, physical, psychological, time and social risk generally create greater involvement, as consumers are unsure about:

- Their buying goals
- Which product or brand is best for them
- Poor consequences arising from the purchase decision.

In the context of online environments, this is known as being in a state of flow. Here, the consumer's attention is focused on a given object (e.g. browsing YouTube videos, Facebook, playing Candy Crush or shopping online) and no longer notices anything happening around them, including time (Finneran and Zhang, 2005).

Hierarchy of effects

The level of involvement will influence the decision-making process. The ABC model can help explain how attitudes are formed and several theories place attitudes as a strong predictor of intentions and behaviour. According to Beatty and Kahle (1988) the starting point for the formation of attitudes can be any of the 3 components identified in the ABC model. Each component has different implications for marketers. This is known as the hierarchy of effects, and Beatty and Kahle (1988) identified four main sequences (Table 4.3).

■ Consumer engagement

Within the marketing and communication literature, the concept of engagement is rooted in five contextual dimensions: consumer engagement, customer engagement, advertising engagement, media engagement and general engagement (Gambetti and Guendalina, 2010). This section focuses on the consumer and will expand on consumer engagement and consider its distinctiveness and similarities with other constructs. Consumer engagement is a multidimensional concept (Brodie et al., 2013; Patterson et al., 2006), comprised of cognitive absorption, emotional dedication, behavioural vigour and interaction with the focal object. **Absorption** relates to the state of being fully concentrated, happy and deeply engrossed while playing the customer's role (overlapping conceptually with the concept of flow). **Dedication**, according to Patterson et al. (2006) refers

Table 4.3: Hierarchy effects and its implications for marketers

Hierarchy and sequence	Example and implications
High involvement Cognitions ⇨ affect ⇨ behaviour	e.g. purchasing a laptop Consumers will engage in a long search for information and develop an affective or emotional connection with the brands available. Marketers give priority to providing relevant information and strong branding.
Low involvement Cognitions ⇨ behaviour ⇨ affect	e.g. milk (repetitive buying) Consumers start with a set of beliefs about the consumption object, but not necessarily a lot of information asthis not important for decision making. Often cognition and the action are very close, and the emotional response is usually developed after consumption (i.e. I did like the milk purchased). Delivering the expected performance for the product at each time of consumption is important for marketers, a consistent taste over and over again.
Behavioural hierarchy Behaviour ⇨ cognitions ⇨ affect	e.g. impulse buying product (new chocolate bar at the counter) In this sequence the consumer acts first and then develops thoughts (beliefs) and feelings about the object. Only once the new chocolate bar has been eaten will the consumer decide if s/he likes it (or not)
Emotional hierarchy Affect ⇨ behaviour ⇨ cognitions	e.g. a special dress / suit Consumers act on emotional triggers. Feelings lead to behavioural outcomes and following the action the person will think it through and form attitudes toward the object. Consider a student looking for a dress or suit for a special occasion, such as graduation. In this context, they may decide to buy the product based on how they feel while wearing it – feeling smart or 'just right'. After purchase, they may start thinking about other uses for the purchase such as wearing to a job interview. They may consider if they have paid the right price. In this hierarchy, feelings trigger the formation of attitudes.

4

to the customer's sense of belonging and is similar to London et al.'s (2007) interpretation of engagement. **Vigour** refers to the customer's level of energy while interacting with an organisation, its employees, the brand or other customers. Vigour is also associated with the willingness to allocate time and effort to this interaction (giving it some similarities with commitment). Finally, **interaction** refers to the various interactions and connections formed between the customers, the organisation/brand as well as among other customers.

Based on the conceptualisation of consumer engagement as a multi-dimensional construct, can you think of a brand or product that you are highly engaged with?

Within marketing, and in particular in online settings, consumer engagement is becoming one of the most desirable behaviours since it can generate positive consequences. Marketing practitioners rank consumer engagement as one of the top priorities of online marketing activities (eMarketer, 2013; Calder et al., 2009). Among the reasons behind this interest are that consumer engagement is associated with consumer trust (Hollebeek, 2011), satisfaction and loyalty (Bowden, 2009) and commitment (Chan and Li, 2010). All are strong indicators of long-term sales, word-of-mouth and brand advocacy.

A behavioural perspective to consumer engagement is shared by marketing practitioners. Haven and Vittal (2008) argue that engagement measures include quantitative and qualitative metrics that can be collected both online and offline. They identify four components of engagement: involvement, interaction, intimacy, and influence. Common metrics used to measure consumer engagement online are shown in Table 4.4.

Table 4.4: Components and metrics for consumer engagement (Adapted from Haven and Vittal, 2008)

Component	Metric
Involvement	Number of visitors
	Time spent on the site
	Visits to physical store
Interaction	Click-through rates
	Online transactions
	In-store purchases
	Uploaded videos/pictures
Intimacy	Sentiment measurement
	Blog posts
	Blog comments
	Discussions in forums
Influence	Brand awareness
	Loyalty
	Affinity
	Repurchase
	Satisfaction ratings.

The decision making centre

Discussion so far has centred around the assumption that customers and consumers are one and the same but in Chapter 1 it was suggested that other influential roles affect the decision-making process and that the consumer or end user is not always the customer. Within a family, parents are the customers who will purchase household products, food, toys, or leisure activities, but all family members, including the children, will influence their choice. Children are highly influential across many category choices and may teach parents about the consumption and use of technology products (Ekstrom, 2007). Joint purchases may be more strongly influenced by one partner using bargaining and reasoning to increase their affect.

■ Business to business decision making

Within an organisation, the number of individuals with influential roles is even greater. Marketers must understand the requirements and determine the most appropriate marketing mix for each 'customer' or member of the decision-making unit or buying centre.

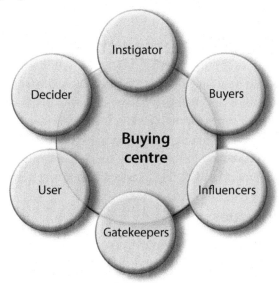

Figure 4.3: Roles in the buying centre

The instigator will be the first to identify the need for a new product or service. An operations manager, for example, considering a new piece of equipment to reduce waste or following up research about new processes. Users will, as the name suggests, be those operating or using the machinery and may be involved in testing it as part of a trial. Influencers include the chief engineer who produces technical specifications and the decider is possibly the financial director who concentrates on the return on investment and affordability of purchase. The buyer is often a purchasing professional whose role is to get the best price and terms. Gatekeepers control the amount of information available to the whole buying centre and the access given to the sales people. They are often overlooked but have great power in the buying centre. Consider, for example, the difficulties encountered by an airline trying to increase business class sales when a personal assistant will not pass on information about airline availability to their boss. The roles highlighted in Figure 4.3 are not fixed and may be shared across people in the organisation or held by the same individual. This makes it extremely difficult for those selling in a business-to-business context. Personal relationships may be needed with all members of the decision-making unit, and relevant benefits presented using the right medium and content. Engineers, for example, will expect technical information presented by someone with equal standing and expertise.

Business-to-business decision making is presumed to be fully rational but is very often emotional, and affective motives impact on the decision-making process, with purchase choices taken to reduce an individual's personal career risk, or based on personal relationships and trust.

Consumers: a global perspective

In a global context, marketers need to consider consumers from different cultural backgrounds, values and beliefs systems if they wish to develop inclusive and effective marketing plans for their products and services. Marketers face the challenges of highly diverse settings, or working in countries with a different cultural environment. This section introduces the concept of values and discusses some of the existing frameworks available to assess differences across cultures.

■ Consumer values

To understand consumer behaviour from a global perspective, marketers must understand the concept of values and different value systems. A value is a belief that one condition is preferable to an opposite one. It is important to note that people can have similar beliefs and behavioural outcomes (e.g. vegetarians) but their underlying beliefs system may be different. One person may decide to stop eating meat due to health concern values, whereas another may do so because of animal activism values. Across different cultures, consumers form and are exposed to different value systems that shape the way they behave.

Companies try to be sensitive about the values held by the people in the countries in which they operate. For example, it is well known that the role of women in different parts of the world differs in terms of rights and equality. In Saudi Arabia, women are not currently allowed to drive or take on certain jobs, and there is gender segregation in most public spaces. Many of these behaviours are driven by the social values held by the country, and not necessarily by laws (Sherman, 2016). Taking this into consideration, in 2012 IKEA airbrushed the women that appeared in their catalogue in an attempt to comply with the value system of that country. Interestingly, this caught the attention of the media and IKEA customers around the world and the company back-tracked from this practice arguing that was against IKEA's values (McCabe, 2012).

4

Figure 4.4: IKEA's catalogue in Saudi Arabia (left), and in the US (right). Source: Sherman, 2016

Think about… If you were the marketing manager for IKEA Saudi Arabia, would you have acted differently? Would this be getting the same level of attention if a Saudi furniture company was adding women in their catalogues for their UK branch?

■ Hofstede's cultural dimensions

Cultural differences are also found at organisational/national level. One of the most prominent studies conducted across multiple countries in this matter is Hofstede's model of national culture (Hofstede et al., 1990). The model consists of six cultural dimensions, and each represents independent preferences for one state over another that distinguish between countries.

Power distance The extent to which the less powerful powerful members of a society accept and expect power to be distributed unequally.	**Individualism vs collectivism** Preference for a loosely-knit social framework, where individuals are expected to take care of only themselves and their immediate family. Compared to collectivist nations.	**Masculinity vs feminitiy** A preference for achievement, heroism, assertiveness and material rewards for success. Its opposite, femininity, prefers cooperation, modesty, caring for the weak and quality of life.
Uncertainty avoidance The degree to which the members of a society feel uncomfortable with uncertainty and ambiguity.	**Long-term vs short-term orientation** Societies scoring low on this dimension prefer to maintain time-honoured traditions and norms while viewing societal change with suspicion.	**Indulgence vs restraint** Indulgent societes allow relatively free gratification of basic and natural human drives related to enjoying life and having fun. Restraint, the opposite means that a society supresses gratification and regulates it through strict social norms.

Figure 4.5: The six dimensions of national culture (Adapted from Hofstede, 2016)

Hofstede's cultural dimensions and implications for marketers

Understanding cultural differences using Hofstede's framework can be of value to a marketer managing brands in different countries. Consider a brand of watches being sold in both the UK and Malaysia. Using Hofstede's framework, the UK would be a more individualistic society and ultimate decision making would be personal, based on the information available to that individual, even though some family and friends may be consulted. Malaysia has a lower level of individualism in comparison and potential buyers are likely to give credence to the opinion and knowledge of their social networks and confer widely before making a purchase decision.

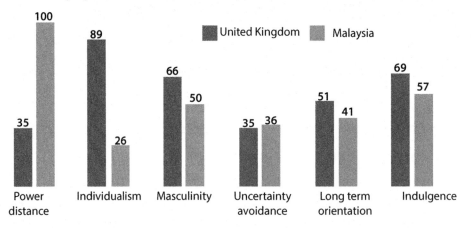

Figure 4.6: Applying Hofstede's six cultural dimensions – UK and Malaysia. Adapted from Hofstede (2016).

Consider how collective or individualistic decision-making will affect the marketing of a product.

Islamic marketing

Muslims are the fastest growing religious group in the world, accounting for just over 23% of the global population in 2010 (Pew Research Centre, 2015). In the UK, Muslims represented 4.5% of the total population at 2.6 million (Office for National Statistics, 2011). It is interesting to note that despite the fact that Muslims as a religious group have existed for centuries, actively engaging in consumption and trade, the interest in the relationship between Islam and marketing is only now of growing interest (Özlem, 2011). Marketing scholars are now considering Islamic marketing beyond 'halal' food and Islamic banking. Wilson (2012) argues that Muslims, like any other consumer segment, love fashion, entertainment, cosmetics and holidays, yet they also exhibit unique and identifiable homogenous traits. To fully understand Islamic marketing, it is necessary to be aware of the principles of Muslim practices and how this translates into marketing practice. Table 4.5 summarises these principles and shows the level of adoption of these practices and their effect on how companies and marketers react.

Table 4.5: Principles of Muslim practices and acts (Adapted from Alserhan,2015)

Halal or permissible comprises of three levels	*Wajib* or duty Failure to perform these duties is a sin (e.g. being honest and transparent)
	Mandoob or likeable Not performing these acts is not a sin (e.g. being helpful or going the extra mile).
	Makrooh or despised/ not preferable Engaging in makrooh does not result in a sin unless it leads to one (e.g. divorce).
Mushtabeh or doubted	Acts that a Muslim should avoid because they might be Haram or may lead to Haram.
	Saudi Arabia clerics issued a fatwa, which is a religious edict that warns people from playing Pokémon Go. This is because parents may use the game to punish and reward their children, while adults could gamble money whilst playing the game (The National, 2016).
Haram or not permissible	All acts condemned explicitly or implicitly in the Islamic religion.

4

There are different levels in which companies and marketers can engage in Islamic marketing. Wilson (2012) identifies six levels of adoption of Islamic marketing practices among marketers and organisations present in Islamic markets (Figure 4.7). At the lowest level, organisations follow the cultural values of their home countries, and disregard completely the values and customs of the Muslim population. At the top of the pyramid, we have Sharia'ah compliant marketers, who follow the practices of Islam at both personal and organisational level.

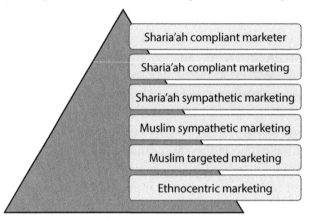

Figure 4.7: Levels of adoption Islamic Marketing practices. Source: Wilson (2012)

Companies demonstrating different levels of adoption of Islamic marketing practices in the UK are growing. Retailer Selfridges has extended opening hours before and during Ramadan, whilst Westfield shopping mall in London has set up prayer rooms and Arabic-speaking concierges (Ilyas, 2015). Several restaurants (e.g. KFC, Nando's, selected Subway stores) and supermarkets sell halal ranges to cater for this increasingly important market segment (Henley, 2014). However, companies implementing Sharia'ah compliant marketing are usually found in countries where Islam accounts for the majority of the population's religion.

Online brand communities and reference groups

Involvement in a brand community is extremely common globally. Brand community is defined as "specialized, non-geographically bound community, based on a structured set of social relations among admirers of a brand (Muniz and O'Guinn, 2001) and might include a community that follows brands on Twitter or Facebook, or a blogger on Instagram. The value that marketers see in being part of or managing brand communities is that they provide a direct channel of communication between the consumer and the brand. This enables business to learn about consumer perceptions, and collaborate with loyal consumers of the brand

Case study: UBER and Careem react to a fire in Dubai Marina

Careem dates back to 2012, when the company was started by Magnus Olsson and Mudassir Sheikha, former consultants at McKinsey & Company. The app operates in and has offices across 14 cities in the Middle East. The company was born in Dubai, and since its creation has been competing face-to-face against its Californian nemesis, UBER, which had been started in 2009 to create a solution to the horrible taxi problems in San Francisco, and had decided to make Dubai the 44th city to join their network in 2013.

On the 20th of July 2016, a fire started at the Sulafa Tower in the vibrant Dubai Marina. As a response to this fire, both UBER and Careem offered support. UBER removed surge pricing, a mechanism that multiplies the price of a ride whenever there is high demand. The reaction to the same situation by the team at Careem was slightly different; they went the extra mile by offering free rides to anyone using the app from Dubai Marina.

Discussion questions

1 What level of adoption of Islamic marketing practices do you think each of the two companies has?

2 Do you think that higher levels of Islamic marketing practices (i.e. top of the pyramid in Figure 4.7) can be a source of competitive advantage outside Muslim countries? Why?

to develop enhanced product offerings (Franke and Shah, 2003; McAlexander et al., 2002). Muniz and Shau (2005) found brand communities influence their members' evaluations and actions. Other evidence suggests that brand communities contribute to the dissemination of information (Brown et al., 2007, 2003; Jin et al., 2009) and foster consumer engagement (Alversia, 2013; Brodie et al., 2011; Gummerus and Liljander, 2012; Lee et al., 2011). In terms of marketing outcomes, online brand communities are effective tools for influencing sales in both company-owned and independent websites (Adjei et al., 2010).

There are many different types of communities; Lesser et al. (2009) suggest a classification based on the purpose of the community (Table 4.6). Some communities are created with underlying utilitarian purpose: to sell and buy products (e.g. local groups to facilitate buying and selling such as Freecycle and eBay). These are communities of transaction. Other communities are based on common interests; a good example of this would be The Student Room forum, an online community where university students can discuss a wide range of topics with an underlying interest around university life. Other communities such as Second Life or the SIMS are commonly used by consumers regardless of their age range. Users can create and adopt completely new personalities and roles, and a strong sense of belonging is also present. Other examples include online gaming including World of Warcraft, where the global online community gathers with the initial intent to settle in an imaginary world called Durotar.

Table 4.6: Community types (Adapted from Lesser et al, 2009)

Communities of transaction Facilitates the buying and selling of products and services, as well as the exchange of information for purchase decision.	**Communities of interest** A group of people interested in a specific topic of interest. Exchange can occur in terms of services, products and information, but focuses on the area of interest.
Communities of fantasy Allows users to create a new personality, environment or story. Users take on their desired roles that may be distinct from their offline environment role.	**Communities of relationship** Communities built around intense personal experiences, often anonymous with masked identities. Examples might include support groups for sufferers from a particular illness.

Are you a member of Facebook for your course or an interest group? Do you follow any brands on Twitter? Are you following a fashion or food blogger on Instagram? If you answered yes to any of these questions, then you are already part of an online brand community. What type of community is it? Are you actively engaged in the community? If so why or why not?

Online brand community influence is strongly dependent on how the consumer perceives the community. The concept of reference group becomes relevant to understand this effect. Reference groups can be defined as "an actual or imaginary individual or group conceived of having significant relevance upon an individual's evaluations, aspirations, or behaviour" (Park and Lessig, 1977:102). Consumers use others as a source of information to make meaning of the world and shape their own beliefs and the influence is stronger when others share the same beliefs or are similar to the consumer in certain relevant dimensions (Escalas and Bettman, 2005). Different types of reference groups can moderate the effect that the group has over certain behaviour (Table 4.7).

Table 4.7: Types of reference groups (Adapted from White and Dahl, 2006)

Membership groups	Usually these are groups an individual currently belongs to, identifies with, and feels psychologically involved with. e.g. Family, peers, Weight watchers, Chartered Institute of Marketing, Pokémon Go groups.
Aspirational groups	Positive groups that the individual identifies with, is attracted to and the individual aspires to be member of. e.g., celebrities such as from Made in Chelsea, but also can be groups that a consumer may realistically join and work towards this effect.
Avoidance groups	Groups that an individual wish to avoid being associated with and does not feel identified with, e.g. 'nerds', a certain football team fan group, Star Wars vs Star Trek fans, etc.

Consider the last time that you were looking for ideas to go and dine out in town. Whom did you ask for advice? It is very likely that you relied on friends or that you went online and read reviews. How did you weigh the advice from all these different sources of information? Was one friend with similar tastes to you more influential? Now think about online reviews. Did you pay attention to the name and gender of the reviewer? Were you looking for social cues to understand if the person reviewing a restaurant is in a similar situation to you? Did you disregard reviews from other types of people?

Summary

This chapter has considered some of the influences on consumer including attitudes, values and culture. It shows that the typical decision-making hierarchy is fluid and that decisions are affected by involvement. They are not always led by a cognitive recognition that a problem exists. Decisions may be made individually but more often than not, the process is influenced by others including social reference groups or members within a buying centre. Marketers need to understand and respond to these complex influences and create full value for all involved.

Further reading

Branthwaite, A., Patterson, S., 2011. The power of qualitative research in the era of social media. *Qualitative Market Research: An International Journal*, **14**, 430–440.

References

Adjei, M.T., Noble, S.M. and Noble, C.H. (2010). The influence of C2C communications in online brand communities on customer purchase behaviour. *Journal of the Academy of Marketing Science*, **38**, 634–653.

Ajzen, I. (1991). The theory of planned behaviour. *Organizational Behaviour and Human Decision Processes*, **50**, 179–211.

Ajzen, I. and Fishbein, M. (1980). *Understanding Attitudes and Predicting Social Behaviour*. Prentice-Hall.

Allport, G.W. (1935). Attitudes, in *A Handbook of Social Psychology*. Clark University Press, Worcester, MA, US, pp. 798–844.

Alserhan, D.B.A. (2015). *The Principles of Islamic Marketing*. Ashgate Publishing, Ltd.

Alversia, Y. (2013). *To Engage or Not: Identifying the Consumer-Based Antecedents of Online Consumer Engagement Behaviour* (SSRN Scholarly Paper No. ID 2331145). Social Science Research Network, Rochester, NY.

Beatty, S.E. and Kahle, L.R. (1988). Alternative hierarchies of the attitude-behaviour relationship: The impact of brand commitment and habit. *Journal of the Academy of Marketing Science* **16**, 1–10.

Bowden, J. (2009). Customer engagement: a framework for assessing customer-brand relationships: the case of the restaurant industry. *Journal of Hospitality Marketing & Management*, **18**, 574–596.

Brodie, R.J. and Hollebeek, L.D. (2011). Response: advancing and consolidating knowledge about customer engagement. *Journal of Service Research*, **14**, 283–284.

Brodie, R.J., Ilic, A., Juric, B. and Hollebeek, L. (2013). Consumer engagement in a virtual brand community: An exploratory analysis. *Journal of Business Research*, **66**, 105–114.

Brown, J., Broderick, A.J. and Lee, N. (2007). Word of mouth communication within online communities: Conceptualizing the online social network. *Journal of Interactive Marketing*, **21**, 2–20.

Brown, S., Kozinets, R.V. and Sherry, J.F. (2003). Teaching old brands new tricks: retro branding and the revival of brand meaning. *Journal of Marketing*, **67**, 19–33.

Calder, B.J., Malthouse, E.C. and Schaedel, U. (2009). An experimental study of the relationship between online engagement and advertising effectiveness. *Journal of Interactive Marketing*, **23**, 321–331.

Chan, KW. and Li, SY.(2010) Understanding consumer-to-consumer interactions in virtual communities: the salience of reciprocity. *Journal of Business Research*, **63**: 1033–40.

eMarketer (2013). Brands leverage influencers' reach on blogs, social, eMarketer. http://www.emarketer.com/Article/Brands-Leverage-Influencers-Reach-on-Blogs-Social/1009695 [Accessed 8.20.14].

Ekstrom, K.M (2007) Parental consumer learning or 'keeping up with the children'. *Journal of Consumer Behaviour*, **6**, 203-217.

Escalas, J.E. and Bettman, J.R. (2005). Self-construal, reference groups, and brand meaning. *Journal of Consumer Research*, **32**, 378–389.

Finneran, C.M. and Zhang, P. (2005). Flow in computer-mediated environments: promises and challenges. *Communications of the Association for Information Systems*, **15**, 82-101.

Franke, N. and Shah, S. (2003). How communities support innovative activities: an exploration of assistance and sharing among end-users. *Research Policy*, **32**, 157–178.

Gambetti, R.C. and Guendalina, G. (2010). The concept of engagement. A systematic analysis of the ongoing marketing debate. *International Journal of Market Research*, **52**, 801–826.

Gummerus, J. and Liljander, V. (2012). Customer engagement in a Facebook brand community. *Management Research Review*, **35**, 857–877.

Haven, B. and Vittal, S. (2008). Measuring engagement: Four steps to making engagement measurement a reality. In Forrester Research (ed.) *Measuring Customer Engagement*, pp. 2 -11.

Henley, J. (2014). Which restaurant chains have gone halal – and why? *The Guardian*, 7 May.

Hofstede, G. (2016). The 6 dimensions of national culture. https://geert-hofstede.com/national-culture.html [Accessed 7.20.16].

Hofstede, G., Neuijen, B., Ohayv, D.D. and Sanders, G. (1990). Measuring organizational cultures: a qualitative and quantitative study across twenty cases. *Administrative Science Quarterly*, **35**, 286–316.

Hollebeek, L. (2011). Exploring customer brand engagement: definition and themes. *Journal of Strategic Marketing*, **19**, 555–573.

Ilyas, S. (2015). How fashion is courting the Muslim pound. *The Guardian*. 2th June.

Jin, X.-L., Cheung, C.M.K., Lee, M.K.O. and Chen, H.-P. (2009). How to keep members using the information in a computer-supported social network. *Computers in Human Behavior*, **25**, 1172–1181.

Lee, D., Kim, H.S. and Jung, K.K. (2011). The impact of online brand community type on consumer's community engagement behaviours: consumer-created vs. marketer-created online brand community in online social-networking web sites. *Cyber Psychology, Behavior & Social Networking*, **14**, 59–63.

Lesser, E., Fontaine, M. and Slusher, J. (2009). *Knowledge and Communities*. Routledge.

London, B., Downey, G. and Mace, S. (2007). Psychological theories of educational engagement: A multi-method approach to studying individual engagement and institutional change. *Vanderbilt Law Review*, **60**(2): 455–481.

McAlexander, J.H., Schouten, J.W. and Koenig, H.F. (2002). Building brand community. *Journal of Marketing*, **66**, 38–54.

McCabe, M. (2012). Ikea apologises for deleting women from Saudi catalogue. http://www.campaignlive.co.uk/article/ikea-apologises-deleting-women-saudi-catalogue/1152795 [Accessed 7.20.16].

Muniz, A.M. and Schau, H.J. (2005). Religiosity in the abandoned Apple Newton brand community. *Journal of Consumer Research*, **31**, 737–747.

Muniz, A. and O'Guinn, T.C. (2001). Brand community. *Journal of Consumer Research*, **27**, 412–432.

Office for National Statistics (2011). 2011 Census data - Office for National Statistics. https://www.ons.gov.uk/census/2011census/2011censusdata [Accessed 7.20.16].

Özlem, S. (2011). Researching Islamic marketing: past and future perspectives. *Journal of Islamic Marketing*, **2**(3), 246-258.

Park, C.W. and Lessig, V.P. (1977). Students and housewives: Differences in susceptibility to reference group influence. *Journal of Consumer Research*, 4, 102–110.

Patterson, P., Yu, T., & De Ruyter, K. (2006). Understanding customer engagement in services. In *Advancing theory, maintaining relevance, proceedings of ANZMAC 2006 conference* (pp. 4–6). Brisbane.

Pew Research Center (2015). *Muslims and Islam: Key findings in the U.S. and around the world*. Pew Research Center.

Sherman, E. (2016). This is how oppressed women are in Saudi Arabia. *Fortune*, 17 March.

Stone, R. N. and Gronhaug, K. (1993). Perceived risk: Further considerations for the marketing discipline. *European Journal of Marketing*, **27**, 39–50.

Van Doorn, J. van, Lemon, K.N., Mittal, V., Nass, S., Pick, D., Pirner, P. and Verhoef, P.C. (2010). Customer engagement behavior: Theoretical foundations and research directions. *Journal of Service Research*, **13**, 253–266.

Vogel, T. and Wanke, M. (2016). *Attitudes and Attitude Change*. Psychology Press.

Wilson, J. (2012). The new wave of transformational Islamic marketing: Reflections and definitions. *Journal of Islamic Marketing*, **3**, 5–11.

Zaichkowsky, J.L. (1985). Measuring the involvement construct. *Journal of Consumer Research*, **12**, 341–352.

5 Market Segmentation, Targeting and Positioning

Lai Hong Ng

It is impossible to appeal to all customers in the marketplace who are widely dispersed with varied needs. Organisations that want to succeed must identify their customers and develop marketing mixes to satisfy their needs. This chapter considers the steps in the target marketing process, including how to divide markets into meaningful customer segments, evaluating each segment, deciding which segment(s) to target, and designing market offerings to be positioned in the minds of the selected target market.

The target marketing process

The target marketing process provides the basis for the selection of target market – a chosen segment of the market that an organisation wishes to serve. It consists of the three-step process of segmentation, targeting and positioning (Figure 5.1). Marketers utilise this process due to the prevalence of mature markets, greater diversity in customer needs, and its ability to provide focus for an organisation's marketing strategy and resource allocation among markets and products (Baines and Fill, 2014).

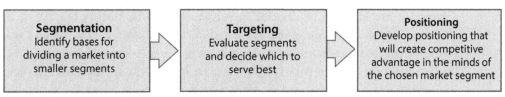

Figure 5.1: Steps in target marketing process. Adapted from Solomon et al. (2013).

The benefits of this process include the following:

- **Understanding customers' needs.** The target marketing process provides a basis for understanding customers' needs by grouping customers with similar characteristics together and for the selection of target market. Segmentation allows marketers more precisely to define customer needs and expectations. Marketers improve their understanding of how, why, and what influences customer buying. Being in touch with customers increases their responsiveness to changing needs and allowing better marketing programmes.

- **Suitable marketing mix.** This process allows marketers to understand customers' requirements of a target market and design a suitable marketing mix that meets their needs. Hence providing effective and efficient matching of organisational resources to targeted segments and promising greater return on marketing investment.

- **Differentiation.** By breaking a market into different segments allows marketers to decide which segment is more appropriate to differentiate its offerings from the competitors.

Market segments need to be protected from competitors. Otherwise, there is a threat that new entrants will establish a foothold and grow market share in a neglected, poorly served segment of a market.

Market segmentation

Market segmentation is the process of dividing a market into smaller groups or segments of customers with distinctly similar needs or characteristics that have implications for different products and marketing mixes. There are many variables available and there is no single best way to segment a market. This section discusses three important segmentation topics: segmenting consumer markets, segmenting online shoppers and segmenting business markets.

■ Segmenting consumer markets

Consumer markets can be divided in various ways and marketers have to try different segmentation variables, alone and in combination, to find the best way to divide the total market into relatively homogeneous segments that are identified by common characteristics (Tynan and Drayton, 1987). These characteristics are relevant in describing and in predicting the response to marketing stimuli by consumers, in a given segment. Segmentation variables include profile (geographic and demographic), psychographic and behavioural (Table 5.1).

Table 5.1: Segmentation variables for consumer markets. Adapted from Perreault et al. (2014).

Geographic	
World region or country	Western Europe (UK, France, Belgium, Germany, Italy, etc.)
	Eastern Europe (Poland, Romania, Slovakia, Ukraine, etc.)
	North America (United States, Canada, etc.)
	South America (Argentina, Brazil, Chile, Peru, etc.)
	Middle East (Saudi Arabia, Iran, Iraq, Jordan, etc.)
	Africa (Egypt, South Africa, Nigeria, Kenya, etc.)
Country region examples	Asia (China, Japan, Malaysia, Thailand, Taiwan, Korea, etc.)
	Australasia (Australia, New Zealand, Papua New Guinea, etc.)
	UK: England, Scotland, Wales and Northern Ireland.
	America: Pacific, Mountain, West North Central, West South Central, East North Central, East South Central, South Atlantic, Middle Atlantic and New England.
	Malaysia: Penang, Perlis, Kedah, Perak, Selangor, Negeri Sembilan, Melaka, Johor, Pahang, Kelantan, Terengganu, Sabah and Sarawak.
	UAE: Dubai, Abu Dhabi, Ajman, Fujairah, Ras al-Khaimah, Sharjah and Umm al-Quwain.
Density	Urban, suburban, small town, rural
Demographic	
Age	Under 6, 6-11, 12-19, 20-34, 35-49, 50-64, 65+
Life stage	Infant, preschool; child, teen, collegiate, adult, senior
Gender	Male, female
Generational cohort	Baby boomer (1946-1964), Generation X (1965-1979), Generation Y (1980-1995), Generation Z (after 1995)
Income	Low, middle, high
Family Size	1-2, 3-4, 5+
Family life cycle	Young single, young couples, young parents, middle-aged empty nesters, retired
Occupation	Professional and technical; managers, officials and proprietors; clerical; craftspeople; supervisors; operatives; farmers; retired; students; homemakers; unemployed
Education	Some high school or less; high school graduate; university graduate, etc.
Social class	Lower-lowers, upper-lowers, working class, middle class, upper-middles, lower-uppers, upper-uppers
Psychographic	
Lifestyle	Sports-oriented, fashion-oriented, culture-oriented
Personality	Extroverts, introverts, aggressive, submissive
Behavioural	
Benefits sought	Convenience, speed, economy, quality, status, performance
Purchase occasion	Regular occasion, gift, special occasion, eating occasion, holidays
Purchase behaviour	Self-buying, brand switching, innovators
User status	Non-user, ex-user, potential user, first-time user, regular user
User rates	Light user, medium user, heavy user
Loyalty status	None, medium, strong, absolute
Readiness stage	Unaware, aware, informed, interested, intended to buy
Attitude to product	Favourable, indifferent, unfavourable

5

Geographic segmentation

The needs of a group of customers in one geographic area are often different from those in another area. Geographic segmentation is frequently used for dividing a market into different regions such as continents, countries, states, provinces, counties or cities (Kotler and Armstrong, 2014). The geographic variables are useful when there are regional differences in consumption patterns. An organisation may choose to operate in one or more areas but has to pay attention to geographic differences in needs and preferences.

Certain food has specific geographic interest. For instance, fish and seafood are marketed more heavily along the coastal areas in Japan, Indonesia, China and Malaysia where supply is fresh all year round.

Demographic segmentation

Demographic variables relate to age, life stage, birth era, gender, family size, family life cycle, income occupation, education and social class (Table 5.1). Demographic variables are popular bases for segmenting consumer markets because consumer needs often vary closely with demographic variables and they are easier to measure, i.e. easier to assess the size of the target market and to reach it efficiently. Marketers can use a combination of geographic and demographic variables identified as geodemographic.

Insight: Acorn

Acorn is a geodemographic segmentation tool, which segments the UK's population – it segments households, postcodes and neighbourhoods into 6 categories, 18 groups and 62 types (CACI, 2014). Acorn and other geodemographic services provide valuable consumer insights helping organisations target, acquire and develop profitable customer relationships and improve service delivery. Visit the Acorn website (http://acorn.caci.co.uk/) to check out the user guide.

Consumer needs and wants change with **age** and their **life cycle position**. Many organisations use this segmentation variable, to provide differentiated products or services for different age and life cycle groups. For example, a toothpaste brand in Malaysia such as Colgate offers three main lines of products

- **Colgate Kids:** designed to make brushing enjoyable so that children will develop great habits for life.

- **Colgate Total 12**: provides busy adults 12-hour protection against bacteria build-up for superior oral health

- **Colgate Sensitive**: targeted to seniors, it provides formula for everyday protection from painful sensitivity.

Gender segmentation has long been used by product categories such as cosmetics, hair colour, magazines and clothing. For example, Schick has increased its efforts to capture the women's razor market by introducing Schick Hydro Silk with five blades and moisturising strips for women. However, they have been criticised for gender-based pricing as both the Hydro Silk for women and the Hydro 5 for men are a similar product, but women are paying more (Willett, 2015). Marketers need to pay particular attention when segmenting markets to be sure that there is a real need for a differentiated product and that the point of difference is not based on stereotypical and superficial factors.

Members of a **generation** are likely to share similar preferences, priorities and viewpoints as they are influenced by the times in which they grow up, such as the music, movies, politics and defining events of that period (Kotler and Armstrong, 2014). Marketers targeting a generation have to know about the characteristics in order to effectively market to them. For example, during the cola war Pepsi's tagline ('the Pepsi Generation') aimed to persuade the youth that its drink mirrored their core values hence leaving Coca-Cola as their parents' drink. Table 5.2 profiles the different periods and features of the different generation cohorts.

Table 5.2: Profiling generation cohorts. Adapted from Kotler and Armstrong (2014).

Generational cohort	Birth range	Defining Features
Baby Boomers	1946-1964	Still largely in the prime of their consumption cycle, they embrace products and lifestyles that allow them to turn back the hands of time.
Gen X	1965-1979	Sometimes seen as falling between the generational cracks, they bridge the technological savvy of Gen Y with the adult realities of the baby boomers.
Gen Y (Millennials)	1980-1995	Raised with relative affluence, technologically plugged in and concerned with the environment and social issues, they also have a strong sense of independence and a perceived immunity from marketing.
Gen Z	After 1995	Immersed in social networks, relying on it for socialising, they are accustomed to auto-correct, emoticons and visuals – preferring a number of screens for multitasking (Mobile phone, tablet, laptop, TV, desktop, portable music player, etc.). They are mature, self-directed and resourceful.

Case study: Generational marketing – PNC's virtual wallet

In early 2007, PNC Financial Services hired IDEO, a design consultancy, to study Gen Y (which PNC defined as people aged 18-34) and help formulate a marketing plan to appeal to them. IDEO's research evidenced that this generation cohort (Gen Y):

(i) they typically do not know how to manage their money and

(ii) they consider bank sites clunky.

With that in mind, PNC rolled out Virtual Wallet that combined three accounts dubbed:

(i) 'Spend' (regular checking),

(ii) 'Reserve' (backup checking that garners interest) and

(iii) 'Grow' (savings) – linked together with a personal finance tool.

Customers can drag money from account to account on one screen. Instead of a traditional ledger, they view balances on a calendar that displays estimated future cash flow based on when customers are paid, when they pay bills, and on their spending habits. Customers also can set various saving rules with a feature called "Savings Engine," which transfers money to savings when they receive a paycheck, and get their account balances by text messages. PNC says it has signed up more than 20,000 Virtual Wallet customers, 65% of them new and 70% in the Gen Y demographic. An added benefit is that Gen Y-ers are cheaper to service than older customers because they rarely call customer service or visit branches.

Source: adapted from Helm (2008)

However, Gardiner et al. (2013) evidenced that some consumers have inexplicit association with their generational label. Generation self-identity congruence is better among baby boomers compared to the younger generations. Hence, marketers should understand the pros and cons of using this segmentation approach.

Income segmentation divides a market into different income segments such as consumer's personal income, household income or disposal income (Baines and Fill, 2014). This is an important demographic variable because it determines the purchasing power of consumers. Automobiles, clothing, cosmetics, financial services and travel markets are heavily income segmented. Another point to note: income is closely related to social class, which is usually determined by wealth, income, education and occupation. Segmentation using income alone may yield segments that are too vague to be of use, hence marketers may consider using multiple segmentation variables, which will be discussed later.

Demographic segmentation is useful but marketers should guard against stereotypes when dividing consumers into meaningful segments. For example, a male segment uses cologne; marketers would not be able to tell whether certain men prefer cologne that express a trendy, mysterious, classy or masculine image. Many researchers suggest the use of both demographic and psychographic segmentations are better predictions in consumer markets (Kerin et al., 2013).

Exercise: Select a market of your choice and use geodemographic segmentation to identify market segments. Explain the profiles of the possible segments.

Psychographic segmentation

Psychographic segmentation divides consumers into different groups based on lifestyle or personality characteristics (Kerin et al., 2013). It can be used independently to segment a market or combined with other segmentation variables.

The products or services customers buy reflect their lifestyles. Marketers often segment their markets by consumer lifestyles and base their marketing strategies on lifestyle appeals. Marketers attempt to group customers according to their way of living as reflected in their activities, interests and opinions. For example, in Malaysia, Astro television uses lifestyle segmentation to target different interest groups including food lovers (Asian Food Channel), sports devotees (Astro SuperSport) and film fans (Astro World of Movies).

Marketers also use personality variables to divide the markets. Often useful when a product resembles many competing products and consumers' needs are not significantly related to other segmentation variables. For example, Mountain Dew depicts a youthful, rebellious, adventurous, go-your-own-way personality and its ads remind customers to 'Do the Dew' (Armstrong et al., 2015).

Case study: Charles & Keith – From a footwear brand to a lifestyle brand

Charles & Keith is a popular Singapore brand known for women's footwear and accessories. Established in 1996 by brothers Charles and Keith Wong, it started out as a simple shoe store at the Amara Hotel. Today, Charles & Keith is an international chain with over 170 franchises worldwide.

Background. The brothers Keith learned the ropes by helping their parents at their shoe store in Ang Mo Kio. In 1996, at the age of 22, Charles opened his own shoe store at the Amara Hotel arcade in the financial district. Keith joined the business in 1998. At the time, it was a small business selling women's shoes made in China and Malaysia.

Customer feedback showed that merely selling shoes bought from wholesale suppliers did not provide sufficient variety of designs or customer choice. Realising that they needed to have an edge over their competitors, the brothers began designing their own shoes. Keith was in charge of designing the shoes while Charles managed sales. The brothers made the business cost efficient by buying materials directly from China instead of wholesalers in Singapore. The strategy proved to be successful, and Charles & Keith went on to establish itself with 12 outlets in major shopping centres and suburban malls in Singapore.

This made the potential of creating a brand that consumers could identify with – leading to the creation of the Charles & Keith brand. A key characteristic of their target market are customers conscious of fashion trends. With this in mind, the design teams travel to key fashion capitals such as Paris and Milan to research designs and spot the next season's trends. Today, the company is well known for its distinctive products and quick in-season turnaround that offers 20-30 new designs in stores every week. The product range now includes bags, belts, shades, tech accessories and bracelets, with Charles and Keith evolving from a footwear to a lifestyle brand.

Source: adapted from Ramlan (2010).

Behavioural segmentation

In addition to understanding demographics and psychographics, it is beneficial to know what consumers actually do with a product. The behavioural bases for segmenting a consumer market include benefits sought, purchase occasion, purchase behaviours, user status, user rates, loyalty status, readiness stage and attitude toward the product.

Understanding the different **benefits sought** by customers is a useful way to segment markets. For example, Sunsilk determined eight benefit segments of shampoo users in Malaysia and offered Sunsilk Co-Creations for each segment – clean and fresh; soft and smooth; perfect straight; smooth and manageable; anti-dandruff; hairfall solution; damage restore; and black shine.

Purchase occasions: Marketers can distinguish customers according to the occasions when they develop a need to buy a product. For example, air travel is triggered by purchase occasions such as business, holiday, relocation or family; Heinz advertises its soups regularly during winter months; and in Malaysia M&M's advertises on occasions such as Christmas, Chinese New Year, Diwali, Eid al-Fitr and Valentine's Day.

User status: Markets can also be divided on the basis of non-users, ex-users, potential users, first-time users and regular users of a product. For example, when Unilever launched deodorant in China, it had to enlighten non-users why they should buy the product. Most Chinese do not recognise the need for deodorant because they believe that people do not suffer from body odour. Therefore, Unilever has to educate non-users to convert them to new users (Kotler et al.,

2011). Other examples include blood banks which cannot only depend on regular donors but must also recruit new donors and remind occasional donors to donate.

Usage rate or **usage frequency** is the quantity consumed and it varies among different customer groups – light, medium or heavy product users (Kerin et al., 2013). For example, Burger King targets its Super Fans (aged 18 to 34) who eat at Burger King on an average of 16 times a month (heavy users). It runs ads that exalt monster burgers containing more meat and more cheese for Super Fans with huge appetites (MacArthur, 2006).

Loyalty status. Customers can be segmented into groups according to the degree of loyalty – none, medium, strong or absolute. Consumers can be loyal to brands (Samsung or iPhone), stores (Isetan or IKEA) and companies (Ford or Toyota). Some customers are loyal to a brand – they buy one brand all the time for IT gadgets such as Samsung laptop, printer, smartphone and tablet. Other customers are somewhat loyal or loyal to two or three brands of a given product. There are customers that show no loyalty to any brand, for example, and they buy whatever is on sale.

Using multiple segmentation variables

Marketers usually use more than one variable to segment the consumer markets. Multiple segmentation variables are used to identify better-defined target groups. For example, benefit segmentation allows marketers to classify customers based upon the benefits they value or seek from a product. Demographic analyses can then be formed to identify the type of customers (e.g. by age, gender or income) in each benefit segment so that targeting can take place (Ahmad, 2003). A bank may identify a group of wealthy retired adults and within that group distinguish several segments based on their assets, savings, risk preferences, housing and lifestyles (Kotler et al., 2011). Such segmentation offers marketers a powerful tool to better understand key customer segments, target them more efficiently and tailor market offerings and messages to their specific needs.

Segmenting online shoppers

Similar to consumer markets, online consumer markets can be identified by considering demographic, psychographic and behavioural variables (Doherty and Ellis-Chadwick, 2010). In an online context, psychographics might include the affinity an individual might have with a type of website – they may frequently visit technology sites or be seekers of news. Behavioural variables might include segmentation using number of visits to the site, whether they use a mobile or PC, the number of transactions per visit, source of visit (e.g. whether they were referred to the site from social media or search engine) and sequencing along with discussions about loyalty and whether they are an active or lapsed customer.

While there are similarities between online and offline shoppers, for example, age, gender, education and income, Bhatnagar and Ghose (2004) provided evidence that segmenting online shoppers based on benefits sought provide more effective marketing information than mere demographic profiling. Online behavioural segmentation or specifically the important benefits that shoppers seek from an online store include convenience, innovativeness, risk aversion, variety of choices, quality, and price (Donthu and Gracia, 1999; Brashear et al., 2009).

■ Segmenting business markets

Like consumer markets, business markets are frequently segmented using multiple segmentation variables. Consumer and business marketers use similar variables to divide their markets. According to Solomon et al. (2013), business customers can be divided using the variables such as:

- Geographic such as by region, country, states, province and density.

- Demographic by industry or company size in total sales and number of employees; whether they are a domestic or a multinational company; the type of business they are in and the production technology they use.

- Behavioural such as benefits sought, user status, usage rate, loyalty status and policies on how they purchase.

For example, demographic. American Express targets segments using company size (in total sales) and number of employees (Kotler et al., 2011).

(i) large corporate customers – corporate card programme which includes extensive employee expenses, travel services, asset management, retirement planning and financial education services;

(ii) small-business customers – created small business network for customers to access the network for everything from account and expense management software to expert small-business management advice and connecting with other small-business owners to share ideas and get recommendations.

Market targeting

Market segmentation tells the organisation which segments of a market are available. Market targeting is the next stage and is where the organisation evaluates the different segments and decide which segment(s) it can serve best by choosing a market targeting strategy.

■ Evaluating market segments

An organisation considers six factors when evaluating different market segments (Armstrong et al., 2015):

■ **Segment size**: Marketers collect and analyse data on current sales and expected profitability for each segment. It is not necessarily the largest segment that is most attractive for every organisation. Smaller organisations may lack the required resources and skills to serve large segments and they may select smaller segments that are potentially more profitable for them and ignored by their larger competitors.

■ **Expected growth**: Marketers evaluate expected growth of various segments. Although a segment size may be small now, it might be expected to grow in the future.

■ **Competitive position**: The current and future competitor strength for each segment is evaluated to show which the most attractive segments are. Segments with fewer competitors are more attractive.

■ **Accessibility**: A segment that is inaccessible to an organisation's marketing actions should not be pursued. Marketers need to examine whether there are specific media and distribution channels that provide access to the chosen segment.

■ **Relevance**: Marketers have to consider whether the benefits of the product or service being offered are relevant or adequately serve the segment needs.

■ **Organisational objectives and resources**: Although a segment has all the right factors mentioned above, the organisation must consider its own longer-term objectives and resources. An organisation should choose segments where superior customer value can be offered to gain advantages over competitors.

During this stage, the organisation must balance its resources and capabilities against the attractiveness of different segments.

■ Market targeting strategy

After evaluating various market segments, marketers then decide which segment(s) to target. A target market comprises of a group of buyers possessing similar needs or characteristics which an organisation decides to serve (Kotler and Armstrong, 2014). There are four target marketing strategies (Figure 5.2) from which to choose (Jobber and Ellis-Chadwick, 2013):

■ **Undifferentiated marketing**: single marketing mix for the whole market.
   A market targeting strategy whereby an organisation ignores market segmentation variables and decides to develop a single marketing mix for the whole

market. For example, Henry Ford exemplified this strategy when he offered the Model-T Ford in one colour, i.e., black. Today, many marketers doubt this targeting strategy because of the difficulties arising when developing a product or service that will satisfy all consumers and often have trouble competing with more focused organisations.

■ **Differentiated marketing**: several potential targets.

An organisation decides to target more than one market segment and designs different offers for each. This strategy exploits the differences between market segments by designing a specific marketing mix for each and thus gains maximum market share of the total market. For example, airlines design different marketing mixes for first class, business class and economy class passengers, including varying prices, service levels, seats, legroom, in-cabin comfort, quality of food and waiting areas at airports. This targeting strategy increases the costs of doing business. Therefore, the organisation must weigh increased sales against increased costs when deciding on a differentiated targeting strategy.

■ **Focused marketing**: single market mix aimed at one target market.

This market targeting strategy is appropriate for organisations with limited resources. The organisation designs a marketing mix aimed at one target market (niche) and is therefore practising focused marketing. For example, Saga Holidays targets the over-50s and is a senior travel expert.

■ **Customised marketing**: individual customers are unique and their purchasing power sufficient – separate marketing mix for each customer.

In certain markets the needs of individual customers are distinctive and their purchasing power is sufficient to make designing a separate marketing mix for each customer viable. For example, Fujifilm Medical Systems design and build medical imaging equipment to specifications given to them by individual hospitals. Nowadays, car companies (such as Audi, BMW, Mercedes and Renault) as well as companies selling trainers (like Nike and Adidas), allowing a product to be built to individual specifications from a range of options, have adopted mass customisation.

Exercise: Give further examples of each market targeting strategy and how it benefits the organisation.

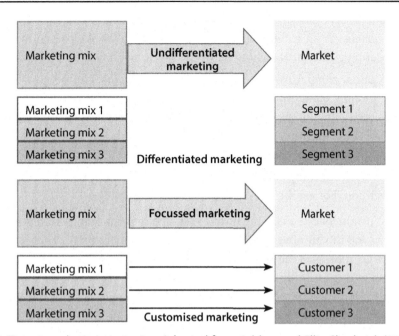

Figure 5.2: Target marketing strategies. Adapted from Jobber and Ellis-Chadwick (2013)

Market positioning

Once segments have been identified and the targeting decision made, an organisation then decides on a product or service position – how to create differential value for the chosen target market and determine what position to occupy in the minds of its customers (Hassan and Craft, 2012; Armstrong et al., 2015). As popularised by Ries and Trout (1981) product positioning is the way a product is defined by customers or the place the product occupies in consumers' minds relative to competing products. Batra et al. (1995) advocate that positioning has been used to indicate the product's image in the marketplace and Ries and Trout (1981) suggest that this product image must contrast with competitors. Hence, the main message in a campaign is to position the product by promoting or communicating the benefits it offers and differentiating it from the competition. The following positioning strategies available to marketers include positioning by:

■ **Product attributes** – a frequently used positioning strategy that associates the product with an attribute, feature or customer need, benefit or solution. For example, Colgate offers benefits of preventing cavity and fresh breath.

■ **Usage occasions** – associating a product with when or how it is used by target market. For example, Kellogg's Corn Flakes was positioned for use as popular breakfast cereal in Malaysia.

- **Users** – associating a product with a user or a class of users. For example, *For Dummies* is an extensive series of instructional books presenting non-intimidating guides attractive to readers who do not have any prior knowledge.

- **Against competitors** – to directly compare against competitor. This allows a reputable competitor's image to be exploited and conveys that the product is better than or as good as a given competitor is. For example, Dynamo, the first liquid laundry detergent brand in Malaysia has launched television ads exhibiting its product benefits against brand X.

- **Away from competitors** – positioning a product opposite or away from competition. For example, 7-UP calling itself the Uncola.

Most products use a combination of the above positioning strategies. However, increasing the number involves obvious confusion and risk. Therefore, focusing on target market is the key goal of positioning, i.e. to only use positioning strategies that appeal to the chosen target market and creating a sense of belonging in the mind that the product is for them. Keys to successful positioning include (Jobber and Ellis-Chadwick, 2013):

- **Clarity**: the positioning idea must be clear and memorable to target market. For example, simple message such as "BMW, the ultimate driving machine"and "Wal-Mart's low prices, always".

- **Consistency**: in message is required to break through the competitive clutter. For example, L'Oréal has benefited from a consistent message (i.e. "because you're worth it") being communicated to their target market.

- **Credibility**: the differential advantage is reliable and credible in the minds of target market. For example, Toyota uses Lexus and not Toyota Lexus as the brand name for its luxury models.

- **Competitiveness**: the chosen differential advantage should offer something of value to the target market that the competition is failing to supply. For example, iPod's seamless downloading of music from a dedicated music store.

Positioning makes a bridge between customers and a product by linking target marketing strategy and the marketing mix required. It represents the position occupied in the minds of its customers and helps determine the image/perception that marketers will try to communicate to customers.

(Re-)positioning using perceptual mapping

One way to positioning a brand effectively is the use of perceptual mapping. This tool generates a two- or multi-dimensional map helping marketers to understand customer perceptions of different brands. The three steps approach include:

1 Identify the dimensions that are key requirements of customers.

2 Discover how customers rate competing brands with respect to these dimensions.

3 Discover where the organisation's existing brand is rated along these dimensions in the minds of consumers.

This tool helps marketers to understand consumer perceptions of different brands in the market and identify gaps in the market. Marketers are helped in choosing a strategy to strengthening an existing brand position, reposition the brand or decide where to position a new product (Figure 5.3).

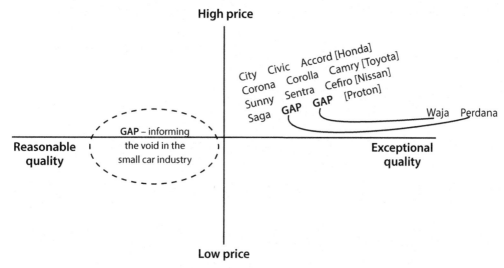

Figure 5.3: A perceptual map of purchasing new cars in the 1980s

As shown in Figure 5.3, Proton (Malaysia's leading carmaker) first introduced Proton Saga as the basic car for lower middle-income earners. Subsequently, the perceptual map has facilitated marketers to introduce a new Proton Waja for middle-income earners and a Proton Perdana for upper middle-income earners. Moreover, the perceptual map has shown a gap for compact/small car where Perodua (Malaysia's leading compact/small carmaker) introduced Perodua Kancil. This model has received high demand since its launch and was popularised in Malaysia then. On the other hand, a flagship example of repositioning is Lucozade changing its target market and differential advantage from a drink that aided recovery from illness, to an energy drink for sports. Therefore, positioning maps make available useful customer perceptions of different brands for marketers involved in developing product portfolios and marketing mixes.

> **Exercise:** Consider a product that you like. How is it positioned and how the positioning is conveyed to you as a customer by the organisation? Is the positioning strategy different from its competitors?

Summary

Choosing suitable target market is crucial to an organisation's adoption and use of the marketing concept philosophy. Identifying the right target market and positioning is the key to implementing a successful marketing mix or strategy. A careful target market analysis places an organisation in a better situation to both serve customers' needs and achieve its objectives.

Further reading

Smith (1956) first introduced the term market segmentation. The roots of early and recent market segmentation research include the work of Wind (1978), Tynan and Drayton (1987), Wedel and Kamakura (2002), Dibb and Simkin (2009) and Quinn and Dibb (2010). Special issues on this topic can be found in the *Journal of Marketing*, *Journal of Marketing Research* and *Journal of Marketing Management*.

The term positioning was first introduced by Trout (1969) followed by his work with Al Ries (1972). Their ground breaking first book on positioning was published in 1981. According to them positioning is not what marketers do to the product but instead what the product is in minds of prospective customers (Ries and Trout, 1981).

References

Ahmad, R. (2003). Benefit segmentation: a potentially useful technique of segmenting and targeting older consumers. *International Journal of Market Research*, **45**(3), 373-388.

Armstrong, G., Kotler, P., Harker, M. and Brennan, R. (2015). *Marketing: An Introduction* (3rd ed.). UK: Pearson.

Baines, P. and Fill, C. (2014). *Marketing* (3rd ed.). UK: Oxford University Press.

Batra, R., Aaker, D. A. and Myers, J. G. (1995). *Advertising Management* (5th ed.). US: Prentice Hall.

Bhatnagar, A. and Ghose, S. (2004). Segmenting consumers based on the benefits and risks of internet shopping. *Journal of Business Research*, **57**(12), 1352-1360.

Brashear, T. G., Kashyap, V., Musante, M. D. and Donthu, N. (2009). A profile of the internet shopper: evidence from six countries. *Journal of Marketing Theory and Practice*, **17**(3), 267-281.

CACI (2014). Acorn User Guide. Available: http://acorn.caci.co.uk/downloads/Acorn-User-guide.pdf [Accessed 7 April 2016].

Dibb, S. and Simkin, L. (2009). Editorial: Bridging the segmentation theory/practice divide. *Journal of Marketing Management*, **25**(3-4), 219-225.

Doherty, N. F. and Ellis-Chadwick, F. (2010). Internet retailing: the past, the present and the future. *International Journal of Retail and Distribution Management*, **38**(11/12), 943-965.

Donthu, N. and Garcia, A. (1999). The internet shopper. *Journal of Advertising Research*, **39**(3), 52–58.

Gardiner, S., Grace, D. and King, C. (2013). Challenging the use of generational segmentation through understanding self-identity. *Marketing Intelligence and Planning*, **31**(6), 639-653.

Hassan, S. S. and Craft, S. (2012). Examining world market segmentation and brand positioning strategies. *Journal of Consumer Marketing*, **29**(5), 344-356.

Helm, B. (2008). PNC lures Gen Y with its 'Virtual Wallet' account. Bloomberg Businessweek 26 November. Available: http://www.bloomberg.com/news/articles/2008-11-25/pnc-lures-gen-y-with-its-virtual-wallet-account [Accessed 8 April 2016].

Jobber, D and Ellis-Chadwick, F. (2013) *Principles and Practice of Marketing* (7th ed.). UK: McGraw Hill.

Kerin, R. A., Lau, G. T., Hartley, S. W. and Rudelius, W. (2013). *Marketing in Asia* (2nd ed.). Singapore: McGraw Hill.

Kotler, P. and Armstrong, G. (2014). *Principles of Marketing* (15th ed.). England: Pearson.

Kotler, P., Armstrong, G., Ang, S. H., Leong, S. M., Tan, C. T. and Yau, O. H. M. (2011). *Principles of Marketing: An Asian Perspective*. Singapore: Pearson.

MacArthur, K. (2006). BK rebels fall in love with King. *Advertising Age*, **77**(18), 1.

Perreault, W. D., Cannon, J. P. and McCarthy, E. J. (2014). *Basic Marketing* (19th ed.). New York: McGraw Hill.

Quinn, L. and Dibb, S. (2010). Evaluating market-segmentation research priorities: targeting re-emancipation. *Journal of Marketing Management*, **26**(13-14): 1239–1255.

Ramlan, N. (2010). Charles & Keith, National Library Board Singapore. Available: http://eresources.nlb.gov.sg/infopedia/articles/SIP_1696_2010-08-03.html [Accessed 12 April 2016].

Ries, A. and Trout, J. (1981). *Positioning: The Battle for your Mind*. New York: McGraw-Hill.

Smith, W. R. (1956). Product differentiation and market segmentation as alternative marketing strategies. *Journal of Marketing*, **21**(1), 3-8.

Solomon, M. R., Marshall, G. W., Stuart, E. W., Barnes, B. R. and Mitchell, V. W. (2013). *Marketing: Real People, Real Decisions* (2nd ed.). UK: Pearson.

Trout, J. (1969). Positioning is a game people play in today's me-too market place. *Industrial Marketing*, **54**(6), 51–55.

Trout, J. and Ries, A. (1972). Positioning cuts through chaos in marketplace. *Advertising Age*, **43**(May), 51-54.

Tynan, A. C. and J. Drayton (1987) Market Segmentation. *Journal of Marketing Management*, **2**(3), 301–35.

Wedel, M. and Kamakura, W. (2002) Introduction to the Special Issue on Market Segmentation. *International Journal of Research in Marketing*, **19**(3), 181-183.

Willett, M. (2015). Men's and women's razors, soaps, and moisturizers are essentially the same — here's why the women's version always costs more. Business Insider 9 April. Available: http://www.businessinsider.my/womens-products-more-expensive-than-mens-2015-4/#5q5MbqybMDIMZYkD.99 [Accessed 13th July 2016].

Wind, Y. (1978) Issues and advances in segmentation research. *Journal of Marketing Research*, **15**(3), 317-337.

6 Products, Services and Ideas

Geraldine McKay

Physical products cannot exclusively satisfy all individual, societal and organisational desires. A range of offerings, including products, services, ideas, experiences, places and people are consumed to provide benefits and meet the varied requirements of potential customers and other stakeholders. Although these offerings are very different propositions, they all come under the consideration of the product concept. This chapter will discuss several product categories, develop understanding of the anatomy of a product and create insight into why products and services must be managed from inception. Products are given meaning and are positioned by both consumers and the organisational family. This chapter concludes by discussing the value created by brands from the perspective of the customer, the organisation and other stakeholders.

What is a product?

A product is "anything that can be offered to a market for attention, acquisition, use or consumption that might satisfy a want or need" (Kotler et al., 2017:226). The product is central to the marketing exchange process. A product that fails to provide required and promised benefits deters dissatisfied current and new customers. Core benefits sought are varied and products become complex mixes of functional features, intangible propositions and ancillaries that augment the offering. This complex mix is known here as the anatomy of the product and consists of:

■ The core benefit offering greater value than competing products.

■ The features and design of the product;

- The augmented product consisting all additional services, guarantees and other elements less fundamental to the core product, but never the less enhancing the offering

- The brand and its associations, pulling together all elements of the product.

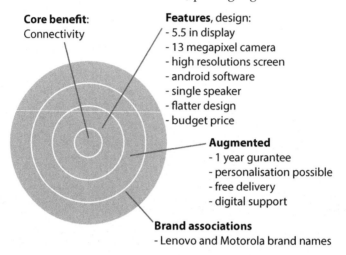

Core benefit: Connectivity

Features, design:
- 5.5 in display
- 13 megapixel camera
- high resolutions screen
- android software
- single speaker
- flatter design
- budget price

Augmented
- 1 year gurantee
- personalisation possible
- free delivery
- digital support

Brand associations
- Lenovo and Motorola brand names

Figure 6.1: Product anatomy – Moto G4 phone

Customers typically rationalise their choices by highlighting their chosen product's superior features, but benefits are often intangible, even for a physical product. An often-quoted example is that the core benefit of a drill is the hole it creates (Kotler et al, 2017). A buyer of a pair of sneakers reports choice based on quality, fit, price, availability, or colour but the main reason for choice springs from the intangible, brand name associations. Ownership of a specific brand makes the purchaser feel good, feel close to a celebrity associated with the brand or offer other social and psychological benefits. Benefits are emotional or functional and product choice made when the full offer provides enough value to justify exchanging resources to obtain these benefits.

> What are the associated benefits of each of the design features of the Moto G4 phone? Are all features important to you as a buyer? How much value is added by the brand names attached?

Services are "deeds, processes and performances" (Wilson et al., 2016:5) and transform physical possessions (such as dry cleaning) or physical bodies and minds (such as healthcare or education). Although services cannot be seen or touched, and so are intangible, most do use physical qualities to help the customer evaluate the offering before and after purchase.

Many physical products augment their offering with additional digital support services. Online ancillary content created by the brand owner is available to product users, employees and other stakeholders. Unilever, for example offers the cleanipedia website with tips on home cleaning, asthma control and others issues, to support sales of their domestic cleaning products. Product fans compliment and supplement this technical and commercial information with contributions and tips of their own.

Ella's Kitchen: Not just food

Ethical brands such as Ella's kitchen, the maker of organic baby and toddler foods, demonstrate the importance of providing service and ideas along with the physical product. The company, set up in 2006 is now sold in over 40 countries. It was named after the founder's first child and uses bright colours, convenient packaging and products oozing goodness. The company website offers several non-product related benefits to build customer connections with the brand– a baby 'foodies' club, feeding, dietary and recycling tips and social media content. It promotes ethical initiatives such as 'no child hungry' and environmental causes. The founder, Paul Lindley suggests, "businesses are waking up to the fact that to engender trust and get people talking about them, they need to have an emotional, as well as a functional, relationship with consumers." (Bacon, 2017). Perhaps this is why Ella's kitchen product is an exciting mix of products, services and ideas that resonates with the needs of new parents.

This is an example of the conceptual logic suggesting that service is now the dominant proposition offered by organisations and economies. This is further discussed in Chapter 1.

Types of products and services

Marketers classify their businesses in terms of the customers they serve, i.e. end consumer or business, so business to consumer (B2C) or business-to-business (B2B) . Within these categories, a product can be tangible such as table salt or intangible such as insurance. Most offerings are, however a mixture of both physical and tangible elements and intangible elements, as shown in Figure 6.2.

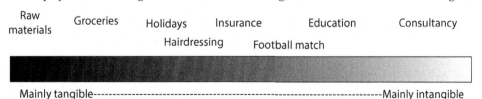

Raw materials   Groceries   Holidays   Insurance   Education   Consultancy

Hairdressing   Football match

Mainly tangible--Mainly intangible

Figure 6.2: The product/ service gradation

Not just products

Not only products and services are marketed and bought. Countries, cities and streets create customer value as holiday and tourist destinations, somewhere to live or a place to locate a company. Football clubs are examples of brands with a tremendous following. Experiences and events such as The Glastonbury Festival of Contemporary Arts offer a range of benefits, such as somewhere to meet people, hear music, try new tastes, experience drama and create memories – so a mix of tangible and intangibles. Getz et al. (2010:30) proposed that "festivals celebrate community values, ideologies, identity and continuity". Within a business context, research into attendance at conferences shows that when deciding to attend, the most important factors were the intangible elements such as networking, and personal and professional development (Mair and Thompson, 2009).

Ideas are products too. Social marketers develop ideas to change behaviour (such as anti-smoking campaigns or encouraging immunisation) to benefit individuals and society. Additionally, politicians, celebrities and other personalities are marketed and all individuals, famous or not, are products to be presented in best light, whether this be at a job interview, or to gain favour amongst friends on social media. Research amongst small and medium enterprises (Resnick et al, 2016) suggests that owners see that their business reflect their personal qualities as the brand, alongside processes and outcomes.

Business-to-Consumer products and services

Table 6.1 shows common categories of business to consumer (B2C) products. Kotler et al (2017) adds a group of products and services that classed as "unsought". This includes services such as insurance, solicitors, funeral services, or physical goods such as fire alarms. These types of products and services may need heavy sales effort to gain the attention of customers who see little pleasure in buying such products.

Durable goods

Some products are infrequently purchased but in frequent use and expected to last for a long time. Termed durable goods, they include household products such as fridges and dishwashers (so-called white goods), televisions and furniture (referred to as brown goods) and cars. Other consumer durables are personal including mobile phones and luxury items such as jewellery. Within a business-to-business (B2B) market, durable goods include capital products such as machinery and plant or other day-to-day equipment such as photocopiers and computers, all essential when running an organisation. These products are relatively expensive and customers have high involvement with their purchase.

Consumables or non-durable goods

Consumables are bought frequently. The risk of purchase is low as they typically cost less than durables and consumers are familiar with the product, price and where to source. Purchasers generally have low involvement and these goods bought without much thought and may be impulse buys. One category of non-durable goods is fast moving consumer goods (FMCG) including grocery and cleaning products.

Some products are classified as durable but are purchased frequently by knowledgeable customers and carry characteristics more akin to non-durable goods. Low cost fashion goods sold through outlets such as Primark and fast fashion items are examples. Additionally, some consumers become highly involved in fast-moving consumer goods purchase, for example, they are buying soap for someone with a skin condition. Therefore, the categories shown in Table 6.1 are a continuum. Consumer products can be categorised in terms of how they are shopped for:

- **Convenience products** such as confectionary, snacks or gasoline. Frequent purchase, with limited effort, these need to be available at many outlets.

- **Shopping products**. The consumer is willing to travel to find precise brand. Gift items fall under this category along with fashion and household durables.

- **Speciality goods** carry very specific features and the consumer is willing to make extra effort to source. Examples include hi-tech products, furniture designs, wedding dresses and even items normally seen as convenience goods such as a speciality regionally produced cheese.

Table 6.1: Classification of types of consumer goods and services

Consumer goods		Products	Product example	Services example
Durable	Speciality goods	Luxury, Professional technology	Designer clothing, DJ headphones	Wedding photographer
				University programme
			Mobile phones	Holiday
	Shopping goods	White goods/ brown goods	Fridges, Furniture	Dentist
Consumable				
	Convenience goods	Fast moving consumer goods (f.m.c.g.)	Detergents, beverages, food	ATMs Telephone credit

■   ## Business-to-Business products and services

With so many well-known consumer brands, it is easy to neglect the importance of the many essential activities performed to make products and services available for consumers. Organisations must procure a range of services and products to ensure that they can operate and fulfil their purpose. Products and services sold between businesses are called business-to-business product (B2B) and can be split into five main categories as shown in Table 6.2

Table 6.2: B2B goods categories

B2B category	Definition	Examples
Equipment goods	Physical items needed to run the operation.	Capital goods - machinery, plant, buildings and accessories including office machinery
Raw materials	Basic and fundamental materials processed as part of the finished item.	Chemicals, food items e.g. hops, grains, sugar, cotton, wood, and minerals, labour.
Maintenance repair and operation goods	Products needed to run the business but not part of the finished item.	Stationary, cleaning products, heating equipment, and services such as energy supplies, telephones and broadband.
Component parts	Finished parts bought complete and incorporated into the final product	Window manufacturers buy in metal furnishings (knobs, catches and locks)
Business services	Specialist services	Marketing agencies, professional services, information systems,

Baines et al. (2017) add semi-finished goods as a category to include raw materials that are converted into products that require further processing to be made into the final goods, such as sheet metal or soy sauce used in food manufacturing.

Service dominance is evident in B2B sectors also. Lean manufacturers require that their raw materials be delivered at the right time. L'Oréal, manufacturers of haircare products, sell a range of professional products such as shampoos and colour to salons and a range of training services. This logically includes hair colour application, cutting techniques and less tangible business services such as how to handle salon emotion, use of digital media and developing communication skills.

Exercise: List the products and services your local hospital needs to help patients get well. The list is likely to be wide ranging and include consumables, human and physical capital goods as well as maintenance, repair and operating materials.

Managing products over time

From inception to development and up to the time when products are no longer popular, products need careful management. This requires decision making across the marketing mix. The product lifecycle (PLC), as it is commonly known, consists of four stages:

■ Introduction

During introduction, the product has no sales but has accrued many development costs and requires further investment in the creation of stock, promotion and assuring distribution. Prices are set without sure knowledge of demand, either low in the hope of rapid market share gains or high to skim profit from early adopters, keen to be innovators. Decisions on promotional spend alongside pricing decisions help position the product. Higher prices make a greater contribution to costs but demand may be deflated.

■ Growth

Ideally sales increase as customers become aware of the product and the company should start to show a profit with market share gains. At this stage, competitors may enter the market and the company will need to react - either by increasing promotional spend, creating additional features and services, or reducing prices (or any combination) to maintain a dominant market position.

■ Maturity

During maturity, sales will be at their highest but will start to level and profit will be falling. Competition is likely to be fierce as companies decide whether to fight to maintain market share or withdraw support for the product, leading to eventual decline.

■ Decline

At this stage, sales are in decline and profitability reduces. The reasons for this are:

■ Other companies growing market share by providing greater value for customers.

■ Customer requirements change and less perceived need for the product, affecting all companies in this market.

■ Companies stay in the market place to defend their position or withdraw their support, letting the product die slowly, dropping it entirely, or selling

6

off their investment. The strategy chosen will depend on the reason for the decline. Where loyal customers exist and there are no substitutes or replacements available for a declining product, a company may strategically decide to extend the product life to maintain the customer base or to keep goodwill.

Not all products will be successful and they can fail at any stage. The PLC does not always run its course. The failure rate of new products is regularly quoted as higher than 80% but this figure is arbitrary when considering the empirical evidence (Castellion and Markham, 2013). Failure varies across product categories and the level of resource invested to support the new product through all stages of the PLC. Although money is essential, particularly in the early developmental stages and during launch/introduction (when no income is generated), other resources and expertise are equally important. Good market research capability, promotion and distribution strategies and market led pricing can affect sales outcomes and companies must allow sufficient time before withdrawal. Short term thinking leads to premature withdrawal before a product has a chance to gain sufficient acceptance.

Last Tweet: The Vine withers

Vine was a video sharing platform that allowed six seconds looping videos. It was loved by a generation of musicians and comics who could share samples of their work through social media.

Twitter decided to cut Vine in September 2016 - just 4 years after its launch. The growth of Snapchat video platforms and a need to increase investor confidence in the company's ability to make a profit. Some products, even when there is a market will ultimately fail.

Not every product follows the same lifecycle curve. Some products gain very rapid growth but then lose popularity very quickly. Such fads, as they are known, include fast fashion items or some diets popularised but latterly discredited. Many products, services and brands have been popular for many years. Barclays bank was established in 1692 and Twining's tea brand is over 300 years old. Colgate toothpaste was first sold in 1806 and still growing, recruiting over 40 million new households to try their brand in 2015 (Kantar, 2016). Converse All-Star trainers have survived since 1917, despite being sold off to other companies, with several regenerations to keep them ever popular. There are many criticisms of the product life cycle concept. It cannot be used to predict success or pinpoint timescales for a product's lifetime. Products can be reinvented or repositioned (Moon, 2005) to extend lifecycles. Managers who assume that a slight reduction in sales is signalling the evident decline of a product, without considering other market factors, may well be tempted to withdraw support from a product, which will ultimately lead to a decline. Dhalla and Yuspeh (1976) suggest that product life cycles are not inevitable and some brands survive many years in different guises.

Despite criticisms of the PLC, markets change and most products will not be successful forever. Marketing just one product is not a sensible strategy and companies typically manage a balanced portfolio of products and services consisting of some fledgling, potentially successful products alongside currently fruitful offerings, creating profit for investment in new product research and development.

Decisions on product range and variety

A company must make strategic decisions about the markets it will serve, the products and services and the number of product lines they offer. Start-ups tend to offer a limited number of specialist products but as they grow, they will increase the number of items and ancillary services by growing organically and developing new products in house or through acquisition. As they grow further, they diversify to reach more markets with a wider 'mix' of products.

Table 6.3 indicates the width and depth of the product lines offered by the Saudi based company, Almarai. The width consists of three-product categories – food, beverages and supplements. Their food category includes four types of food (each branded separately). The Almarai dairy line is shown as five products deep. Product managers decide on the width of each product line, including the range of flavours offered and pack size variety. As an example, their cheese range includes cream cheddar sold in five sizes of jar, from a huge 900 grams catering size to a one serving pot.

Variety allows a company to serve many markets with different tastes but does create enormous complexity necessitating sufficient resources and marketing capability to maintain individual product strength without cannibalising other products in the range. Unilever, the well-known Anglo-Dutch company were highly diversified with many product lines, crossing the household goods, personal care and food sectors. More recently, they have divested from several sectors by selling off products and brands across the business. As consumers return to eating dairy products such as butter they decided in 2017 to sell their margarine and spread business, which had been part of their core range since 1929. The value of the Flora and Stork brands was estimated at £6 billion. The decision to rationalise the number of product lines and brands enables them to focus on serving key markets.

Table 6.3: Example of product range width and depth

Almarai Product Mix Width						
Depth	Food				Beverages	Food supplements
	Almarai Dairy	Alyoum Poultry	Lusine Bakery	7 days Snacks	Almarai	Nuralac
	Desserts	Fresh poultry	Cup cakes	Swiss roll	Fresh dairy	Nuralac Plus Baby formula including premature, anti-regurgitation, lacto free
	Cheese-cakes	Whole chicken	Breads	Cake bars	Long Life dairy	Almarai Nurababy infant cereal
	Cheese	Chicken pieces	Burger buns	Wafer sticks	Fresh Fruit juices	Nuralac Plus Suregrow- infant and children range
	butter	Marinated range	Croissants	Apple strudel		
	ghee	Minced chicken	Puffs	Croissants		

Discussions about product range and variety accompany essential decisions about how the product or service is to be presented to market and this requires a clear strategy on branding.

Branding decisions

Figure 6.1 shows the anatomy of the product and suggests that the brand is the final layer of the product anatomy, the outer skin that encapsulates all features, benefits and promises of the product. Not all products are brands and not all brands are products. So, what is the difference? This section will consider the main approaches to branding and outline the branding decisions made within an organisation.

■ Why brand?

Branding is an important concept for consumers and companies alike. Brand names "identify, label or symbolize abstract values such as quality, status, or reputation and are a means for differentiating one product, service, manufacturer or retailer from another" (Hollenbeck and Zinkhan, 2005). Brands create value to consumers by:

- Ensuring consistency of product quality and therefore reducing risk at purchase.

- Identification, saving consumer time when choosing a brand.

- Providing differentiation from other available brands and a reason to buy.

- Reassuring the consumer, as rand choice will provide social and/or individual benefits.

For a company, brands are valuable assets. A successful brand offers protection against failure as loyal customers repeat purchase, and a strong brand name, with associated values can ease the route to market for new product lines sold under the same trusted brand. Companies often charge a premium, higher price for a branded product. Potential economies across promotional spend arise when a brand name is used across many products. Heinz crosses several categories and every time the brand name is seen, it incrementally creates awareness across the range. A strong brand can deter competitors from entering a market, offers legal barriers against copying of name and protected features. Such protection is not failsafe and fake branded products are popular amongst some customers. Each year customs officials destroy thousands of fake handbags, trainers, food and drink, medicines and cigarettes. PwC (2013) research highlights the issues faced by brands targeted by counterfeiters. In the UK, more than half of the population have purchased a fake and 20 % of 18-24 year olds do not think buying counterfeit goods is morally wrong.

How to brand

Brands are not born readymade. Brands are combinations of name, logo, design, or symbol with an association to a specific company. Initial decisions about brand features, quality and brand values, pave the way for the long-term direction of the brand. Once launched, the consumer will shape the future of the brand by developing a relationship with the brand. According to Keller (2009), brand resonance occurs when companies have developed:

- Brand salience – the brand springs to mind when the customer is considering buying from a category.

- Brands that live up to performance promises and are consistently positioned.

- Active loyalty between the consumer and the brand

- An understanding of customer judgment and feelings.

■   Brand names

The name should convey something about the brand proposition and create an image to help the consumer position the brand. New product name choice therefore becomes very significant and must consider the offering and whether the name is already being used. The Google search engine was to be named BackRub, but the founders decided that a shortened version of "googolplex" (meaning large numbers) was better. Brand names should be researched amongst the target audience but some names have performed extremely well without being tested.

Table 6.4: Brand names types

Names built on provenance - the founder or the birthplace.	Coutts Bank Birdseye - Clarence Birdseye Speyside Glenlivet Water Christian Dior Liz Earle	Indicates brand heritage. Service companies use founder's name to signify personal service and expertise. Qualities associated with a place transfer to the brand. Some brands use foreign sounding names.
Descriptive names which say something about the brand	I can't believe it's not butter Rentokil Airbus Flipchart	Eases market entrance but potentially difficult to extend into another category
Puns and unusual spellings	Blu Tak The Codfather (Fish and chip shop) Toys R Us	Get noticed, create a sense of fun.
Invented names that have no original meaning	Diageo Accenture Kodak Ikea	No previous associations, awareness building required.
Acronyms or Numbers	HSBC PlayStation 4	Suggests hi-tech. Acronyms easy to remember.

There are several 'rules' that determine whether a potential brand name will work or not. The name should be short, easy to pronounce and remember, be distinctive and create some meaning. It should translate into different languages without difficulty. The Vauxhall car brand Nova was not used in Spanish speaking companies because it translated as "it doesn't go" and Bran Buds cereal had its name changed in Sweden because it meant "grilled farmer." In Portuguese Nescafe means "it is not coffee" (Usunier and Shaner, 2002). A Belgium chocolate maker more recently changed the name from Isis to Libeert to avoid an association with the Islamic State.

Some brands have done extremely well as exceptions to the above rules. Hyundai, (pronounced like Sunday) means modernity in Korea and created an advertisement based on the difficulties that foreigners had with pronunciation. Many Westerners struggle with the pronunciation of the well know Chinese electronic manufacturer Haier. Airbnb is known as Aibiying in China, means, "welcome each other with love", and is easier to pronounce.

Some brands prefer to use a name that says something about corporate values. Innocent yoghurts and soft drinks portray that their pure ingredients and Virgin was named by founders who saw themselves as inexperienced in business. Nowadays names that work on social media or are derived from commonly searched terms is essential. Like all brand assets (logo, trademark, tag line, colour) a good brand name needs legal protection. Brand managers may use experts in semiology to help research their name. Even vowels and consonants carry associations and this is evident in brands ending in 'a' which sound feminine.

Brands names may be changed to achieve global economies of scale but alterations need careful consideration and supportive communications effort. In Australia, the attempt to change Vegemite to iSnack caused outrage with the public and it swiftly changed it back.

6

Classical roots

Many brand names are derived from Latin or Greek. Nike is the Greek goddess of Victory; Sony arose from the Latin word sonus (sound) and Volvo from the Latin word meaning, "I roll". Canon arose from the name Kwanon, the Japanese name for a Buddhist goddess of Mercy. Samsonite luggage is named after Samson – a very strong biblical figure.

Names should be long lasting and potentially extendable into new categories. Therefore, choosing a brand name is a strategic decision and shapes the future of the brand's reach (how many markets will it serve). The next section will consider other strategic decisions about brand architecture.

■ Brand architecture

Brand architecture describes how brands are structured within an organisation. Some companies can be described as a house of brands, where each brand is given its own brand name. Others can be classed as a branded house where each of the products are branded under one name.

House of brands

Brands may start as single product offerings but as companies grow, they may offer several brands in the same category to reach more segments. Known as a multi-branding strategy, each brand offered has its own name. Table 6.3 shows that Almarai offer croissants under two brand names – Lusine and 7-day. Unilever offer over 20 laundry detergents. It is perplexing that companies offer multiple brands within the same category but this situation arises when a company grows through acquisition. Within the Unilever portfolio, each individual brand is differently positioned, with one detergent aimed at those with sensitive skin, another for families and a third positioned as an economy brand, with some unique to a particular region. Multi-branding strategies spread risk, offer wider reach and may deter competitors from launching into a category. However multi branding creates complexity with each brand requiring support, and consequently brand managers internally compete for resources. This can lead to cannibalisation – where one brand in the portfolio steals market share from another, particularly when segments are not clearly defined and many companies are actively rationalising by deleting less profitable brands.

The branded house

Some companies sell all their products under the single corporate brand umbrella. This is common in B2B markets and many services. It is useful because the trust and recognition gained for the brand can extend to new markets and there is an opportunity for a consistent brand message. Good examples of this approach to branding are Standard Life, Barclays, JCB, intel, Virgin and Sainsbury.

Family branding

Known as multi-product branding, part of the name comes from the parent brand joined with a brand name signifying a different category. Thinking of Heinz Weightwatchers foods or Kellogg's Brand Buds, the core qualities of the family brand are subsumed into the sub brand and the goodwill transfers. This is known as the halo effect. Companies such as Mondelez are moving closer to corporate branding, by featuring their corporate name more strongly on packaging.

■ Brand equity

Brand equity is the difference that a brand creates for customers over an equivalent non-branded, generic product. It might attract a price premium because customers see extra value within the brand. Although brand equity is often seen as a financial measure, it is also about added value created in terms of consumer loyalty, respect and how salient or relevant it seems to be for the consumer. Much of the work undertaken on brand equity uses early work by Aaker (1991; 1996) and Keller (1993; 2008) to quantify brand value.

Several companies provide auditing services to brands including the brand consultancy and advertising agency Young and Rubicam who measure brand strength along four dimensions (Kotler et al, 2017):

- **Differentiation** – why and how does the brand stand out from the crowd?
- **Knowledge** – what do customers know about the brand?
- **Esteem** – how much is the brand respected?
- **Relevance**- how important is the brand in meeting consumer needs?

Measuring brand equity and value allows brands to benchmark against similar companies and act as a diagnostic to set strategic marketing priorities. Interbrand (2016) create an annual ranking of the best global brands. In 2016, Apple topped the list with a brand value of over $178 billion. Companies like Coca Cola and Pepsi have weakened brand value compared to technology giants and are possibly affected by healthy eating trends. Although rankings are fascinating, there is some concern that brand equity measurement is of little practical use (Christodoulides and de Chernatonay, 2010).

Product and branding futures

Products exist in a dynamic world and continue to develop to keep up with customer needs. This section will consider some trends affecting all products and brands: internationalisation, the move against brands and the importance of co-creation.

Increasingly, global companies own local brands. In 2010, Kraft Foods acquired the British chocolate manufacturer Cadbury and the sale received a great deal of negative political, public and press comment. Several western brands are Chinese owned, including the London Taxi Company, Volvo, Club Med and several football clubs. Sometimes brands are positioned differently across international markets. The malted drink Horlicks (owned by Glaxo Smith Kline) wakes you up in India but in the UK, it is positioned as an aid to sleep. International brand owners decide whether to go global with their brand, keeping all aspects the same, stay local, maintaining local characteristics, or combine strategies, known as *glocalisation*. American brands Avon and Heinz brands are assumed British in the UK.

For society, the growth and proliferation of brands is a mixed blessing. Branding can push up product quality, provide choice for consumers, employment for workers and many brands adopt an ethos of social responsibility.

However, brands are criticised for creating over-consumption, suggesting difference where there is none, being wasteful of resources, increasing prices, encouraging trade up, fostering greed and creating psychological and other problems for consumers who cannot own the 'essential' brand. Naomi Klein (1999) brought the anti-branding movement to mainstream attention and the movement has gained strength through online communities (Hollenbeck and Zinkhan, 2006), rejecting consumerism, certain brand practices and brands in general.

Most brands do not want to be seen to be doing harm. A responsible corporate brand can attract the best employees (Ind and Horlings, 2016) and will use brand values to demonstrate credentials to all stakeholders including shareholders. Brands remain strong if they can develop and maintain their relationship with customers. Brand meaning is created by consumers within their own social environment, but they are influenced by what is said by brand owners and others. The co-creation paradigm is highly relevant to brands and increasingly facilitated by the accessibility, reach and interactivity of social media. Consumers can generate meaning, new ideas and creative content with, or without the blessing of the brand owner.

Summary

This chapter has considered that products are not just physical items but a mix of intangible and tangible features, including the brand. Product offerings include ideas, experiences and personalities and when they fail to live up to expectations are destined to a short lifecycle. Strategic product decisions about branding, range and reach are fundamental to business success and the ultimate goal is to ensure that the full offer provides value for all.

Further reading

Brunswick, G.J and Zinser, B.A. (2016). The evolution of service dominant logic and its impact on marketing theory and Practice: A review, *Academy of Marketing Studies Journal*, **20**,120-136

Charts the chronological evolution of the S-D logic and its impact on marketing theory.

Usunier, J-C. and Shaner, J. (2002). Using linguistics for creating better international brand names, *Journal of Marketing Communications*, **8**(4), 211-228

A summary of global brand naming.

References

Aaker, D. (1991). *Managing Brand Equity*. The Free Press

Aaker, D. (1996). Measuring brand equity across products and markets. *California Management Review*. 38(3), 102-120.

Bacon, J (2017). Ella's Kitchen founder Paul Lindley on why ethical brands will endure Marketing Week. 15 Feb, https://www.marketingweek.com/2017/02/15/ellas-kitchen-paul-lindley-ethical-brands-endure/

Baines, P., Fill, C. and Rosengren, S. (2017). *Marketing*, 4th Edition, OUP

Castellion, G. and Markham, S.K. (2013). Perspective: new product failure rates: influence of argumentum ad populum and self-interest. *Journal of Product Innovation Management*, **30**(5), 976–979.

Christodoulides, G. and de Chernatony, L. (2010). Consumer-based brand equity conceptualisation and measurement: A literature review. *International Journal of Market Research*, **52**(1), 43-66

Dhalla, N.K. and Yuspeh, S (1976). Forget the product life cycle concept! *Harvard Business Review*, January

Getz, D., Andersson, T.D. and Carlsen, J. (2010). Festival management studies. *International Journal of Event and Festival Management*, (1) 29-59.

Hollenbeck, C.R. and Zinkhan, G.M. (2006). Consumer activism on the internet: the role of anti-brand communities, in *Advances in Consumer Research* Vol.33, C. Pechmann and L. Price (eds.), Duluth, MN: Association for Consumer Research: 479-485.

Ind, N. and Horlings, N. (2016). *Brands with a Conscience*. Kogan Page

Interbrand (2016) Best Global Brands 2016 Ranking. Available at interbrand.com/best-brands/best-global-brands/2016/ranking/

Keller, K. L. (1993). Conceptualizing, measuring, and managing customer-based brand equity. *Journal of Marketing*. **57**(1), 1-22.

Keller, K. L. (2008). *Strategic Brand Management, Building Measuring & Managing Brand Equity*. Pearson.

Keller, K. L. (2009). Building strong brands in a modern marketing communications environment. *Journal of Marketing Communications*. **15**(2-3), 139-155.

Klein, N. (1999). *No Logo*. Harper Collins

Kotler, P., Armstrong, G., Harris, L.C., and Piercy, N. (2017) *Principles of Marketing*. 7th Edition. Pearson

Mair, J. and Thompson, K (2009). The UK association conference attendance decision-making process. *Tourism Management*, **30**(3), 400-409

6

Moon, Y. (2005). Break free from the product life cycle. *Harvard Business Review*. May

PwC. (2013). Counterfeit goods in the UK. Who is buying what, and why? https://www.pwc.co.uk/assets/pdf/anti-counterfeiting-consumer-survey-october-2013.pdf

Resnick, M.R., Cheng, R., Simpson, M., and Lourenco, F. (2016). Marketing in SMEs: a '4Ps' self-branding model, *International Journal of Entrepreneurial Behaviour & Research*, **22**(1), 1-20.

Usunier, J-C. and Shaner, J. (2002). Using linguistics for creating better international brand names, *Journal of Marketing Communications*, **8**(4), 211-228.

Wilson, A., Zeithaml, V.A., Bitner, M-J., and Gremler, D.D. (2016) *Services Marketing: Integrating customer focus across the firm*. McGraw Hill.

7 Price

Graham Pogson

"How much?" is a phrase heard the world over, between shopkeeper and customer, in organisations and in general conversation. Prices can start at no monetary value; Gillette patented his razor and blade system (for shaving beards and moustaches) in 1904, but was said to have given razors away, knowing that customers would buy his disposable blades and that he would make a profit in this way. Although this story turned out to be a myth (Picker, 2011) some products are still given free as an incentive to purchase more with the ultimate aim of making a profit. Price is about value to the customer. Organisations that are able to continuously offer the right mix of goods and services at the right price will create the best customer value and are more likely to be successful.

First considerations

When buying a product, price may not be the first consideration. The features and benefits of the product may be prioritised and if the product solves a particular problem then price may become a secondary factor. This alludes to the concept of utility, which in an economic sense is the sum of benefits gained from consumption (Dibb et al 2012), which often decline through further consumption (Free, 2010). Eventually, as one navigates through the buying process, the price of the product will become of some importance. At its narrowest, price "is the amount of money charged for a product or service" (Armstrong and Kotler, 2013:285). However, money is not the only thing that might need to be sacrificed to buy a product. For example if the purchase is an iPhone, the benefits of an Android phone will be foregone. Equally, if the purchase is an Android phone, the benefits of an iPhone would be lost, unless both are purchased with consequent costs. A broader appreciation of price includes money and the other elements of value given up to buy a particular product. Dibb et al. summarise price as "the value placed on what is exchanged" (Dibb et al., 2012:593). This concept of value can be expressed in diagram form:

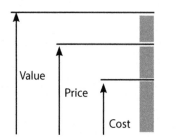

Value – Price = Consumer surplus
Price – Cost = Profit margin
Value – Cost = Value added

Figure 7.1: The components of value

Brassington and Petitt (2006:1221) propose that value is "a customer's assessment of the worth of what they are getting in terms of a product's functional or psychological benefits". This implies that the benefits of a product can be converted into a sum of money for each customer as expressed in Figure 7.1. The marketer's task is to use the marketing mix to communicate maximum value to the customer, allowing the price to be set to minimise the consumer surplus element and enhance the profit margin for the organisation at the same time.

Exercise: Find two or three further definitions/explanations of 'value' to check and enhance your understanding of this concept.

At first glance, the idea of free products seems to be at odds with the value diagram above. However, Osterwalder and Pigneur (2010: 96) use the term '*Fremium*', coined by Jarid Lukin, to explain business models that combine free but basic services with premium services that must be paid for. This works well with an internet based business where the cost of each extra user to the organisation is virtually zero and examples include LinkedIn, Strava and Dropbox. Incentives can be given by the organisation (Kumar 2014) for users to refer friends and this is more likely to work when the basic service is free. Upgrade options are then offered from which the organisation can obtain revenue.

The word *price* is the general term but other names have been developed over time to indicate price in different contexts. Table 7.1 gives a selection of these:

Table 7.1: Alternative terms used for price. Adapted from Dibb et al (2012)

Product/service context	Term used	Product/service context	Term used
Accountant	Fee	Parking Violation	Fine
Ad-hoc payment for service	Tip	Payment for labour	Wages
Estate agent	Commission	Reserving goods and/or services	Deposit
Government services	Tax	Travel e.g. Bus, train or plane	Fare
Insurance	Premium	Use of equipment or property	Rent
Loans, mortgages	Interest		

Exercise: Is there any alternative terminology used within your region not shown in Table 7.1?

Considering the other elements of the marketing mix, they all represent a cost. Price, on the other hand, represents the opportunity to obtain revenue for a product. This revenue gathering is governed by the following equations:

Total revenue = Volume sold × Unit price

Profit = Total revenue − Total costs

These equations form the financial bedrock of the pricing decision. Note that organisations who do not seek to make a profit, such as government organisations and charities, still need to cover their costs and preferably make a surplus to cover future investments. Using a formula makes price setting seem a totally rational and therefore mechanical or scientific process, however this chapter will demonstrate that price is much more involved, incorporating a rational process but embodying emotion too.

Approaches to pricing

Firms determine their approach to the pricing of their products based on their marketing strategy and their understanding of the context in which the product is centred:

Figure 7.2: Factors that influence price

All cost and no returns

James Dyson produced around 1000 designs and spent around £2 million to develop a successful prototype of his bagless vacuum cleaner (Tidd, 2013). He tried, unsuccessfully, to promote this product to existing manufacturers (his preferred customers) for them to buy a licence to make the cleaner. Having invested the time and money in trying to sell licenses, he eventually manufactured the vacuum cleaners himself.

The market, industry and firm are all located within the external environment. Changes in the external environment can have huge effects on a product, hence its price in the market. The external environment can be understood through the well-known PEST (or PESTEL) model.

Political

Economic

Social

Technological

Political changes are wide ranging and include, for example, changes in the levels of tax imposed on some products and this in turn will affect the product price. For example children's shoes in the UK are not subjected to Value Added Tax (VAT) (HM Revenue & Customs, 2014), whereas adults' shoe price must include VAT. If a future UK Government were to review this situation and impose VAT on children's shoes, their prices would have to be increased by the VAT rate.

Changes in the global economy, the regional economy (e.g. the European Union), the economy of a country and even the local economy can result in a change in people's ability to pay for products. The 'credit crunch' at the end of 2007 led to a financial meltdown in 2008 and a global recession in 2009 (BBC, 2009) affecting the income of many millions of people. This led to the growth of discount supermarkets such as Aldi and Lidl in the UK to the cost of more established supermarkets such as Tesco and Asda.

Changes in fashion (sociocultural) and technology (technological) also affect the ability and willingness of people to pay for products.

The customer needs to feel that they are gaining the maximum value from the product(s) they intend to purchase and so the firm's task is to balance this value with price (and the other elements of the marketing mix) to achieve a fair exchange. Several approaches are used to achieve this balance. Baines et al.(2011) refer to four pricing orientations: cost, demand, competitor and value whereas other authors, for example Armstrong and Kotler (2007) and Dibb et al. (2012) use approaches similar to cost competition and market as considered here.

Exercise: Identify and explain one element from each of the overlapping layers that would affect the price of a new car.

■   Cost-based pricing

This method of pricing is one of the easiest to implement and includes the price and cost elements from the value diagram in Figure 7.1. It does not consider the extra element of customer value and so is predominantly an internally based mechanical process. The first task in cost-based pricing is to identify the costs that arise from producing, distributing and selling the product, and then an appropriate price can then be calculated to allow a profit to be made.

Costs can be classified as fixed or variable. Fixed costs must be paid by the organisation whether anything is produced or not and include rents, rates, utilities (for heating and lighting), loan interest and salaries. Variable costs rise in proportion with production and are related to each unit of production. For example the parts used in production (the individual components that make up a car, the milk for a litre of ice cream for example), the power used in production and the labour used in each process. Investment in larger plant can reduce unit costs assuming that economies of scale apply where unit costs reduce as an organisation becomes more experienced in its chosen industry. The addition of fixed and variable costs produces total costs and this can be used in the production of a bBreak-even chart, which occurs when total costs meet revenue. This is illustrated (Figure 7.3) for a zero emissions motorcycle:

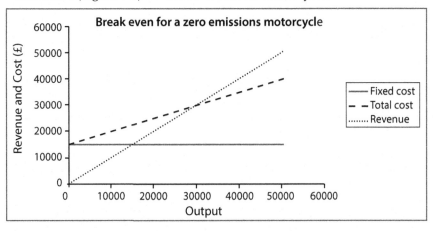

Figure 7.3: Revenue and costs graph for a zero emissions motorcycle

Exercise: Considering Figure 7.3, identify the break even revenue and output for the zero emissions motorcycle

If insufficient motorcycles are sold to make a profit, costs could be lowered by buying cheaper parts, reducing labour costs, achieving economies of scale and/ or the price could be raised to 'shift' the revenue curve to the left and dropping the break-even output. Either way the break-even chart can be used as a forecasting tool to calculate break-even output using alternative product prices in the calculation.

Mark-up pricing (or cost-plus pricing) is another cost based approach. Costs must be calculated and a mark-up is then applied, usually by adding a percentage to the total cost of the product.

■ Competition-based pricing

Successful use of competition-based pricing depends on the organisation having a good working knowledge of both internal and external factors. Armstrong and Kotler (2013:291) define competition-based pricing as:

> *Setting prices based on competitors' strategies, prices, costs and market offerings.*

A useful way to illustrate each of the factors is to tabulate them as shown in Table 7.2. This hints at the complexities of this approach. A thorough understanding of the industry is needed whether it is a monopoly, monopolistic, perfect or oligopoly (Brassington and Pettitt, 2007). The organisation needs to anticipate the responses of competitors to price changes in the market (Baines et al., 2011). Some organisations will use benchmarking (Jobber and Fahy, 2006) to set prices at above, the same as, or lower than the competition. When price is the primary means of competition, an organisation strives to be the lowest cost producer to have the greatest chance of success. This is more pertinent as prices are easily compared online.

Milking the market?

Farmers in the UK who produce milk are 'price takers'; they have no or very little power over the price offered to them by milk processors, who then sell the milk to supermarkets and other retailers. As a result of the price war between supermarkets (Mintel, 2015), the supermarkets reduced the price they paid to milk processors and in turn, the milk processors reduced the price paid to the farmers. The milk market is in the maturity phase of the product lifecycle. Many farmers decided to leave milk production, as they were unable to cover their costs. Is there anything that the milk farmers could do about their situation other than leave the industry?

Table 7.2: Factors involved in competition-based pricing

Factor	Importance to the organisation	Difficulties
Organisation Costs	A thorough understanding of an organisation's costs will indicate where costs can be cut if reduction is deemed necessary. Costs will rise if the organisation decides to differentiate its product(s). Remember that: Profit = Total Revenue – Total costs	The expertise needed to ascertain and allocate costs accurately is needed.
Competitors strategies and pricing tactics	Knowledge of competitors' pricing strategies allows the organisation to set a competitive price and to respond to price changes.	Competitors' current prices are usually visible in the market but future intentions will not be known. Prices not generally known during competitive tendering.
Market offerings (degree of differentiation)	If the products in the market are homogenous, (e.g. some agricultural products) it is likely that 'me too' pricing will be in operation: all organisations will charge a similar price. If there is differentiation between products, customers will judge if extra features and benefits create enough value for a higher price to be charged.	When all competitors set the same price, a reduction by any one competitor can result in a price war; prices fall below costs and only the strongest survive in the market. Organisations must invest in the other elements of the marketing mix to differentiate their product and charge a higher price.

Customers will use the price information that they have and balance the price against other factors that are of value to them, e.g. service, delivery time, packaging, in order to choose the product that gives them the best value. The internet increases price transparency to consumers and competitors alike and the best deals found through search engines and price comparison sites, and this can be automated through virtual personal assistants. Online price increases and decreases can also be automated, depending on demand and competitor pricing. This means that pricing becomes much more dynamic with competitors reacting to price changes rapidly to maintain and gain market share.

■ Market-based pricing

This is a more multi-faceted approach than cost-based or competition-based pricing. Market-based pricing involves a knowledge of costs (internal to the organisation), the rest of the marketing mix elements (product, place and promotion as a minimum), a knowledge of competitors and their products (external to the organisation) and a knowledge of what is important to the customer and therefore the factors that contribute to customer value. It also embodies the ideas of supply and demand and requires answers to questions such as "what is the total supply to the market just now?" and "does the level of demand justify our entry to this market with our product?"

For a comprehensive review of demand elasticity see Klein (2010); a brief review is given here.

The 'classic' demand curve relates price to quantity demanded (purchased):

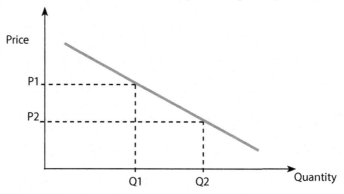

Figure 7.4: The classic demand curve

The graph in Figure 7.4 relates to any 'normal' product. As the price is reduced from P1 to P2, the quantity demanded will increase from Q1 to Q2. A change in anything other than price or quantity will lead to a 'shift' in the curve rather than 'movement along the curve'.

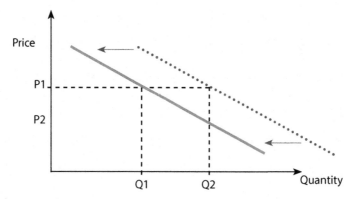

Figure 7.5: Shifting the demand curve

Imagine that the upper line in the graph (Figure 7.5) is the current demand curve for children's shoes. A change in taste/fashion away from children's shoes e.g. to trainers, would cause the demand curve to 'shift' to the left as indicated by the two arrows. The lower curve now represents the new demand for children's shoes. This shift in the curve means that at any price the quantity of shoes demanded will have reduced. The price is P1 with the quantity demanded reduced from Q2 to Q1. It can be seen that there will be a corresponding shift to the right of the demand curve for trainers.

Luxury products are examples of goods that are described by a different demand curve called a 'boomerang demand curve':

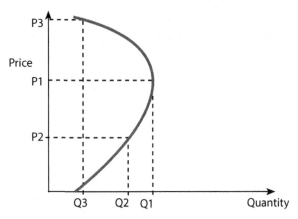

Figure 7.6: The boomerang curve

Figure 7.6 shows that a decrease in price from P1 to P2 results in a decrease in the quantity demanded from Q1 to Q2, the opposite to the classical demand curve. This indicates that part of the value of this type of product is in its relatively high price and so a lowering of the price lowers the value to the potential consumer. The curve bends round like a boomerang (as its name suggests) at higher prices indicating that the price can still be too high for a luxury product and that marketers need to set the price of such a product using an understanding of the boomerang curve amongst other factors.

Exercise: List three products that could behave in the manner illustrated by the boomerang curve.

The demand curve is used to determine the sensitivity of the demand for a product to a price change. For some products, even a slight change in price will lead to a large change in quantity demanded; these products are said to have a high elasticity of demand and the demand curve is quite steep. An example of this is the UK motor insurance market where "a one per cent price reduction online can drive up to a 50 per cent increase in volume" (Bertini and Ham, 2013: 49). Conversely, the quantity demanded for products with a low elasticity of demand changes only slightly (i.e. a flatter curve) with a change in price.

Table 7.3: Summary of factors considered in market-based pricing

Factor	Importance to the organisation	Difficulties
Cost	Organisation needs to know its costs	Needs up to date information of all costs
Marketing strategy	The vision created, defining the direction for the organisation has clear implications for all marketing activity.	Strategies take time to develop and this can be problematic in any market where there is rapid change.
Marketing mix	Product, place and promotion can all influence the final price of a product	Changes in any marketing mix element can affect the price that can be charged in ways that are not always expected.
Demand	Basic economic understanding is important, e.g. is the demand curve a 'classic' curve or another shape such as the boomerang curve	There are many factors that determine the shape and movement of a demand curve
Perceived value	Higher perception of value allows a higher price to be charged	Consumer perception is influenced by many factors external to the companies control
Elasticity of demand	How much does a change in price affect demand?	Can be difficult to determine especially as prices can change quickly, especially in ecommerce.
Supply	Both over- and under-supply affects price.	External factors such as supply of raw materials may influence this
Product lifecycle	The whole marketing strategy, including pricing is affected by the position of the product in the lifecycle.	Changes in any of the PEST factors or the external environment can render a product obsolete in a short time span, e.g. VHS recorders and computer floppy disks are now obsolete in most markets.
Type of Market	Business to business (B2B) transactions are very different to Business to Consumer (B2C) sales. Consumer to Consumer (C2C) may be based on set prices, negotiated prices or auction through third party platforms such as EBay	B2B transactions often require long-term relationships and contracts between the parties involved.
External environment e.g. PEST	The organisation should be continually updating itself and be a learning organisation by scanning its environment for potential changes that will affect demand and supply	Changes in legislation affecting the sale and use of a product can be difficult to forecast.

> **Exercise**: Table 7.3 is not exhaustive. Identify other factors that influence pricing within an organisation.

Pricing for different situations

All organisations need to know how to set a price for their product(s) and the three pricing approaches in the previous section have addressed this. However, the market place is very dynamic with new products being introduced, incumbents leaving the market, others seeing a gap in the market for their offering, and product withdrawals as they near the end of the product lifecycle. Pricing for the introduction of new products and existing markets are now addressed.

■ New product introduction

The dilemma here is whether to take the risks associated with being first to market with a product or to wait for others to enter the market so that they take the risk but potentially reaping the rewards. An organisation introducing a product that is completely new to the market has a choice of two approaches, 'skimming' or 'penetration' (see, for example Baines, 2011; Brassington and Pettitt, 2007; Kotler et al., 2005) and the approach adopted depends on an organisation's marketing strategy and objectives.

7

The **skimming** approach to product introduction assumes that it is possible to segment the market with the segment willing to pay the highest price for the new product targeted first. Successive segments are targeted (skimmed) at progressively reduced prices until the desired market has been served. The initial product offering must be of high quality or be sufficiently unique and innovative to justify the premium price; later products can be of lower quality to keep costs down. The diffusion of innovation model (e.g. Kotler 2005; Brassington and Pettitt 2006) is one segmentation method that could be considered. Skimming works well for technology products, e.g. Apple's iPhone, where some consumers (innovators and early adopters) are happy to pay a higher price for a new model of phone than are the early majority, late majority and laggards.

Market **penetration** depends on setting a low initial price to drive high sales volumes and capture a large share of the market. This approach relies on high sales volumes leading to a lowering cost per unit resulting in break-even and profit. Once high sales volumes are achieved, along with resulting falls in costs, the organisation may be able to reduce prices more and further increase market penetration. EasyJet and Ryanair have used this strategy, introducing flights to and from smaller airports at low prices compared to national carriers such as

British Airways, Malaysia Airlines, and Emirates. This method also depends (Armstrong and Kotler, 2013) on the market being price sensitive and that low prices will be a barrier to entry for other organisations.

Exercise: Look at one of the low cost airlines operating in your country to see what destinations the company serves and then search for flights using one of the flight comparison sites, e.g. Skyscanner, to see which company is cheapest. Would price be your first consideration if you were booking one of these flights?

Jobber (2006:201) combines skimming and penetration to produce a matrix with promotion and price for the axes. The speed of skimming/penetration can be affected by increasing or decreasing the amount of promotion used. For example, if a new product has been introduced and the rate of penetration is too low, the organisation can increase the original promotional budget to accelerate the rate of penetration. To achieve slower skimming and potentially higher revenues an organisation could limit the amount of promotion e.g. through niche/specialist magazines most likely to be read by the target market.

■ Existing markets

In this case, there is at least one market incumbent and there may be many more depending on the market structure and product under consideration. An organisation that is already serving a market, with one or several products, inherently has different choices to make compared to an organisation that has developed a new product to enter an existing market. Each should have a clear marketing strategy that includes determination of price along with the rest of the marketing mix. The major options for a new entrant are (Porter, 1985 in Johnson et al., 2008) through cost advantage (leading to the ability to charge lower prices) to achieve market penetration or through differentiation of the product allowing the organisation to charge the same or preferably higher prices than the competition.

Cost advantages can be used to enter a market and achieve market penetration. The organisation prices their product below that of current offerings in the market to gain a share of the market that is large enough to achieve marketing objectives, cover their costs, make a profit and use this position to make further price cuts and achieve a higher market share. Ryanair use their low cost model to enter existing markets. Entering a market using the differentiation approach requires that the product has some unique feature or benefits in comparison to the products currently in the market and that potential customers value these product differences sufficiently to pay a higher price. Fitness watches are a recent product that depends on differentiation. There are many possible features from stopwatch and step counting functions to heart rate measurement, altitude, recovery advice, race prediction and multi-sport capabilities, e.g. swimming, cycling and running. Companies such as Polar, Suunto, Garmin and Tom Tom each differentiates itself using a particular mix of features, making it more difficult for consumers to compare watches on price, and thus allowing the companies greater discretion on selling price.

When a product is part of a product range, (also called product line or product mix), the organisation has to consider how to set the price for each of the products within the mix. Armstrong and Kotler (2007) call this a 'product mix pricing strategy' and propose several possibilities for product mix pricing:

Table 7.4: Product mix pricing strategies. Adapted from Armstrong & Kotler (2007)

Product mix strategy	Explanation and example
Product line pricing	Differences in price between products depending on features and benefits; mobile phone contracts
Optional-product pricing	Extra products that can be added to the main product; addition of onion rings to a meal
Captive-product pricing	Captive products must be used with the main product; Gillette razors and blades
By-product pricing	Products produced along with the main product but of low value; sawdust is a by-product of the timber industry
Product bundle pricing	Bundles of products sold together; a McDonald's Happy Meal

Further pricing decisions

Even once an organisation has developed its marketing strategy, determined its approach to pricing and applied these factors to its situation (new product or existing market), there are still further pricing decisions needed. For example, organisations selling their products in different countries need to develop a strategy on international pricing. It is possible to set one price and charge this throughout the world as Boeing do with their aircraft (Armstrong and Kotler, 2007), however most organisations will determine prices based on their approach to pricing as discussed earlier, applied to the local market conditions. Price changes can be initiated in response to market conditions and competitors will then have to tactically determine what they should do to respond to these price changes.

These strategic and tactical pricing decisions are summarised below along with sources where fuller details can be found:

Table 7.5a: Strategic pricing decisions

	Explanation	Consequences
Differential pricing (Dibb et al 2012)	Different prices are charged to different buyers of the same product based on segmentation	A single price is much simpler but does not encourage demand across different segments that may otherwise be excluded from the offering. For example, reduced prices to the elderly and students
International pricing (Armstrong & Kotler, 2007)	Products can be sold at the same price in all countries or prices determined for each country	Different costs for different markets (due to economic conditions, laws and regulations, tariffs and transport) make charging the same price difficult. Price is used to position a brand in a different way depending on the country, e.g. some international brands are seen as luxury in one market but standard elsewhere
Discount pricing (Armstrong & Kotler 2007, Brassington & Pettitt 2007)	Several discounts and allowances can be applied, e.g. trade discounts, quantity discounts, cash discounts, early payment discounts.	Every discount applied has the potential to reduce the profit on the product. Early payment discounts can lead to better cash flow offsetting any loss in profit
Transfer pricing (Brassington & Pettitt, 2006)	Component parts and products are transferred between plants within an organisation with a special pricing policy.	There is no ideal method to set transfer prices. Some buyers source parts and products from outside their own organisation. There may be taxation implications depending on the geographic region/country that the organisation operates in
Psychological pricing	Prices are changed to influence the customer decision making process	Customers may not understand the psychological tools used by the marketer e.g. pricing at £2.99 instead of £3.00.

Table 7.5b: Tactical pricing decisions

	Explanation	Consequences
Initiating price increases (Jobber 2006)	Cost increases and a need to reduce demand due to emerging shortages are two reasons for raising prices. 'Price jump' or 'escalator' options can be used.	Loss of market share (depending on competitor response) could lead to reduced profits.

Initiating price cuts (Brassington & Pettitt 2006)	Prices may be cut to improve market penetration, clear stock or to defend market share	Knowledge of the elasticity of demand for the product is required. Any sales increase must offset any loss in profit. Consider the likely response from competitors
Responding to competitors' price changes (Kotler et al., 2009)	Should an organisation follow price rises/cuts made by competitors? This is complex and varies with the situation, e.g. stage in product lifecycle, competitors' intentions, price elasticity and resources. It is better to anticipate possible price changes rather than to have to respond at short notice.	If the product is differentiated, some latitude in response is possible with no response required given sufficient differentiation. Otherwise, price reductions will be matched. For homogenous products, price rises may be reversed if the leader faces enough opposition from competitors.

Exercise: Explain the difference between discount pricing and a price cut.

■   Psychological effects of pricing

7

Pricing has an extremely important role in positioning a product or service in the consumer's mind. Higher prices are often seen as an indicator of higher quality and may increase the brand's overall success, as well as providing surpluses that can be used to incentivise distributors and promote the brand. Reductions in price can stimulate demand but might also suggest to consumers that the product is going to become obsolete or that the product is in decline.

■   Ethical issues

The ethics associated with the determination of price are set within the broader issues of the laws that apply. The major ethical issue with price is the level at which it is set. Prices need to cover costs for the organisation and allow for a profit but they must also be fair. The following is a sample of ethical issues associated with price:

Table 7.6: Ethical issues

Issue	Example	Justification
Price discrimination (Alternatively, differential pricing, see Table 5a.	Finding out that your fellow air passenger has paid $180 for their seat when you have paid $1100 (Elegido, 2011). Lower prices for different segments such as student special prices.	Although this practice may lack transparency, some discover how to pay the lower price. In the case of flight prices, airlines hold a few seats until the last few days before a flight and these carry a premium price to offset the risk of not selling the ticket(s)
Transfer pricing	In July 2010, Italian law decreed that transfer pricing documentation must be made available to tax authorities by multinational enterprises (MNE's). (Martinelli, 2010)	This improves transparency. Non-provision of the required documents can result in severe penalties
Dumping: when products are sold in a country other than their origin at below cost	Tata Steel decided to sell its UK operation due to several economic factors, one being the very low prices of steel from China (BBC News, 2016)	China's steel producers were looking for other markets for steel due to lower demand in 2015/16. Some argued that the price for this steel was 'unrealistically low' (BBC News, 2016)
Pricing transparency	"Traditional haggling over prices in open markets is visible for all to see. With many modern information technology-based systems of individual pricing, the results are less visible." (McMahon Beattie, Palmer, & Yeoman 2011: 61)	A lack of openness in pricing leads to mistrust by consumers, so e-retailers need to ensure that their pricing is as transparent as possible to retain and increase customer trust. Many online auction sites now provide postal costs and credit card fees up front, so they are not hidden. Customers discuss price paid on social media and review sites

Forecasting

Forecasting is an essential part of the marketing planning process (Brassington and Pettitt, 2006) and the marketing function is responsible for preparing the sales forecasts (Kotler 2006). It can be very difficult, even at an individual product level, to forecast demand as discovered by a producer of the starter ballasts for fluorescent lighting tubes (Mentzer, 2012). When a fluorescent light is switched on, there is a slight delay before the light responds; this is due to the starter ballast 'starting' the light. These starters were sold in small numbers over time but a sudden spike in demand overwhelmed production capabilities. The company found that the 'small number' sales were due to households and organisations replacing starters as they failed. The larger orders were for office and factory re-fits where hundreds or thousands of starters were being replaced with new, highly efficient starters to save electricity. The company were unable to forecast this mixed demand but overcame the problem by offering contractors a discount if they ordered their starters five weeks before needed. This allowed the company to schedule production to meet demand and to reduce costs.

Both quantitative and qualitative methods can be used in the production of a forecast and forecasts can be produced at the levels of external environment, industry/market, organisation/firm and product; see Figure 7.2, illustrating this hierarchy. Qualitative methods include management judgement, sales force surveys, panels of experts and scenario techniques (Brassington and Pettitt, 2006). Any of these methods once selected must be carefully carried out and they all carry a risk of being wrong when the external environment changes unexpectedly. Reliance on management judgement alone would be particularly risky, as management will inherently have their own motivations and filters based on experience and incentives. Quantitative methods, by their nature, appear to be much more reliable as they are based on numbers and calculations. However, these methods often use historical data on which to base projections of demand into the future and cannot take complete account of changes in the environment that will affect demand.

Summary

It is clear from this chapter that price setting is a complex part of the marketing process. A good understanding of the concepts of price and value helps set appropriate price for a product. Cost, competition, or market-based approaches are adapted to the situation, depending on whether the market is new or existing. Further strategic and tactical decisions are necessary and must consider the market, the product and what customers value all within an ethical context. Developments are continually taking place that affect the price setting process, particularly the rise on of online and digital approaches.

References

Armstrong, G. and Kotler, P. (2007). *Marketing An Introduction* (8th ed.). Harlow: Pearson Education Limited.

Baines, P., Fill, C. and Page, K. (2011). *Marketing, 2nd Edition.* Oxford: Oxford University Press.

BBC. (2009). *Global recession timeline*, BBC News, 9 September. http://news.bbc. co.uk/1/hi/business/8242825.stm. [Accessed 24 February, 2016].

BBC News. (2016). *Britain's steel industry: What's going wrong?* BBC News, 30 March. http://www.bbc.co.uk/news/business-34581945. [Accessed 17 May, 2016].

Bertini, M. and Ham, T. (2013). *The right price, at the right moment, to the right customer.* London Business School, 18 April. https://www.london.edu/faculty-and-research/lbsr/the-right-price-at-the-right-moment-to-the-right-customer. [Accessed 10 May, 2016].

Brassington, F. and Pettitt, S. (2006). *Principles of Marketing, 4th Edition.* Harlow: Pearson Education Limited.

Brassington, F. and Pettitt, S. (2007). *Essentials of Marketing, 2nd Edition.* Harlow: Pearson Education Limited.

Dibb, S., Simkin, L., Pride, W. and Ferrell, O. (2012). *Marketing: Concepts and Strategies, 6th Edition.* Andover: Cengage Learning EMEA.

Elegido, J. (2011). The ethics of price discrimination. *Business Ethics Quarterly,* **21**(4), 633-660.

Free, R. (2010). *21st Century Economics: A Reference Handbook.* http://hw.lib.ed.ac. uk/vwebv/holdingsInfo?bibId=353449: Sage Publications, Inc. doi:http://dx.doi. org/10.4135/9781412979290

HM Revenue & Customs. (2014). *VAT rates on different goods and services.* Gov.UK, 4 February: https://www.gov.uk/guidance/rates-of-vat-on-different-goods-and-services#clothing-and-footwear-protective-and-safety-equipment. [Accessed 24 February, 2016].

Jobber, D. and Fahy, J. (2006). *Foundations of Marketing, 2nd Edition.* Maidenhead: McGraw-Hill Education.

Johnson, G., Scholes, K. and Whittington, R. (2008). *Exploring Corporate Strategy, 8th Edition.* Harlow: Prentice Hall.

Klein, K. (2010). Supply, demand, and equilibrium, in *21st Century Economics: a reference handbook.* (R. Free, Ed.) Los Angeles, California, USA: Sage. doi:http://dx.doi.org.ezproxy1.hw.ac.uk/10.4135/9781412979290.n7

Kotler, P. &. (2006). *Marketing Management, 12th Edition.* New Jersey: Pearson Prentice-Hall.

Kotler, P., Keller, K., Brady, M., Goodman, M. and Hansen, T. (2009). *Marketing Management: 1st European Edition*. Pearson Education.

Kotler, P., Wong, V. and Armstrong, G. (2005). *Principles of Marketing, 4th European Edition*. Harlow, England: Pearson Education Limited.

Kumar, V. (2014). *Making 'Freemium' Work*. https://hbr.org/2014/05/making-freemium-work. [Accessed 25 May, 2015].

Martinelli, M. (2010). New Italian Legislation on Transfer Pricing Documentation. *International Tax Journal*, **5**, 17-83.

McMahon Beattie, U., Palmer, A. and Yeoman, I. (2011). Does the customer trust you? In U. McMahon Beattie and I. Yeoman, *Revenue Management: A Practical Pricing Perspective*. London: Palgrave Macmillan.

Mentzer, J. &. (2012, May). *Sales Forecasting Management: A Demand Management Approach, 2nd Edition*. Thousand Oaks, California: Sage Publications Inc. doi:http://ezproxy1.hw.ac.uk:2078/10.4135/9781452204444

Mintel. (2015). *Added Value in Dairy Drinks, Milk and Cream*. Mintel Group Ltd. http://academic.mintel.com/display/715792/

Osterwalder, A. a. (2010). *Business Model Generation A Handbook for Visionaries, Game Changers, and Challengers*. New Jersey: John Wiley & Sons Inc.

Picker, R. (2011). *The Razors-and-Blades Myth(s)*. Retrieved May 18, 2015, from The University of Chicago Law School: http://www.law.uchicago.edu/faculty/research/randal-c-picker-razors-and-blades-myths

Ryanair. (2016). *Welcome to Ryanair*. Ryanair, 27 April. http://corporate.ryanair.com/news/news/160427-3-new-newcastle-routes-to-gdansk-warsaw-wroclaw-launched/?market=en. [Accessed May 10, 2016].

Tidd, J. B. (2013). *Managing Innovation: Integrating technological, market and organisational change*. Chichester: Wiley.

7

Promotion: Marketing Communications

Kitty Shaw

Promotion is how an organisation communicates with its customers and other stakeholders. Organisations use many promotional tools to achieve a range of objectives including increasing awareness of their product or service offering; communicating brand values; and building relationships with their customers and other stakeholders. Promotional tools or the marketing communications mix include advertising, sales promotions, public relations, sponsorship, direct marketing and personal selling. These tools are used across a range of media including print, television, radio, digital channels and the internet, as well as personal communications.

The choice of communication tools and media will be determined by the organisation's marketing strategy and the segmentation, targeting and positioning approach that supports this strategy, as discussed in Chapter 5. This chapter begins by discussing the role of promotion as part of the broader marketing strategy; how promotional tools support the delivery of this marketing strategy; and how the effectiveness of these communications in delivering marketing strategy is measured. It then discusses marketing communications theory and how this informs modern marketing practice. The remainder of the chapter provides a more detailed discussion on individual promotional tools.

Planning marketing communications

Communication strategy is driven by the organisation's marketing strategy and the segmentation, targeting and positioning approach that flows from this. The strategy will determine the organisation's high-level communications objectives and key messages, along with the audiences or stakeholder groups it wants to target. This in turn helps to determine the best promotional tools and media to deliver key messages to these target audiences. For example, an organisation wanting to increase sales will identify specific market segments that it will target to generate sales, either as new customers or to increase its 'share of wallet' among existing customers. It may then use research to establish the most effective promotional tools and media to reach its target audiences. Effective marketing communications planning needs to be driven by data, including the organisation's own SWOT (internal strengths and weaknesses; external opportunities and threats), market analysis and a detailed understanding of target audiences. Figure 8.1 illustrates how an integrated and data-driven marketing communications planning process should work.

For example, the investment company Standard Life identified that many of its target audiences for investment products regularly travel through major UK airports and railway stations linking the financial centres of Edinburgh and London. The company commissioned a series of billboard advertisements to be displayed in Edinburgh and London airports and a selection of London train and tube stations, which financial sector commuters are known to pass through.

Effective marketing communications planning needs to be integrated so that a consistent image is delivered across all audiences and media. While companies may target a number of different audiences and stakeholder groups using a range of communications channels and media, they need to represent a consistent set of values and core messages to establish their identity and positioning so that all audiences know who they are and what they stand for. This is known as *integrated marketing communications* (IMC). If organisations present very different images to their customer groups this undermines credibility and leaves positioning unclear. Organisations must develop a strong positioning, which supports their overall marketing strategy, and resonates with their target audiences.

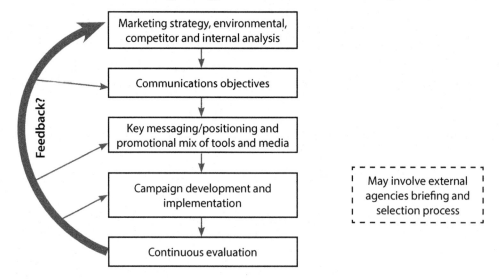

Figure 8.1: The marketing communications planning process

The first stage of communications planning is to establish the communications objectives, which will be derived from the marketing objectives. For example, if the overall objective is for growth through new markets, this may generate a number of communications objectives including establishing the brand in these new markets and promoting specific products or services to target segments. Alternatively, a company seeking growth from its existing markets will want to use communications to reinforce brand values and strengthen relationships with existing customers. Fill (2013) identifies four purposes of marketing communications, to differentiate, to reinforce, to inform or to persuade. This model, known as DRIP for short, is illustrated in Table 8.1.

Table 8.1: The four purposes of marketing communications. Adapted from Fill (2013:15)

Task	Explanation
Differentiate	To make product or service stand out from the competition
Reinforce	To consolidate previous customer experiences and messaging
Inform	To draw attention to product or service and its features
Persuade	To move potential customers towards purchase decision or further enquiry

Many organisations seek to differentiate themselves from their competition by stressing their Unique Selling Points (USPs), which might be based on product features and their associated customer benefits or more psychological benefits arising from intangible brand benefits.

Having established the communication objectives, the organisation then needs to translate these into key messages for the positioning it wants to establish and then work out the best communications mix to deliver these objectives. This involves marketing research to inform the development of creative work which will then be tested to ensure that the message and positioning is understood by the target audiences. Often more than one set of messages will be developed to suit distinct audience groups. Having developed the messaging the next step is to determine the promotional tools to be used and the media. These decisions involve several factors including the available budget and cost of each tool, the level of control over messaging and targeting, the perceived credibility and the potential geographical reach or dispersion of each tool (Fill, 2013). Table 8.2 illustrates how the various promotional tools compare across these key criteria. These factors need to be considered alongside the suitability of each tool for the communications objective and their relevance and effectiveness in reaching the target audiences. For example, national newspaper and magazine advertising is still a significant choice for international brands, but is only appropriate for companies with large budgets, and careful consideration needs to go into the selection of publications used to reach the relevant audiences for the brand and meet objectives.

Table 8.2: Selection criteria for tools in the marketing communications mix. Adapted from Baines et al. (2011)

	Primary task	Cost	Control	Credibility	Geographical reach
Advertising	Differentiating, informing	High	Medium	Low	High
Sales promotions	Persuading	Medium	High	Medium	Medium
Public relations	Differentiating, informing	Low	Low	High	High
Direct marketing	Persuading, reinforcing	Medium	High	Medium	High
Personal selling	Persuading	High	Medium	Medium	Low
Digital	Informing, persuading	Low	High	Medium	High

A further challenge for companies in determining the best communications approach is that both audiences and the media through which marketers reach them are increasingly fragmented. Previously media planners would have been able to predict consumers likely reading habits based on demographics, profession or home address. As society becomes increasingly diverse and consumers lead more individual lives, it is increasingly difficult to identify significant groups of consumers with similar lifestyles or media preferences. At the same time the proliferation of media and channels available both on and offline makes it much more challenging for marketers to identify communications tools and media guaranteed to reach and resonate with their target audiences. It can be argued that digital is really a communications channel and not a separate tool. Advertising, sales promotion, Public relations, personal selling and direct response can all be undertaken digitally.

As with any planning activity, it is important to be able to measure the effectiveness of the marketing communications plan. As illustrated in Figure 8.1, the feedback loop is a critical part of the process in informing future planning and ongoing amendments to communications activities to improve effectiveness. Vast ranges of measures are used to monitor the effectiveness of marketing communications from consumer brand recall or awareness to the number of website hits. These measures may be deployed on an ad hoc basis or tracked over a set period, which covers the period of campaign activity and immediately afterwards. Often measures are devised on the basis of what can be measured from available management information rather than what should be measured. However, marketers should develop measures that reflect their stated communications objectives.

As discussed media and audience fragmentation requires communications campaigns to potentially use a variety of tools and media, encompassing both on and offline methods and both free and paid-for media which are intended to work together to deliver the stated communications objectives. While measures for each tool can inform enhancements to these individually, a more holistic approach is required to measure the effectiveness of the campaign with a focus on outcomes rather than communications outputs (Young and Aitken, 2007).

According to Kliatchko (2008), marketers should make more use of metrics that link their activities to business results. This might include increased sales or enquiries from targeted groups and this is supported by research, which indicates that attitudinal, and awareness measures used are not always linked to business outcomes because of the artificial nature of the research setting (Heath and Nairn, 2005).

Along with informing future planning, these measures also help to prove the value of marketing activities, which can be called into question whenever there is pressure on company budgets.

Communication theory and recent developments

Early communication theory is based on a linear model of communication developed by Wilburr Schramm (1955). This linear model considers a message source, such as a product provider, encoding a message, transmitted to a receiver who then decodes or interprets the message and gives feedback. In marketing communication terms, an organisation encodes its messaging into marketing materials, such as advertising which the consumer as the receiver interprets and may or may not then act upon the message. Consumer action, in terms of expressing interest or making a purchase acts as feedback to the provider. In the model both the sender and receiver are situated within their own realms of understanding or perceptual worlds, however the model does not take account of other people who may influence how the consumer receives and interprets the message.

To address the limitations of the linear model, a two-step model (Fill, 2013) has been developed which takes greater account of the role of others in influencing how people receive and interpret messages. This model particularly stresses the role of two influential groups – *opinion leaders* and *opinion formers*, in shaping consumers' attitudes and responses to marketing communications.

- Opinion formers are those who have a professional interest in a subject. They may write a blog or newspaper column on a given market or inform others through talks and training sessions. Travel websites such as TripAdviser may be regarded as opinion formers as they are actively involved in assessing services and products and providing opinions, which others will seek out.

■ Opinion leaders are those who belong to the same group as the consumer and so are able to exert influence from within a target customer group as a result of having a common bond with other consumers. An example would be the forum PC Advisor, where computer users share queries and opinions with other users. Opinion leaders here could have significant influence on take-up of new software or hardware releases.

Social media has significantly increased the importance of both opinion formers and opinion leaders and the extent of their influence since consumers use social media to seek out or to share opinions and reviews of companies and their products or services.

A limitation of the two-step model is that while it takes account of opinion formers and opinion leaders it still presents a fairly linear view of communications with consumers receiving messages from mass media channels, which are set against messages they receive from opinion formers and leaders in a given market.

The interaction model of communications (Baines and Fill, 2014) views communications as a more iterative and interactive process where messages flow not only between organisations, consumers, opinion leaders, and opinion formers, but also between consumers who interact on social media and with friends and family in forming an opinion on a product or service. In this model mass media channels such as advertising are just one of numerous message sources influencing consumers as they exchange opinions between themselves and are exposed to opinions and reviews from multiple sources. This model more accurately reflects the realities of modern marketing, where consumers are often well informed and less likely to take any advertising messaging at face value, but to consult other sources, including discussing their previous and prospective purchases with friends or family, or looking on social media for product reviews and comparisons. Word of mouth and e-WOM are increasingly important elements. This model also reflects that consumers are not just passive recipients of messages, but will also actively seek information and will respond to messages from both providers and other consumers.

In planning marketing communications, companies need to take account of this interactive model of communications and consider how their planned communications effort will interact with other messages and communications in the consumers' environments. It is much more challenging for companies to control how their communications are received. Any one piece of messaging will be fighting for the attention of consumers among hundreds of other images and messages encountered in a day and is also likely to be queried or undermined by alternative views or issues in the media and elsewhere.

Exercise: Can you remember when you last made a significant purchase? How many different sources of information can you think of that may have influenced your decision. How important was the advertising or other information from the provider?

Digital marketing

Digital marketing is an increasingly important part of the marketing communications mix and encompasses a broad range of activities and media including internet marketing, email marketing, social media marketing and mobile marketing. Digital marketing therefore forms an integral part of the other marketing communications tools as it encompasses advertising, direct selling and sales promotions, which may also use digital channels. Baines and Fill (2014) point out that terms such as e-marketing and digital marketing are often used interchangeably when in fact there are several separate digital marketing tools used. Table 8.3 below sets out the main elements of the digital marketing mix.

Table 8.3: Digital marketing activities. Adapted from Baines and Fill (2014), Brodie et al. (2013) and Jutkowitz (2014)

Activity type	Explanation
Internet advertising PPC, display ads	Advertising using the internet to increase website traffic by encouraging recipients to click through to a web page. This includes display advertising on home pages, social media advertising on Facebook and Instagram, rich media advertisements, pay-per click and post-roll advertising on YouTube.
Search marketing	Techniques used to raise the profile of a webpage in the results of search engines. Known as Search Engine Optimization (SEO), this includes paid entries in search engines, contextual advertising and ensuring that web pages contain frequently used search words.
Email marketing	The use of email and other electronic means to send marketing communications directly to targeted groups. This is used to encourage repeat purchase and build relationships with customers. This can be a very effective way of targeting specific customer groups, but can only be used where customers have opted-in to receive electronic communications.
Mobile marketing	Similar to email marketing but using mobile devices such as smart phones to engage with an audience often with interactive content.

8

Viral marketing	Online marketing intended to encourage consumers to pass a message on to others, hence the expression 'gone viral'. Often used with entertaining or emotional content such as YouTube clips, promoted tweets, Buzz feed.
Online retailing	Selling to customers online from a website for delivery or collection from a local store.
Advergaming	Online games and videos used to promote a product or brand. Also used by not-for-profit organisations to promote causes and ideas.
Social media marketing	Using social networking sites for marketing purposes either by generating content that users will share or by building engagement with target groups through interaction with the brand.
Content marketing and online PR	Publishing content online which consumers will find informative, useful or entertaining in order to position the brand as a trusted or respected source of knowledge in its field. A means of engaging consumers with the brand without being seen to try to sell. There may be ethical considerations here.
Marketing automation	Using software to automatically manage customer interactions from lead generation to email marketing, campaign management and analytics.

Digital channels have driven something of a revolution in marketing communications. Channels such as social media marketing have enabled and encouraged much greater consumer involvement and interaction in communications. These channels allow consumers not just to comment on communications but also to co-create brand content through brand forums and other interactive tools. This increased interaction has been found to play a role in building consumer brand engagement (Schau et al., 2009).

A further advantage of digital marketing methods is that they can be tailored and targeted to address specific audiences. They are more flexible than other communications tools as web pages can be updated more easily than print or other media to respond to changing market conditions or competitor activities. This can be very important in fast moving markets.

It is thought to be unlikely that digital channels and communications tools will replace more traditional marketing communication tools and media, but they are an increasingly important part of the mix for many companies, and this is evident in the shift of marketing budgets towards increased spend on digital media and away from television and print (West, 2014). The sportswear company Adidas, for example, has moved from its sponsorship of major sporting events to focus on promoting the brand through social media in line with a strategy of building the brand at grassroots level with fans (Thomasson, 2016).

The key disadvantage is that internet penetration is still low in some markets and among some population segments, including older consumers and those in lower socio-economic groups. Digital channels therefore have a limited reach in some markets.

Advertising and sales promotions

Advertising has been used throughout history to deliver messages. From Ancient Egyptians placing messages on stone slabs (MacDonald and Scott, 2007) to bus stops with digital advertising in high streets today, advertising has been part of our lives and an important way for organisations to try to get our attention.

Today advertising takes many forms, from printed media to television and radio; outdoor advertising on billboards; in train stations and elsewhere and increasingly online and on social media. From everyday items from bus tickets to coffee cups and outside spaces such as the hulls of ships all sorts of spaces are used to promote brands. Even within television, advertising takes many forms. As well as advertisements shown in program breaks, products placement is used to promote brands as part of storylines and providers may also sponsor whole programs or series so that their brand or products get maximum exposure during broadcasting.

Figure 8.2: Pasta advertising in Hamburg, by Jung von Matt Advertising Agency Germany

A recent development is the use of interactive advertising. Social media and the internet have enabled providers to produce advertisements that customers can interact with, but interactivity is also used in print advertisements in magazines. Peugeot for example, produced a magazine advertisement that asked readers to hit the image of the car featured. This activated a small airbag, contained within the next page and was a novel means of promoting the safety of the cars.

The main advantage of mass advertising is that it can be an effective means of reaching a large audience. However, it is a very broad-brush approach and not so useful for delivering targeted messages or reaching niche audiences. Media scheduling and buying experts make it possible to influence the sort of audience that will be exposed to an advertisement, but only to a limited extent. Advertisers generally consider a very broad audience, both in terms of whom their advertisement will appeal to and whom it might offend. A further weakness of all advertising is that exposure does not equal awareness or impact. While thousands of people may walk past an advert on a station billboard, only a small proportion of them may actually be aware of it and fewer will actually appreciate its messaging, with even fewer acting upon it. Other challenges for advertisers come from the proliferation of television channels available, which limits the potential reach of any one and the option exercised by some consumers to skip the advertisements when viewing digital recordings of programs.

> **Exercise**: In how many different places have you come across advertising today? List as many of them as you can. How many of these can you remember paying attention to/reading?

■ Regulation and ethics

In the effort to make sure that their advertisements are seen and noticed among vast numbers that consumers are exposed to on a daily basis, organisations need to consider a number of risks to their brand from producing materials that may cause offence or breach local regulations. In the UK, advertising is regulated by the Advertising Standards Authority, or ASA (www.asa.org.uk). The ASA enforces the UK Advertising Codes and can force organisations to withdraw advertisements, which are breach of these. Promotions also need to take account of other regulations such as data protection legislation. In an online environment there is a temptation for advertisers to use more risqué messaging or images because the audience may be younger but advertisers must consider that these may also be seen by children or other groups for whom they are offensive.

Internet advertising regulation

Visit the Internet Advertising Bureau digital policy guide (Available at: http://www.iabuk.net/policy/digital-policy-guide) to see how on line advertising is regulated. Can you think why on line advertising is more difficult to regulate?

■ ## Sales promotion

Sales promotion is a popular form of marketing activity in consumer retail markets, where companies will create special offers to increase sales. These are most commonly used to drive short-term sales but may also be used to reward and build engagement with existing customers, by offering deals, which are exclusive to them; to increase awareness or trial purchase of a new product range, or to challenge the activities of competitors or new entrants.

They are used both on and offline and take many forms from special bundled packages of goods and services, to buy-one-get-one-free (also known as BOGOF) discount coupons and free samples. To be effective, sales promotions are best deployed as part of an integrated campaign to increase awareness or sales.

While sales promotions can be effective in driving short-term sales, evidence suggests that they do not lead to longer-term increases but to one-off purchases by consumers who may only return to retailer when similar promotions are available.

Public relations

■ ## Public relations

PR is the Swiss army knife of marketing communications – it includes a number of different tools, which can be used creatively to get a message across; to create buzz or hype around a brand or proposition by generating publicity; or correctively to solve problems. Positive publicity generated through public relations activity is more than a 'nice to have' but can also improve sales (Spotts et al., 2014). The skill in public relations is in understanding the organisation's different stakeholder groups and knowing which tools to use when. The remainder of this section discusses the different public relations tools and how they are used. PR is now commonly run through digital media, with companies and customers producing relevant content that may be seen by all stakeholders.

■ ## Media relations

Media relations is what many people think of as public relations. Media relations involves managing the organisation's relationship with the media and trying to influence how the organisation is portrayed in the press and other media, both on and offline.

Most large organisations will have a press office, whose role is to engage with relevant media, journalists and editors and has three elements to it. First, they need to manage an ongoing dialogue and relationship with key media contacts. This helps to ensure that key journalists understand the organisation's positioning and are more likely to report any news about the organisation accurately. It also means that they will ask the organisation for their viewpoint when they have a story about the organisation or sector rather than just reporting it. An important part of this is identifying who the key media are and which journalists are most influential. This may involve considering which news channels or other media your key stakeholder groups look at. For example, in financial services, there are a few key publications such as the *Financial Times, Money Marketing* and *Financial Adviser* that companies will try to engage with.

Having built a relationship with key media contacts, the organisation is more able to approach the press and other media to proactively deliver its messaging through planned news content. For example, a company planning a new product launch will want to maximize publicity for the new product and getting good news coverage of a launch is a very effective way to do this. Having a good relationship with key media outlets in the sector will help with this, as anyone can write a press release but many will be ignored and not all will result in useful news coverage. Companies may also hold media briefings where they will invite journalists to hear important announcements such as new product developments or changes within the business. Again, having a good relationship with the right media contacts is important in ensuring that the target media channels attend a media briefing.

A third element of media relations is troubleshooting when things go wrong. Again, having a good relationship will help with this but other key elements are responding quickly to queries and understanding public and media concerns and addressing these, rather than offering bland responses, which do nothing to allay public concerns. Trying to ignore a problem or gloss over important issues will not work with increasingly knowledgeable and connected consumers and other stakeholders. Several organisations have suffered from trying to ignore public concerns and have suffered significant business impacts from poor communications in times of crisis including Volkswagen, Toyota and BP.

■ Sponsorship and celebrity endorsement

Sponsorship and celebrity endorsement are increasingly popular aspects of public relations as there seems to be a growing public appetite for news and images of latest celebrities. Sponsorship is where an organisation pays either a sportsperson, or event, a sum of money and in return have the brand associated with the successful attributes of that person or event. This will usually involve the company's logo being displayed on the sportsperson's clothes or equipment.

Sponsorship can be a very effective way of getting brand awareness through exposure to huge international television audiences and associating the brand with the success of the sportsperson. Standard Life Plc. sponsor the UK tennis star Andy Murray for example and will have their logo broadcast around the world on his shirts every time he plays. In 2014, Standard Life Investments wanted to build its profile as a global investment house and used its sponsorship of the golf's Ryder Cup to promote the company as world class. Large banners were erected outside Edinburgh and Heathrow airports, which were both pinch points for people travelling to the Ryder cup with the strapline 'World Class as Standard'. This outdoor work was supported by a digital campaign that positioned the company as world class. In this way, the organisation used sponsorship to support key promotional objectives and reach a target audience of high net worth individuals from around the world.

However, sponsorship is an expensive option and carries risks. There are several examples of companies cancelling sponsorship deals where their sportsperson has behaved badly and the brand then risks being associated with negative publicity.

Celebrity endorsement is where a company recruits a celebrity to proactively endorse their products either in advertising or in other publicity. Like sponsorship, this carries some risks.

The key to success in both sponsorship and endorsement is to choose celebrities or causes which are relevant to your brand values and to which key stakeholder groups can relate. Standard Life Plc. for example list the criteria for sponsorship on their website. These include aligning with the group's aims and values and having a global reach to endorse the brand's position as a global provider.

8

Exercise: Consider an example of a sponsorship or celebrity endorsement deal that has been cancelled by an organisation. What do you think an organisation will consider before terminating an agreement?

■ Government relations

An important stakeholder in many markets is the government and the regulatory bodies established to monitor industry sectors. It is therefore important for organisations to maintain good relations with relevant government departments and regulatory bodies. These relationships can be invaluable for organisations in influencing legislation, regulations or trade deals, which may affect their sourcing of materials, production methods, marketing or profitability. In an increasingly global marketing environment, organisations may have to manage these relationships with governments and regulators in a more than one country if they have international operations.

This is particularly the case in highly regulated industries such as financial services; those of national interest such as utilities; and those affected by international trade agreements. Companies may manage these relationships by joining industry bodies, which lobby government on behalf of a sector. They may also have their own government relations manager or team who are responsible identifying in advance any emerging threats or opportunities in the regulatory environment and formulating the organisation's response to these.

Exercise: Consider a recent event where an industry body has been lobbying your Government on an issue. What were the implications of the issue for that industry? What communications activity was used and was it successful?

Direct marketing and personal selling

Direct marketing is a more targeted and personal approach to marketing communication, where communications are sent to existing and prospective customers. Companies use databases to identify groups of consumers who match the profile of their target consumer segments. This may be based on demographic information such as age, home address, and membership of specific interest groups or previous purchases of related products. For example, someone who is a member of a gym or a sports club would be a target for companies offering sportswear and equipment. Companies selling garden equipment may target consumers living in specific streets within affluent suburbs of major cities.

Direct marketing has traditionally involved using physical mailshots of letters or catalogues sent to customers' and prospective customers' home addresses, but is also now increasingly conducted through email marketing. Advanced data-mining technology allows organisations to build up quite sophisticated pictures of the consumption patterns and lifestyles of consumers. This in turn enables specific targeting of direct marketing offers. The supermarket giant Tesco was one of the first companies to adopt this approach, which is now widely used. Apple for example will approach customers who have bought a laptop two years ago with an offer to trade up to a more recent model. The main advantage of direct marketing is that it enables organisations to target consumers that it thinks will be interested in its offering and to tailor materials for different consumer segments. A downside is that some consumers who are attractive prospects to several companies can be bombarded by approaches from different companies or several from one company.

Exercise: Thinking of any mailshots which you received recently, either in hard copy or electronic, can you guess why these companies have targeted you personally?

Personal selling is another form of more targeted marketing and involves selling through personal interaction between the customer and a sales person working for the organisation. As this is the most labour intensive form of marketing communications, personal selling is most common in markets where individual transactions are of high value, such as cars or in B2B markets. The main advantage of personal selling is that the organisation has the customer's undivided attention while they are interacting with the sales representative, and that the communication interaction can specifically address the needs and concerns of that individual customer or prospective customer. The disadvantages of personal selling are that it is very expensive and has limited geographical reach. A further disadvantage is that personal selling gives organisations limited control over how their messages are delivered because of the human element involved. Problems here can range from inconsistency of messaging to the use of unethical methods by some salespeople to secure sales.

Summary

To conclude, marketers have many options in terms of the communications tools and the media they use. Organisations must have a robust understanding of their target audience needs, their own capabilities and the market environment and be able to consider the strengths and weaknesses of each of the available options in order to assess the most suitable methods to achieve their stated communications objectives.

Further reading

Danaher, P. and Rossiter, J. (2012) Comparing perceptions of marketing communications channels. *European Journal of Marketing*, **45**(1/2), 6-42

Drumwright, M.E. and Murphy, P.E. (2009). The current state of advertising ethics: industry and academic perspectives, *Journal of Advertising*, **38**(1), 83-107

Voorveld, H., Neijens, P. and Smit, E. (2011) Opening the black box: Understanding cross-media effects. *Journal of Marketing Communications*, **17**(2), 68-85

References

Baines, P. and Fill, C. (2014) *Marketing* (3rd Ed.), Oxford: Oxford University Press.

Baines, P., Fill, C. and Page, K. (2011). *Marketing*, 2nd edition, OUP

Brodie, R.J., Ilic, A., Juric, B. and Hollebeek, L., (2013) Consumer engagement in a virtual brand community: An exploratory analysis, *Journal of Business Research*, **66**(1), 105-114.

Fill, C. (2013) *Marketing Communications: Brands Experiences and Participation* (6th Edition) Harlow, UK Pearson Education Limited.

Heath, R. & Nairn, A. (2005) Measuring affective advertising: implications of low-attention processing on recall, *Journal of Advertising Research*, **45**(2), 269–281.

Jutkowitz, A. (2014) The content marketing revolution. *Harvard Business Review*, July 1.

Kliatchko, J. (2008) Revisiting the IMC construct. *International Journal of Advertising*. **27**(1), 133-160.

McDonald, C. and Scott, J. (2007). A brief history of advertising, in *The Sage Handbook of Advertising*, London, Sage, pp. 17-34.

Schramm, W. (1955) How communication works, in W. Schramm (ed.) *The Process and Effects of Mass Communications*, Urbana Il: University of Illinois Press.

Schau, H.J., Muñiz, A.M. and Arnould, E.J., (2009). How brand community practices create value. *Journal of Marketing*, **73**(5), 30–51.

Spotts, H., Weinberger, M. and Weinberger, M. (2014) Publicity and advertising: what matter most for sales? *European Journal of Marketing*, 48(11/12) 1986-2008

Thomasson, E. (2015) Digital Marketing helps Adidas cut ties to sports bodies. Reuters News [online]. Available at http://www.reuters.com/article/athletics-corruption-marketing-idUSKCNOV51J6. [Accessed 02/02/16].

West, G. (2014) Digital markcting budgets to increase by 17 per cent in 2015 says Gartner, The Drum online. http://www.thedrum.com/news/2014/11/04/digital-marketing-budgets-increase-17-cent-2015-says-gartner. [Accessed 30/07/16].

Young, A. and Aitken, L. (2007) Measuring marketing communications: concentrate on outcomes not outputs. *The Marketing Society*. Available at https://www.marketingsociety.com/the-library/measuring-marketing-communications-concentrate-outcomes-not-outputs. [Accessed 11/06/16].

9 Place and Physical Distribution

Carrie Amani Annabi

Physical distribution decisions are vitally important to the overall marketing strategy. Physical distribution, also known as 'logistics', consists of all activities involved in moving the right amount of the right product to the right place at the right time at the right price. Physical distribution is the combined term used for the connected functions that include transportation, holding inventory, warehousing and storage, handling the product, including picking and packing it in the warehouse ready to meet the order processing, and then physically transferring the product from the producer to the end customer. This can be direct or through an intermediary such as an agent, wholesaler, retailer or distributor. Marketers decide the most appropriate channels for their products and services to reach their target market. Additionally, they must consider how to manage relationships across the supply chain and how to ensure that physical distribution activities create value for consumers.

It is wise to differentiate between a marketing channel and a distribution channel. A marketing channel is the transfer of ownership between organizations and communication flows between those organisations but a distribution channel is concerned with the transport of products between physical locations.

Physical distribution considers the delivery of goods to the final customer and takes account of inventory control: how much to order, when to order and where to hold the product. Distribution is about product scheduling, warehousing and transportation choices. In logistics, this is known as the supply chain. If you imagine that the customer is standing downstream waiting for the product to reach them, then everything else is upstream. The terms upstream and downstream are frequently used in logistics to talk about the product or service in relation to the next customer in the supply chain.

The ten Ps of distribution

Distribution channel choices directly impact all marketing decisions and vice versa. The chosen channel must take into account target market needs, be accessible and provide the appropriate level of service in order to sell and distribute the product and meet after sales requirements. This can be shown in terms of the ten Ps of distribution: Product, Place, Payment, Price, Processes, Packaging, Positioning, Promotion, Profit and Physical evidence.

The **product** is strongly tied to selecting the correct marketing channel intermediaries. If the product is mass-produced, and mass-sold with a mid-price-range, then it is likely that it would need to be delivered to a wide variety of places. Perishable and convenience products like milk need specialist chiller handling and daily deliveries to supermarkets and a range of convenient outlets, whereas popular toys might only need to be delivered on a weekly basis to both specialist and other stores where they might be bought on impulse. In contrast, durable goods such as electronic items or furniture (classed as shopping goods) require less frequent delivery to fewer locations since consumers are willing to travel to specialist outlets to view and gain access to pre- and post-sales advice. High-cost, top-of-the-line products that are sold through high-end department and specialty stores may only need deliveries every couple of weeks or have delivery patterns triggered by product demand. Pricing in such stores will reflect the higher levels of service and sales offered whereas mass merchandising markets (such as Wal-Mart) provide customers with low prices.

Aspects of the **place** are covered above but there are also online e-demand business models that provide same day delivery (Asos), next day delivery (Amazon) and pre-booked delivery slots (Tesco online shopping). Online shopping is increasingly popular, with anything from high-end luxury goods through to fast food being ordered online. Some of these carry a cost implication for the customer and others are built into the product attributes. For example, Asos offer high fashion and even same day accessibility within some cities with a safe return option. Agents can act as channel intermediaries and also provide home delivery. This is seen with Virgin Vie Home or Desert Diamonds products. In these examples the agents meet customers in private, often home settings, where a host throws a get-together and attendees are encouraged to sample products and make orders that are honoured either at the time of booking or shortly thereafter.

There are implications for the number of stopping points between a manufacturer/producer and the end customer, as each step can create a delay and can add costs to the overall delivery process. Sometimes these delays have only negative consequences but at other times, each stopping point might provide additional services that are valued by the customer. Such value added services and the functions in the distribution channel are discussed later.

Payment and payment terms are among the advantages offered by intermediaries in that can provide value added services to ensure that the manufacturer and consumer are not involved directly with each other regarding the financial transaction.

Many organizations have used **processes** as a way of creating competitive advantage. For example, Dell Computers, who deliver direct to the customers' homes, have also customized the product line to meet customer expectations with software and warranty options. Another innovative aspect of their operations is that online customer orders trigger inventory and production, with customers paying in advance of delivery. Online processes have developed services that speed up customer delivery and transaction ease in ways that offer significant competitive advantage over bricks and mortar (an organisation that possesses physical buildings, warehouses, storage facilities or shops) businesses. One such example is the US broker Charles Schwab, whose online financial services have seen investors look to them in the same way as they used to consider banks for holding their savings. Transaction ease and process visibility can provide a product with a distinct market position.

How products are **packaged** affects how well those products can be showcased or delivered throughout the length of the channel chain. Packaging is not just about how the product looks (that is branding), but how easily it can be handled in single and multiple units. The packaging should provide the product with protection during its journey and ensure that it can be stored, stacked and racked in the most effective way. Packaging adds value for the consumer in terms of product information. Often packaging contains barcoding for pricing process ease. Everyday items in supermarkets are often in shelf-ready packaging (SRP), or retail-ready packaging (RRP), which has allowed a range of products to be delivered to a retailer in ready-to-sell outer packaging that can be put directly on the shelf without requiring further handling, thus reducing costs. With shelf space at a premium it makes sense that space is optimized by ensuring the product is packaged to maximize space. Supermarkets and other retailers use merchandising units (MUs). MUs are off-fixture displays holding things such as a large number of egg boxes and they can be pre-filled by the manufacturer or co-packer, and delivered to supermarkets ready for immediate display and sale. European Union (EU) legislation has regulations on packaging; the Packaging and Waste Directive sets out recovery and recycling targets and deadlines for EU Member States and obliges them to address the recovery and recycling of used packaging.

9

In the US, the Federal Trade Commission (FTC) reported that the practice of paying for **position** is 'widespread' within the retail industry. Some retailers charge fees to position products in prime locations and allocate scarce premium shelf space, particularly in supermarkets. Retailers argue that this can balance the failure risk of stocking a new product line. Also termed a 'slotting fee' it has been reported in areas such as supermarkets, book and music stores. Slotting fees can include payment for special displays at the aisle-end, setting books out on tables within bookstores or **promoting** songs at music store listening posts. This can be part of a promotional approach. However, there is no point promoting a product that is not available for sale or promoting a product for the wrong reason.

Ten green cars sitting on the line...

One classic example of misplaced promotion is the cautionary case of the green Volvo. At one point Volvo had a large number of green cars sitting at the manufacture point. Despite encouraging distributors to push these cars, very few people seemed to want to buy a green car. Volvo decided to price green Volvos significantly lower than other colours. Unfortunately, the marketers forgot to tell the manufacturing plant of their great plan. When green Volvos began to sell, the high volume of sales triggered an increase in green car manufacture to meet the new demand. Promotional activity can be a good thing as it definitely increased green Volvo sales. However, because the whole company was not aware of the promotional plan it meant that instead of selling off unpopular stock, it created unrealistic production forecasts. Promotion decisions must link inventory, demand, forecasting and delivery. That promotion caused even more problems since it diverted production away from making Volvos in more popular colour choices that potentially sold for a higher price.

Profit drives most distribution decisions. Choosing a distribution channel is generally a long-term decision so profitability can depend on making the right selection. Profit is what is left after all costs are deducted from the selling price. Distribution channel costs include the direct costs (e.g. materials and labour) and indirect costs (picking, packaging, storage, processing and delivery) as well as the overheads (which might include the place, such as the warehouse or depot).

Physical evidence relates to the way that a product is perceived in the marketplace. Consumer perceptions of tangible goods are created through the visible touchpoints that the consumer comes across when buying the product. Within physical distribution, this includes all elements that draw the customer to the product. In retail outlets, this would include the shop layout and signage, customer service and the ability to try before you buy. For the newer e-commerce channels, it involves the ease of the online transaction, and how the product is packaged and presented on dispatch, through to the image created by the delivery staff as they transport the product to the consumer. Physical distribution has an impact on whether the pricing reflects the quality of the product and the dispatch (e.g. same or next day delivery) reinforces the choice of distribution channel.

All of the ten Ps within the distribution channel are inter-related.

Table 9.1: The Ten Ps relative to distribution channels

The Ten Ps	Definition
Product	Something tangible or intangible, such as an item or service that provides a solution that meets a customer need.
Price	The amount of money that the customer pays for the product or service in order to own or procure it.
Place	Place is expanded to placement to incorporate physical distribution. It is essential to provide access to the product in a place that is available to and valued by the target customers. Distribution channel strategies might be intensive, exclusive, or selective and owned, contractual or franchised.
Processes	Systems that affect the execution of the distribution and placement service. Processes draw together the sales channels, payment systems, physical distribution and other procedures (such as warranty) that create an effective means of serving the customer in the fastest time and with minimal friction between the touch points.
Packaging	Packaging includes the wrapping and boxing that gives the product its finished look (branding). It protects the product during its physical journey through the touch points up to delivery and makes it easy to handle and present on display.
Position	Where the product is placed in relation to other similar products that are offered in the marketplace. An advantageous position allows a product to stand out from competitors within a category, although unusual positioning might help the product standout to consumers. Some products are placed in refrigeration (even though they do not need this for shelf life) to create the perception of freshness.
Promotion	How a product is presented to attract the target market and create a demand. This is also a way of establishing 'brand' or 'identity'.
Profit	The amount of money available after all costs have been deducted from the selling price.
Payment	How the financial transaction is executed to allow the customer to own the product, including the smooth transaction at point of sale, the payment terms through intermediaries (interest free or interest-bearing loans that allow the transaction to proceed.
Physical evidence	Physical evidence affects how the product is seen in the marketplace and how the organisation perceives its presence and business. It incudes how the buying experience feels, either through face-to-face sales or via the online portal all the way through to the product's journey until delivered to the end customer.

9

The distribution channel

A distribution channel is designed to facilitate smooth product flow from the manufacturer to the consumer and to eliminate either bulk storage or stock-outs so that customer demand is met.

■ Functions in the distribution channel

The following section evaluates the various functions that can take place within the distribution channel. These are not assigned to specific intermediaries because the functions are steps that the product goes through at different stages of time, place, and ownership transfer, to make that particular product available when and where the consumer wants it, in a required packaging and quantity.

The distribution channel goes through various logistic activities, including undertaking delivery, to maintain efficient product flow whilst trying to eliminate unnecessary transactions. Wholesalers and retailers buy in bulk to gain economies of scale. It is generally cheaper to package and ship product in large quantities. However, the next customer in the supply chain generally wants to buy in smaller quantities and not everything bought by the wholesaler or retailer is distributed onwards in the supply chain to their next customer, so they need to break-bulk. Breaking bulk is splitting large lots of product into more manageable individual shipments ready for delivery.

Another vital role offered by intermediaries is to provide assortment. Typically, retailers offer to sell an assortment of products rather than just offering one product line. For example, a supermarket carries thousands of different products made by hundreds of different manufacturers but they may only deal with a handful of different wholesalers. The retailer assortment of different brands, different sized packages, or, if clothes then different sized clothing, with different designs and colours, provides customer choice value and saves them time an effort in sourcing goods.

Warehousing is provided by some wholesalers/retailers to allow for holding stock already broken down into manageable quantities, which means that the products will be available when the customer requires them. Holding inventory allows the merchandiser to use their floor space for selling product rather than holding it in storage. By holding inventory for merchandisers, it also allows value-added services to be offered – such as specialized packaging or *kitting*. Kitting is where items are linked together – for example, a promotional mug to be sold off as boxed with coffee or a paintbrush to be sold attached to a paint pot.

Intermediaries can also provide additional facilitating functions such as acting as a financier or securing credit for customers, conducting market research to establish trends or offering other market information such as an evaluation of suppliers.

Other aspects that intermediaries may undertake include those of transportation and distribution, which involves moving the product from where it is made/ is warehoused to where it is to be displayed and even onward to the end customer after it is purchased.

■ Reverse logistics

Increasingly EU legislation has grown the need for reverse logistics, which is returns management of a product for whatever reason; it may be defective or it may simply be unwanted. It can be thought of as pushing the product back upstream, and the process is not as simple as reversing the supply chain. The product may be resold as is or it may require refurbishment to have utility value. Parts of the product may be recycled for another use and the packaging recycled, reduced or reused. All these facets may necessitate the need for an intermediary. This can add costs to the process.

More thought currently tends to be placed on ensuring that the end customer receives the product in an optimum time, than in considering how to effectively take back the product. Product returns range from 5% to 35% depending on the product and sector, so this ultimately adds to costs. Reverse logistics has a range of hidden costs such as labour. For example, return handling or logging the reasons for return. This could be faulty or just not wanted by the prospective end user. It is important to know whether the reason for the return relate to product features or for other personal reasons.

Another issue that may add to costs is that the end customer wants to know that the item has been returned to ensure that they are no longer invoiced for it. Personnel are required to track the visibility of the item through its return shipment and answer customer queries. Larger customers sending back a volume of returns may calculate their own credit for the returned goods and deduct this amount from future invoices, which leads to difficulties in reconciling payments with invoices. Equally, the data relating to these returns needs to be fed into forecasting systems. If forecasts on the percentage of returns are wrong then accurate forward forecasts are likely to be distorted since there is no accurate information on current stock levels.

If the product is not faulty, it could be resold through a different channel. Therefore, it becomes what is known as a 'grey good'. A grey good is the selling

9

of a commodity through distribution channels that are legal but unintended by the original manufacturer. This is also called a 'parallel market'. If returns and credit reconciliations are not handled promptly or a grey market emerges that is not aligned to the original product, it could lead to brand toxicity. Unsatisfied or frustrated end customers have an expectation that organizations should stand by their products for the entire lifecycle.

Hedge buying leads to un-happy return

Better returns policies from leading retailers have led to customers 'hedge buying'. This is where they buy goods at full price, knowing that they can be returned if the price is reduced. Consumers also buy in multiple sizes and colours to try at home. It is estimated that the cost of handling returned goods is twice as much as getting the goods ready for delivery. The cost of goods being returned following internet sales is now costing UK e-tailers £20billion per annum. Up to 25% of fashion goods sold are returned in the UK and around 10% of other goods such as electricals and household goods (KPMG, 2016). The figure is even higher in Germany where 70% of goods are likely to be returned. Each returned item passes through up to seven different processes and can be unsaleable. Marketers therefore need to make sure that they provide as much information as possible for consumers to make correct choices at point of sale and reduce the levels of returns.

Sources: Ram (2016); Clancy (2016)

■ E-commerce within the distribution channel

E-commerce has increased the importance of physical distribution because it presents a challenge relating to fulfilling orders in a timely manner. Indeed, customers expect to shop online for next or even same day delivery. Late or awkward deliveries can create customer dissatisfaction and this can lead to the loss of that customer and potentially to reputation damage since the wider customer base is connected through social media. Marketing must understand distribution issues as products and services cannot be sold or delivery scheduled without a full overview of what it takes to get the product from the manufacture point to the end user.

Marketing channels

Physical distribution is the link between producers/manufacturers and final marketplace and customers. The type of market has implications for distribution choices, as customers may be individuals, or another business.

The consumer needs somewhere to complete the transaction, whether this is online or offline. This is why channel intermediaries are important in marketing. The path that a product follows to market frequently involves interaction with intermediaries or external organizations that bridge the point of production and the point of sale.

Most producers/manufacturers rely on intermediaries to reach the consumer and in doing so they create either one or a range of distribution channels to achieve this. In simple terms, a distribution channel is nothing more than the various organizations that work together to ensure that the product is available for the consumer.

The number of different types of intermediary that can ease the journey of the product to the end consumer include:

- **Agents** (known as jobbers, brokers or dealers in certain industries). This intermediary legally acts on behalf of the manufacturer or wholesaler to seek business. They do not take legal ownership of the products, or hold stock, or undertake other roles expected of an intermediary. This is a common role in service industries such as insurance and many universities deal through agents to increase the numbers of international students applying. Companies may initially use agents to make contacts and start business in international markets.

- **Wholesalers**. These stock a variety of products, from different competing manufactures and sell them (usually in bulk) to the next player in the distribution chain who generally will go on to resell the item to their customer. UK examples include Booker and Macro who sell to 1.3 million retail, catering and other business customers, who then sell on these goods to their customers. Dubai is establishing an international Wholesale City that will provide a physical and digital space for wholesalers across all sectors including food, electronics, chemicals, textiles, appliances, machinery and equipment.

- **Retailers** tend to be the last intermediary in the chain and sell direct to end consumers. They may buy direct from manufacturers or deal with a wholesaler depending on how much volume they buy. A proposed takeover of Booker by the giant retailer Tesco will increase the retailer's power over competing convenience stores who buy from Booker. In some markets such as car sales, the retailer is known as a distributor. Retailers vary in terms of the number of product lines (assortment width) or categories offered and the number of varieties of products or brands within that line (assortment depth). Clothing stores, for example offer a narrow assortment with lots of depth. Some stores pride themselves on a high level of service, whereas others gear toward self-service. Table 9.2 summarises the main types of retailer.

9

Table 9.2: Retail store classifications (adapted from Baines et al (2017)

Type of store	Assortment	Service/ Price	Example
Department	Broad and Deep	High	Macys, Harvey Nichols, Sogo, Harrods, Galeries Lafayette
Discount	Broad but shallow	Low	Pound world, B & M, Dollar store
Speciality	Narrow but deep	High	Foot Locker
Supermarket and superstores	Broad and deep	Low to medium	Tesco, Careffour, Giant, Spinneys
Convenience stores	Narrow and shallow	High to medium	Co-op, 7-Eleven, Circle K

Companies must decide how many and the type of outlet to reach and this will depend on the product, the company's strategic ambition and their level of resources. Products positioned at the higher end maintain some of their cachet through limited availability in high-end stores, which complement the brand with superior service, product knowledge and sales skills. Fast moving snack products need to maintain wide presence and be available in convenience stores, supermarkets and electronic kiosks. Shoppers look for a hedonic and pleasurable shopping experience for some of the time, but seek utilitarian value that comes from accessibility, convenience and saving money on other occasions.

■ Direct or indirect selling

Companies can of course sell direct to their end user, to maintain total control over the whole process but potentially reduce the reach. As most companies do not have the expertise to carry out all of the functions offered by the distribution channel to reach end consumers, they will benefit greatly from using channel intermediaries. There are four basic distribution channel choices with channel intermediaries and the greater the number of intermediaries the longer the length of the channel is said to be.

Figure 9.1: Channel length

Manufacturer	Consumer			
Manufacturer	Retailer	Consumer		
Manufacturer	Wholesaler	Retailer	Consumer	
Manufacturer	Wholesaler	Jobber/ broker/ dealer/ agent	Retailer	Consumer

Channel length

→

Longer channels tend to offer less control over how the product is sold, priced and promoted and the remoteness from the customer can make it more difficult to understand end customer needs.

Figure 9.2 shows distribution systems with and without intermediaries to help indicate the intensity of deliveries required when a producer deals directly with the consumer.

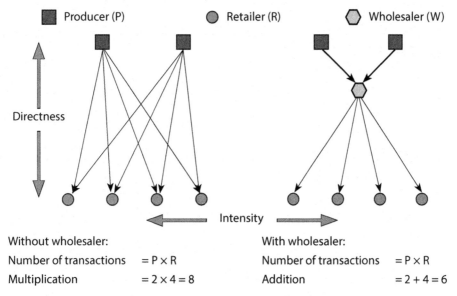

Figure 9.2: Distribution systems with and without intermediaries. Adapted from McKinnon (1989)

For calculating the deliveries for 100 producers and 500 consumers

Without wholesaler:　　　　100 x 500 = 50,000 transactions

With wholesaler:　　　　　　100 + 500 = 600 transactions

There are almost 99% fewer deliveries for the producer to make if they use a wholesaler as an intermediary.

The decision to use channel intermediaries in the physical distribution channel is based on a the ease of transaction, the logistical implications of reaching the consumer and the added value services such as offering finance that the intermediary might then offer the consumer in order to complete the sale.

■ Ease of transaction and logistical implications

Ease of transaction: Intermediaries can create exchange efficiency by reducing the number of contacts required to facilitate the market exchanges. They have more experience than manufacturers in these areas because it is a core competency and intermediaries are usually more effective at performing these tasks than the producer or consumer would be. Certainly, technology has enabled manufacturers to reach consumers much more efficiently, but retailers are also closely linked with manufacturers through vendor-managed inventory (VMI) so that they can arrange for regular deliveries to reach the consumer.

The **logistical implications**: The product needs to be stored, picked, packed and sorted at various locations to ensure the product reaches the consumer in the planned timescale.

■ Added value services

These can include a wide range of services, for example, arranging and paying for storage that helps financially support the marketing channels and providing finance options such as purchase agreement plans and higher purchase (HP) payments to the consumer to ensure that the sale can progress.

Together, these functions performed by the intermediary ensure greater market coverage, reduce the cost of coverage, increase the availability of cash flow in the distribution channel, and increase end-user convenience. A producer can bypass an intermediary by elimination or substitution, but the tasks performed by the intermediary cannot be eliminated. With increasing internet and e-commerce routes there has been a shift in the role that channel intermediaries play. Intermediary reduction, where traditional intermediaries are driven out of the market or eliminated, is known as *dis-intermediation*. They may be forced to differentiate and re-emerge in the electronic marketplace, which is called *re-intermediation*, or entirely new channel markets for intermediaries will be created through e-commerce, and this is termed *cyber-mediation*.

Re-intermediation of travel services

Several online travel agencies (OTA) have entered the market, which has increased complexity within the online distribution network. As a result, hospitality managers are faced with new marketing challenges concerning publicising and selling their services. This is an example of re-intermediation, which leads to a plethora of available online channels in addition to existing traditional distribution channels. Consequently, there is an enlarged distribution environment. The net result is that competition is increased and customers look for more added-value services from the online buying experience. Therefore, to stay competitive within the totality of the tourism experience, OTAs need to provide a 'one-stop-shop' since the competitor is only one click away.

Omni-channels

The growth of online transactions has made a significant impact on the physical distribution operations and has led to omni-channels, sometimes called hybrid channels. This has altered the traditional design of almost every aspect of retail supply chain processes, including how warehouses are operated, how products are picked, packed and dispatched, order fulfilment and delivery, as well as creating further issues for physical distribution with free shipping, last mile delivery, product returns (a component of reverse logistics) and cross-border transactions.

Omni-channel shoppers present a distribution challenge for retailers because consumers often seek the ability to choose their preferred delivery date and time for delivery. Additionally they want the same versatility for the uplift of their inbound packages picking up the product that they have decided to return. Since one of the conveniences of online sales is a trouble-free returns policy, increasingly consumers are only willing to purchase if there is the ability to have free return shipping.

Another trend being driven by Amazon, eBay, and Asos is the same-day delivery trials. The omni-channel consumer is demanding a seamless customer experience across all customer touchpoints. Consumers want to buy from anywhere and they want to take possession of it at a location that suits them (whether it is in a store, at their workplace or at their home) and they equally want to return it anywhere. This has huge implications for physical distribution channels and the following only demonstrates some of these alternatives:

- Buy online and ship the product from a store to the consumer

- Buy at a store and ship the product from a distribution centre to the store

- Buy at a store and ship the product from a different store

- Collect return product from a consumer and return to a store

- Collect return product from a consumer and return to a distribution center

- Collect return product from a consumer and return to an alternate destination

Transportation needs to be flexible enough to allow for late changes in outbound and inbound shipping processes, yet still leverage the existing transportation replenishment network. Retailers have to select the stores that are closest to the consumer in order to meet their delivery expectations. It is not unusual for online fulfillment centres to be located in a different place to the distribution centers. It is also difficult to forecast the number of returns and decide if these inbound packages should be part of a transport service delivering or if it should be a separate service.

Managing relationships across the supply chain

When making decisions on place and physical distribution, marketers may have an ideal strategy in mind, but the final choices are dependent upon the relationships that can be established and maintained throughout the supply chain. Only then can the right goods and services reach the customer in the right place at the right time. Any producer or service supplier that wishes to use an intermediary to reach the market must consider the following factors:

- Does that intermediary have the right reach? The intensity (or number) of distributors will depend on whether the strategy is for local, regional, national or international presence and how far a customer is willing to travel to access your product.

- Is the end consumer willing to buy from that intermediary? Some retailers hold dominant positions and so a listing with them becomes essential.

- Do shoppers want to see that product sold alongside competitive products or would they prefer, or be willing, to go to an exclusive outlet?

- Does the retailer offer the right image and style to complement the brand? A brand positioned at the high end of the market must choose a retailer already serving that existing market.

- Is the retailer able to support the brand at point of sale and with appropriate promotional efforts?

- Does the retailer requires specialist training to sell the product and meet customer service requirements?

Even if a particular retailer meets the above conditions, they must be willing to stock the product and negotiations are necessary to ensure that all parties (consumers, retailers and producers) get value from the relationship. Some important distributers may have established relationships with competitors; some may insist on exclusivity; others may require a large amount of financial and other incentives to stock the brand, such as slotting and listing fees, point of sale materials, advertising support, in-store training for sales staff or commission payments and additional discounts. In short, although the end consumer is the ultimate user of the product or service, the first job of any producer is to make sure that they create a strong business to business relationship with their customers (distributor, agent, retailer and so on) who are the next links in the supply chain.

Links between the supply chains can be strengthened so that the system becomes a vertically integrated marketing system. Contractual relationships, which stipulate the terms and conditions and responsibilities of each part of the chain, can ensure that goods and information flows are established to ensure that the system works efficiently and effectively. Alternatively, there are times when one member on the distribution chain buys the next organisation up or down steam so that a retailer owns the distribution centre or a manufacturer owns the retail outlets. This gives greater control and assures that the information required to make the distribution successful also flows up and downstream. Finally, integration is obtained when one member in the supply chain has enough power to control the whole system. This is known as an administered vertical marketing system.

Managing the full process can be difficult, but is essential to avoid the conflict that can arise when any one link in the chain becomes too powerful and the others feel they are not getting sufficient value from the relationship. Retailers hold a great deal of power over manufacturers and UK supermarkets have been criticised for acting in ways that are unfair, such as buying land for retail development and keeping it empty (to prevent competitors from establishing branches), delisting products at short notice, insisting on sale or return, or discounting brands too harshly. Care of distributor relationships should therefore be a priority so that conflict is avoided

Summary

This chapter has introduced physical distribution channels and addressed a range of important issues that need to be considered by a marketer wanting to get their goods and services to the right target markets at the appropriate time and as efficiently as possible. The Ten Ps of Distribution cannot be seen in isolation – each interacts with the others to affect the channel decisions made. Each member of the distribution channel performs essential roles to create customer value by increasing market coverage and maximizing the flow of cash and information in the distribution channel. A company that embraces these opportunities and successfully manages physical distribution activities will gain competitive advantage and offer real customer value.

9

Further reading

Hübner, A., Kuhn, H. and Wollenburg, J. (2016) Last mile fulfilment and distribution in omni-channel grocery retailing: A strategic planning framework, *International Journal of Retail and Distribution Management*, **44**(3), 228-247.

Murray, C.C. and Chu, A.G. (2015). The flying sidekick traveling salesman problem: Optimization of drone-assisted parcel delivery, *Transportation Research Part C: Emerging Technologies*, **54**, 86-109.

Stangl, B., Inversini, A. and Schegg, R. (2016) Hotels' dependency on online intermediaries and their chosen distribution channel portfolios: Three country insights, *International Journal of Hospitality Management*, **52**, 87-96.

References

Baines, P., Fill, C. and Rosengren, S. (2017). *Marketing*, 4th edition, OUP

Clancy, (2016) Most online clothes shoppers send something back, BBC (May 30) http://www.bbc.co.uk/news/business-36395719

McKinnon, A.C. (1989) *Physical Distribution Systems*, London: Routledge.

Ram, A. (2016) UK retailers count the cost of returns, FT (January 27) http://www.ft.com/cms/s/0/52d26de8-c0e6-11e5-846f-79b0e3d20eaf.html#axzz4GIPF645o

10 Competitive Marketing Strategy and Planning

Alastair Watson

A marketing strategy enables the business to organise its marketing activities to create and increase sales, make a profit or surplus, and engage with stakeholders so that they are satisfied with the business activities. Naturally, a marketing strategy requires levels of planning from conception to execution. Throughout the following pages, the different types of marketing strategy will be discussed, depending on the situation and needs of the business, along with an evaluation of the conditions required for globalisation. Once the strategic approaches have been detailed, the top-level strategy is implemented through a systematic and integrated marketing plan.

Business strategy

It is important from the outset that the organisation understands the key factors, which have roles in achieving a sustainable competitive advantage. Chapter 2 developed understanding of competitive advantage, and the factors that affect an organisation's capability of operating competitively in the market environment. The key players in a business strategy are the company itself, its customers, and market competitors, demonstrated in the *strategic triangle* (Ohmae, 1991; Jobber and Ellis-Chadwick, 2013).

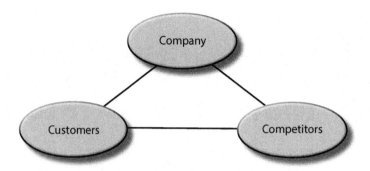

Figure 10.1: The strategic triangle. Adapted from Ohmae (1991:39)

Competitive behaviour

Competition is the driving force for change and is often seen as the heart of healthy economic pursuits in a thriving marketplace. Without competition from other manufacturers or service providers, operators survive through sacrifice: they deliver their goods or services to the consumer with satisfactory levels of product or service quality and limited desire and ability to excel. Competitive behaviour can manifest in a number of different forms, which can encourage healthy behaviour amongst competing organisations. The following section will discuss *conflict, competition, co-existence, cooperation,* and *collusion* (Kotler and Keller, 2016).

Conflict characterises aggressive competition whereby the objectives of each operator identifies a strategy to force the other out of the marketplace, and indeed perhaps out of business. As a result of financial recession, many retailers have since gone out of business because of conflict from their competitors. Borders, the leading book retailer faced much competition and was unable to compete with the likes of Amazon (both its multimedia book section, and hard copy marketplace), and discounted book sales in mainstream supermarkets such as Asda, Tesco, and Sainsbury's. Borders eventually ceased to trade throughout 2011, although franchised stores still operate today in the United Arab Emirates, and trading re-commenced in Singapore during 2013 (Borders books: Back in Singapore, 2013).

The objective of **competition** is not necessarily to stop others in the market, but to ensure that your organisation trades better than they do. Higher sales, improved profits, and increased market share results from beating the competition but there are limits to aggressive tactics. Healthy competitive tactics do not destroy the underlying structure of the industry but understand that overall profits being extracted from operations may be affected. Whilst short-term price promotions are often used, the longevity of these must be managed to ensure that this type of marketing activity does not harm overall profitability.

Co-existence can take different forms. Sometimes businesses do not fully appreciate that they are operating within the same market, due to the definition of market boundaries. Consider Mont Blanc and Cross: both are producers of fine quality writing tools. These operators may ignore competition from the jewellery market by defining their product as writing tools, rather than taking a market-centric approach and understanding that they are also competing in the gift market. They might ignore the serious competition from organisations such as BIC or Zebra, who both produce affordable writing solutions such as ballpoint pens. Finally, companies may recognise a sector of the marketplace which their competitor has entered (perhaps geographic, market segment or differentiation of product technology) and avoid activities which may cause harmful conflict.

Cooperation occurs when two or more operators decide to combine skills or resources to overcome problems and make the most of new opportunities in the market. By forming this type of strategic alliance, or joint venture, it is possible to create a better competitive advantage for future trading. An example of this would be the work by Shell Petroleum, Airbus, and Rolls-Royce who collaborated to produce alternative fuels (GTL Jet Fuel) used in the engines which can be found on the Airbus A380 aeroplane (World's First Commercial Passenger Flight Powered By Fuel Made From Natural Gas Lands In Qatar, 2009).

Finally, **collusion** sees organisations forming an agreement to inhibit further competition. This type of competitive behaviour is more likely to be found where there are a small number of suppliers in the marketplace, where the product or service price is relatively low, or where tariff barriers are in place, which can restrict trade. Recently, Amazon and Apple Books have created a sector in the book market for e-books. In 2009, Amazon sold books at an average price of around seven Euros which caused upset amongst publishers who thought that this would impair the printed market, and see sales fall as they had in the music business through physical media (CDs, vinyl, etc.). Apple brought the iBook platform to the market, with terms agreed with publishers, which caused consumers to switch from Amazon to Apple. This was identified as collusion, which was deemed detrimental to the industry and an example of anti-competitive behaviour from Apple towards another industry provider.

10

Developing strategic objectives

Throughout history, marketing strategies have been likened to those in military warfare (Ries and Trout, 2005; Kotler and Singh, 1981) with competitors viewed as enemies, and so the principles of military strategy are sometimes applied to marketing in the business world. Whilst developing a competitive marketing strategy, the organisation must choose which objectives it wishes to achieve. Marketing strategy theory delivers us five objectives, any of which can be achieved, depending on the form of strategy considered appropriate to its business model.

■ Build objectives

Build objectives are attractive when trading in a growing market. As markets grow in general, each company has the opportunity to appreciate sales growth, regardless of the position of other operators. In growing markets, competitors may retaliate if they do not meet their targets although it is unlikely that this will have as large an effect as it would have had in a situation of no-growth. Build objectives in a growing market are sensible, as many new customers are attracted to products and services offered. Over-capacity or over-provision can be a benefit, as it will eventually be sold. Whilst brand identity may not yet be established, the organisation should begin to build brand loyalty, enabling them to maintain the expected sales growth.

Build objectives, when applied to a mature (or no-growth) market permit the exploitation of competitive weaknesses. Companies might win on service or additional features or different positioning. Google ousted other search engines when it entered the market and Apple beat Microsoft and other competitors by concentrating on easy use and design. Similarly, it is possible that the organisation uses its own competencies to succeed in the market. Marks and Spencer, and Sacoor Brothers Clothing (UAE), both trade in the knowledge that they offer a retail environment, which presents goods that are perceived to be of high quality when compared to many of their direct competitors.

Build objectives can be achieved in four ways: market expansion, winning market share from competitors, merger or acquisition, or through strategic alliances. Market expansion occurs when the organisation seeks to gain new users of the product/service, or by increased frequency of sale. For example, Kellogg's, the traditional breakfast cereal manufacturer entered new markets when they created their breakfast cereal bars, allowing consumers to eat breakfast on the move. By changing terminology of products and removing 'breakfast' from the title (i.e. simply 'cereal') this has also, in essence, changed the group of products to something which can be perceived as usable at other times of the day – creating a 'new' use for cereal. To increase sales frequency, we sometimes rely on persuasive tactics when communicating with the consumer. Kellogg's, by creating a new range of products (cereal bars), and opening cereal up as a snack to be enjoyed throughout the day, have experienced sales growth of their leading brands.

If it is not possible to expand the marketplace, then build strategies imply that to grow market share, the organisation must achieve this to the detriment of competitors. It is possible to achieve greater market share through product, distribution, promotional innovation, and penetrative pricing, for which Kotler and Singh (1981) have designed several attack strategies, as shown in Figure 10.2.

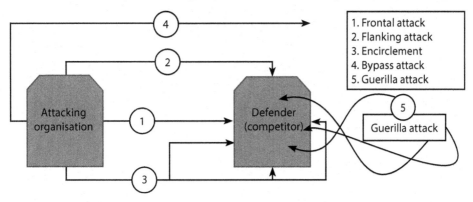

Figure 10.2: Attack strategies. Adapted from: Jobber and Chadwick-Ellis (2013:746)

A frontal attack occurs when a challenger takes on their competitor (defender) head on. For success, the attacker must have a sustainable competitive advantage over the competition. Virgin Atlantic challenged British Airways and American Airlines transatlantic flights based on their approach to continual service improvement and innovations such as video screens to every passenger seat, and their speedy check-in services at certain Upper-Class Wing operations (see Benady, 2009). A frontal attack based on cost leadership will allow an attack on market leaders where a low-price strategy is used. Budget airline Ryanair used cost-leadership in the short-haul market to undercut more traditional carriers (e.g. British Airways and Lufthansa). In this instance, customer value is key to building a differential advantage and must be sustainable to delay the defender ability to retaliate. Challengers must also consider their other business activities and consider whether they can match or beat all other activities such as after-sales service in order to gain a foothold in the market place.

Frontal attacks are more likely to be successful if there is an opportunity to restrict the market leader's ability to retaliate. This may include patent protection, technological advancements and lead times, thus inhibiting retaliation

10

costs. Patent protection makes it difficult for the competition to imitate products, and organisational pride may inhibit imitation as it shows they have lost face in the market and are slow to develop their own technology.

Without sufficient resources, the attacker may not be able to withstand retaliation attempts by the market leader. Hooley at al. (2007) discuss the situation of IBM who launched a competitive attack on Apple. Whilst IBM was slow to develop products in the personal computer market, they created a product, which was more powerful than Apple's machine. IBM also worked with software houses and persuaded them to produce a wide range of software, which would only operate on their platform. This, in turn, offered IBM users a wider choice of operable programmes compared to those available for the Apple operating system. IBM had secured large financial resources due to cashing in on their mainframe products, which allowed them to engage in powerful promotional activities aimed at business users. Their differential advantage, initial ability to match Apple's support functions, and Apple's slow response to retaliate saw IBM become the market leader. IBM did, however, fall foul when cheaper, clone systems were able to operate the software which had been developed for the IBM PCs. Table 10.1 shows some other companies who engaged in head-to-head attack strategies.

Table 10.1: Marketing head-to-head examples

Companies	Market
Zara – Forever 21	Clothing
Coca-Cola – PepsiCo	Soft drinks
Chiquitos – Hungry Horse	Casual dining, branded restaurant
Apple iPad – Samsung Note	Tablets
Dell – Lenovo	Personal computers
Ford – Renault	Motor cars

Considering Figure 10.2, a flanking attack occurs when the attacker identifies a market segment in which their competitor is weak, or vulnerable. This may include geographical areas or segments of the market where the defender has little representation. In the UK, the dominating major supermarkets had opened larger stores in out of town areas, whereas smaller operators such as NISA or McColl's opened small, convenience stores offering more local availability. Now the large supermarkets have retaliated by broadening their range of stores to offer imitation convenience stores called Tesco Metro, Sainsbury's Local, etc.

Can you think of other examples of companies using flanking attacks? Why was it important for the company to do this, and what benefits did they realise?

Another approach experienced recently is the move toward ethical consumerism, and brands which take pride in their ethical values. This pursuit has already bought successful results. Green & Blacks produce organic chocolate bars; Pret A Manger make sandwiches using only natural ingredients which are not exposed to chemicals or preservatives; Ben and Jerry's have strong ethical beliefs in the production and marketing of their ice cream products. Retaliation to flanking attacks is also common and when Mars introduced their range of ice creams to threaten Unilever, their competitor then launched a range of premium brands including Magnum and Gino Ginelli. In addition to this, Unilever had a number of exclusivity deals with retailers who were prevented from stocking competitors' ranges.

An encirclement attack occurs when a competitive assault is launched against the defender from all sides. They will hit every market with as many combinations of products as possible. This can be seen in the watch market where some manufacturers produce a high number of designs that will appeal to as many consumers across the board as possible. Seiko have an extensive range, which varies in price and style, to cover many consumer demands from everyday affordable, to technically advanced GPS controlled watches costing thousands of pounds. By doing this they attack a range of competitors, from Swatch and Timex, to TAG Heuer.

When the attacker sidesteps the competitor, this is known as a bypass attack and is often seen when a business introduces new technology to the market. In the competitive world of gaming and games consoles, Sony has kept ahead of competition by introducing Virtual Reality (VR) aspects into the existing PlayStation range. However, Microsoft is continuing to develop VR, albeit in a new console, and not currently to be integrated in the substitute X-Box console.

Finally, a guerrilla attack is a tactical approach whereby the attacker avoids a full-on blow with one product, or campaign, and makes many small moves to avoid predictability. This may include repeated discount strategies and promotions, or substantial media advertising projects. These may be the only strategies available to a smaller company who wishes to take on a large competitor. This tactic makes the company known to the defender, without a full campaign that might have otherwise encouraged a frontal retaliation. However, a no-retaliation response can ever be guaranteed!

Another consideration for achieving build objectives is merger or acquisition. In this move, the organisation either works together with, or acquires, their competitor's business. This permits the support and development functions to be combined, in turn avoiding the costs being incurred to better oneself against the competition, and the need for expensive marketing strategies and advertising

10

campaigns. Clear objectives must be set out prior to engaging in merged practices, to avoid conflict and any disparity in culture, both organisational and at personal levels, particularly when working globally. There are, of course, further benefits, as detailed in Table 10.2.

Table 10.2: Avoiding conflict with merger and acquisitions

Conflict	Objective
Reduce over-capacity & increase market share/efficiency	Acquiring company plans to eliminate capacity, to gain market share form the acquired business, and become more efficient
	Often difficult to implement as generally involves large companies with incompatible embedded values and processes.
	Care to be taken that any organisational issues do not outweigh the benefits of merger/acquisition.
Geographic expansion	Both companies will benefit from geographic expansion into foreign markets with each partner potentially gaining a foothold in each other's trading markets.
Product/market expansion	Permits expansion into different markets. When Cadbury acquired Green & Black chocolate, they gained share in the ethical market.
Research & development	Enables research or development skills to be acquired, along with their output. Grows in-house expertise, enabling market position to strengthen more quickly.
Exploiting industry convergence	When an emerging industry is identified, the company attempts to gain position by acquiring existing businesses.

Strategic alliances are a further method to achieve build objectives. Here, the company engages in a long-term agreement with partners, to achieve competitive advantage. Normally the partners will operate by means of a joint venture (a company owned by both) and benefit from the use of each other's research and development, or other expertise. A recent example of this is the Fiat/Chrysler initiative, whereby the proposed electric version of the Fiat 500 car is powered by an electric motor developed by Chrysler. The Italian producer owns a majority share of the US giant, Chrysler. An important reason for engaging a strategic alliance is the desire to learn additional skills from the other partner. However, there is risk, in that industrial or corporate developments and secrets may be leaked, and one partner may inadvertently lose some of its core capabilities to the partner. Table 10.3 summarises the key conditions and strategic focus of build objectives.

Table 10.3: Attractive conditions and strategic focus: Build objectives

Conditions and focus	Marketing activity
Attractive conditions Growth markets Exploitable competitive weaknesses Exploitable corporate strengths Sufficient corporate resources	Product- maintain benefits and service Price- penetrative, lower prices Promotion- broaden reach using good range of promotional activities Place- widen distribution to reach growing market
Strategic focus Market expansion (new users, new uses, increased frequency of use) Winning market share (innovation, penetrative pricing, attack) Merger/acquisition Strategic alliances (what can you learn from this)	

■ Hold objectives

When a company defends its current position against attackers, it will engage hold objectives. A classic example of this defensive position being adopted would be by a market leader, in need of maintaining their position against others. Retaining position as leader, the company is able to generate positive cash flow from its products and use that to grow and develop other areas of the business. In addition, market leaders may find themselves more able to enjoy other benefits due to their position: bargaining power with suppliers and distributors, positive brand recognition and awareness from consumers that should ease the introduction of new products.

Hold objectives need the defending business to keep close eye on their competitors, and monitor activity in the market. This means that strategies can be changed, engaged, or even let be if no serious activity is apparent. If attack is likely, and a defence is required, the organisation is faced with a number of strategic options (see Figure 10.3).

Position defence is likely to be utilised when the defender has a good range of products, and wishes to fortify their existing position in the market. The products will need to be priced and promoted competitively and are likely to have differential advantage, which are not easily imitated by competitors. Some leaders will rely on their brand name to provide a strong defence; however, this will not always guarantee success. Land Rover fully believed in their brand image as market leaders in the four-wheel drive vehicle industry, and did little initially to develop products. They soon saw competition in the form of Subaru, Mitsubishi, and Audi (to name a few), who subsequently developed their own technology, and created ranges of smaller, fun, and competitive vehicles using four-wheel drive.

10

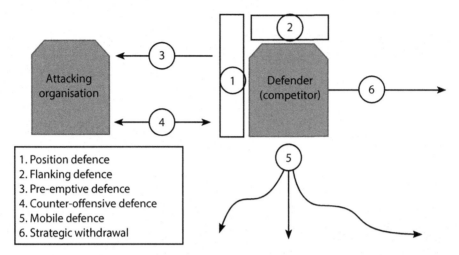

Figure 10.3: Defence strategies. Adapted from: Jobber and Ellis-Chadwick (2013:754)

A flanking defence involves the defence of an otherwise unprotected segment. If it remains unprotected, there is every possibility that new entrants see an opportunity to gain experience, and then engage their own attack strategy against the market leader. Whilst the segment may be unattractive, it would make sense to defend this and avoid activities from new operators. However, defence must be serious, even if the segment is not part of the core business. If products brought to this part of the market are not properly developed, or of poor quality, then competitors may trump the leader and take hold of the marketplace. An additional move against small, yet successful attackers may be for the defender to acquire the competition to gain their market share.

By deciding that the best form of defence is to attack first, we experience a pre-emptive defence. By striking first, we may see continual product development, which can be appreciated typically in electronic consumer goods including computer products, smartphones, and MP3 players.

A counter-offensive defence involves the defender choosing one of three different options: a head-on counter attack, go for the attacker's cash cow, or decide to encircle. Head-on counter measures would see that defender match or surpass what their competitor has done, and may involve heavy discounting or increased promotion – both costly efforts. The defender may also choose to compete by offering increased technological advancement and innovation, such as Apple's iPod and iPhone to the MP3 and mobile communications industry. Attacking the competitor's cash cow will affect the attacker's resources by firstly reducing the cash flow from a main product, subsequently affecting the ability to develop and build resources in other areas of the business. Encirclement involves the defender perhaps launching new brands to compete with an attacker in the market.

A mobile defence can be sensible when the major market comes under threat. To become more competitive, the company may choose either diversification or market broadening. If diversification is chosen, then the company may enter other markets with new products. Market broadening occurs if the company opts to broaden their business definition, for example, the film industry which has many operators who have moved their business activities from purely movie production into entertainment and retail businesses, with activities such as Disney Stores, theme parks, and television production. Table 10.4 summarises the key conditions and strategic focus of hold objectives.

Table 19.4: Attractive conditions and strategic focus: Hold objectives

Conditions and focus	Marketing activity
Attractive conditions Market leader – mature or declining market Costs outweigh benefits of development	Product – Maintain differentiation Price – competitive in the market place Place – maintain distribution relationships through existing channels
Strategic focus Monitor competition Confronting competition	Promotion – broad spectrum of activity maintaining awareness

Strategic withdrawal needs the company to identify its key strengths and weaknesses. It should maximise its strengths, whilst reducing its weaknesses. Interestingly, Nokia once marketed its paper, rubber, and cabling products, but shifted its business practices to focus on computers, telecommunications, and consumer electronics. This defence strategy enables the business to concentrate on its core competencies, and is effective when diversification develops a market range that is too broad.

Consider companies who have strategically withdrawn products from the market? Why would they do this, and what impact did it have on the consumers, competitors and their supply chain?

10

■ Niche objectives

Niche objectives help a company to pursue a small market segment, or sub-segment, and avoid competition from the major market players by focussing on a very specific or specialised area. Boutique hotels are an example of this, concentrating on the quirks and specific needs of specific consumers. However, many of the market leaders have started to copy this aspect of the hotel industry, with companies such as Hilton, who developed several versions of their "art and tech" inspired bedrooms, to attract those who desire the special touches offered by boutique operators, combined with the brand identity of a leading operator.

Niche strategies are often attractive to smaller businesses that may only have a small budget to fight market leaders that dominate the industry. It is important, though, that there are segments within the marketplace, which will support the revenue strands required. This is created when the market demands are generally, but not fully, met by the industry leaders. These segments will be of little interest to the major players, but give room for profit of the smaller, more specialised businesses.

Market knowledge, and segmentation, is of importance in this instance, and the business owners/managers must be aware of where the potential pockets of profit are. Research and development must focus on getting to know the customer closely to create a differential advantage through the coordinated marketing mix. Table 10.5 summarises the key conditions and strategic focus of niche objectives.

Table 10.5: Attractive conditions and strategic focus: Niche objectives

Conditions and focus	Marketing activity
Attractive conditions Small budget Small company Strong leaders hold majority share of market	Product – highly differentiated Price – high to reflect differences Place – specific, available in specialty stores, perhaps limited online activity, perhaps only direct C2B Promotion – very focussed, directed to specific consumers
Strategic focus Segmentation Differential advantage can be achieved Smart R&D Small, focussed, specific consumer needs	

> Can you describe an organisation, which offers a niche product to the market place? Remember, this may also include the service sector (tourism, hospitality, for example).

■ Harvest objectives

These are appropriate when a company is trying to improve profit margins from each unit, which may result in a sales drop. Even if sales to decline, the aim is to achieve a higher profit in the short-term to create positive cash flows, which can be used throughout other areas of the business. Harvest strategies can be used in mature or declining markets to extract more profit. They can also be sensible in growth markets if costs are higher than the existing benefits achieved. The first step in implementing harvest objectives is to stop all research and development spending. The only costs in this instance should be changes to raw materials or manufacturing costs, to achieve higher profit. It is likely that product lines will be limited to a small number of distributors, and marketing and promotion budgets will be slashed. The company may also take the opportunity to increase the product price. Table 10.6 summarises the key conditions and strategic focus of harvest objectives.

Table 10.6: Attractive conditions and strategic focus: Harvest objectives

Conditions and focus	Marketing activity
Attractive conditions Mature or declining market Growth market – costs of development exceed benefits Loyal customers Future products will create large profit	Product – as it is. No spend on R&D, no changes made. Place – no development of network/ channels Price – potential to increase and experience higher marginal profit due to reduced costs and inflated sales price Promotion – cut back! Spend less!
Strategic focus No R&D spend Reformulate product Rationalise manufacture Reduce marketing spend Increase price?	

■ Divest objectives

A company drops products from its range, usually after harvesting and when the losses exceed any profit from the product or service. Products which have a low market share, or are in declining markets are candidates to be divested. Care must be taken when divesting to ensure that the removal of one product does not adversely affect the rest of the company portfolio, or any complimentary products which its sales compliment. If a divest strategy is chosen, it is important to withdraw from the market quickly to minimise cost, although if the product (or its rights) can be sold, some return may be appreciated. Table 10.7 summarises the key conditions and strategic focus of harvest objectives.

Table 10.7: Attractive conditions and strategic focus:: Divest objectives

Conditions and focus	Marketing activity
Attractive conditions Loss-making products Drain on profit Low share of declining market Removing product has no effect on others	Product – no changes Place – withdraw as soon as possible depending on distributor relationships Price – no change, perhaps cut to sell final stocks Promotion – zero, unless special offers/ discounts to rid the organisation of stock
Strategic focus Get out – quickly! Minimise further costs	

10

> What are the benefits to the organisation of closing a business unit, or removing a product from the marketplace? Can you think of any examples?

Global marketing strategy

Competing internationally has its pros and cons. Whilst domestic markets are a known quantity, the risk associated with going global can create greater profits, better brand awareness, and ultimately market growth. International expansion can appeal for several reasons (Table 10.8).

Table 10.8: Reasons for global marketing strategy

Reason	Description
Saturation	If the domestic market is saturated, then international expansion may be the only route to develop the business further. Aldi expanded its activities from Europe to Australasia and beyond.
Domestic market	When the domestic market is small, international trade is the only option to a company, which must broaden its scope to survive. Domestic electronic companies have found success by taking their products abroad. Dyson who designed and manufactured niche vacuum cleaners in the UK now export globally to raise brand awareness, and increase sales and profit.
Low-growth	As domestic markets experience slow growth identification of new opportunities in overseas markets with more buoyant economies, or are experiencing development. With the growth of the middle classes in China, BMW and other motor companies have exploited demand for luxury cars.
Customer demand	In some industries, customers expect suppliers to have a global presence. This could be caused by ex-pat communities who yearn for domestic products abroad, or by international clients who expect a global presence from the supplier.
Competitive focus	Attack strategies may involve companies targeting competitors who have entered domestic markets. Some operators in an industry feel the need to follow competitors who have already engaged international operations.
Cost focus	Markets can be inhibited by the costs of production. For example, minimum wage, and logistic efforts to obtain materials, may cause operators to look further afield for cheaper solutions to manufacture, or deliver customer services.
Balanced portfolio	Generally, different countries will experience differing growth rates. Marketing products and services internationally may offset decline in one market, with growth being appreciated in another.

■   Entry strategies

Indirect export

Independent distributors are used within the domestic market. This may include export merchants or agents, piggybacking on other producers' facilities, or cooperative organisations, who manage the export activities of many domestic businesses.

Direct export strategies

This happens when the business manages their activities internally. Often this will require setting up contracts abroad with distributors and logistics firms, using domestic sales teams abroad, and perhaps setting up a marketing department overseas.

Cooperation

With this strategy, the organisation may enter a license agreement with foreign producers who can produce and market the product or service in the international market, accessing the technology and know-how of the original operator. Quite often, this will be contracted, giving the foreign licensee sole right to produce and market the product. An alternative to licensing would be a franchise, whereby the company offers the franchisee access to certain aspects of the product, at a cost. Coca-Cola is a well-known case of franchising – they sell the product syrup, and right to use the trademark to franchisee who can then produce and market the famous drink in their country.

Joint venture

This is a partnership between domestic and international companies, and is beneficial when there are restrictions to entering the marketplace. By working with an international player in the overseas location, the domestic operator can access the market, share costs, and of course profits.

Direct investment

The organisation sets up their own overseas operations. It requires investment to create new facilities, which will reproduce the domestic business activities, or acquisition of existing amenities from overseas competitors.

10

Implementing strategy - the marketing plan

Strategy needs to be operationalised and implemented and this requires marketing objectives to be determined and a marketing plan to be designed.

Figure 10.4: Marketing strategy implementation process. Adapted from: Jobber and Ellis-Chadwick, 2013: 814)

The marketing plan is a working document that defines the marketing activities required to achieve marketing objectives. Marketing activities must be planned and coordinated to maximise customer value and be effective. As well as being effective, the plan should also be as efficient as possible so the timing of activities and the amount of resource required to carry out each activity must be detailed along with an indication of who is responsible for implementing aspects of the plan.

Each element of the marketing mix will detail its own activity schedule that feeds into the marketing document.

The plan stems from the marketing strategy, which should outline the marketing objectives. Marketing objectives are quantified with the timescale for completion clearly stated and should be achievable through the marketing actions stipulated.

All plans require sufficient resourcing and the main methods for choosing the marketing budget outlined in Table 10.10. Budgets, allocated across the marketing mix will vary according to the industry, organisational goals and current brand recognition.

Table 10.9: Outline marketing plan

Situation/ context analysis	Internal strengths and weaknesses, external opportunities and threats, including market trends, competitors	
Marketing objectives	Quantified and timescales made clear	
Target markets	Clear description of target markets using relevant segmentation criteria	
Marketing mix	Product plans	
	Price plans	
	Promotional plans	
	Place plans	
Budget	How much to be spent, allocated to each part of the mix	
Measurement	Linked to the objectives	
Timescales and people	Responsibility for each activity – internal or using external specialists	

Table 10.10: Setting the marketing budget

Method	Based on	pros/cons
Objectives and task	What is required to achieve marketing goals	Regards promotion as an investment not a cost. The link between spend and outcome is not usually so clear.
Matching competitors	Assumes that the amount spent = customer impact and value.	Difficult to estimate competitors' spend. Assumes competitors have same objectives.
Percentage of sales	Marketing is seen as a cost	Higher sales increase budget. Reverse approach might be more suitable.
Affordability	The company can only spend what it has	This strategy may limit growth.

10

Once a plan is ready it becomes a working document, often referred to and checked to ensure the company is on track. Although a plan may be adapted, planning puts the organisation in control and encourages a proactive approach to competitive environmental changes. The very act of planning does not ensure success but without a systematically researched and produced plan then failure is more likely.

Implementing strategies involves, to some degree, the implementation of change. Key to the success is having the cooperation of top management, to support the model of change required. Changes must be monitored and this cyclical process includes strategy creation, determining the strategy to be adopted, the implementation of strategy itself, and then a review process. The review process may identify a need for further change, which can restart the overall process with a new or tweaked strategy (see Figure 10.4).

Summary

A marketing strategy, whether employed locally or globally, has the potential to either make or break an organisation. By eyeing the competition closely, whilst paying attention to the forces within the market, it is possible to have an overview of what is happening or about to happen to the firm and its products or services. With expertise applied with knowledge, one may choose to take steps to alter the strategic plan in order to maintain a key position in certain sectors, or within the overall marketplace.

A clear understanding of the organisation's position and future plans must be understood when developing a marketing strategy, so that the appropriate offensive or defensive action may be made. Planning of future products, and perhaps the demise of certain items within an existing portfolio, must consider the actions of the firm, and the reaction of consumers within the market. Similarly, the skills, expertise, and proposed future must be clear to those devising and executing the decisions necessary if deciding to 'go global'. Knowledge and understanding of competitors and market places, and the need for specific products and services beyond the domestic market should be fully considered alongside the overall strategic planning and capabilities of the organisation before embarking into foreign fields.

Further reading

Jobber and Ellis-Chadwick (2013), *Principles and Practice of Marketing*, McGraw Hill, Chapter 21.

Hooley, G., Saunders, J., Piercy, N. and Nicoulaud, B. (2007). *Marketing Strategy and Competitive Positioning*, London: Prentice-Hall, 224.

Kotler, P. and Keller, K. (2016) *Marketing Management, Global Edition*, Boston: Pearson.

Ries, A. anbd Trout, J. (2005) *Marketing Warfare: 20th Anniversary Edition*. New York, McGraw-Hill.

References

Baines, P., Fill, C. and Page, K. (2011) International market development, in *Marketing* (2nd ed), Oxford: Oxford University Press, pp.245-284.

Benady, D. (2009) Trouble in the air for Virgin (airlines), *Strategic Direction*, **25** (3).

Jobber, D. and Ellis-Chadwick, F. (2012) Competitive marketing strategy, in *Principles and Practice of Marketing* (7th ed). London, McGraw-Hill Higher Education.

Jobber, D. and Ellis-Chadwick, F. (2012) Global marketing strategy, in *Principles and Practice of Marketing* (7th ed). London, McGraw-Hill Higher Education.

Jobber, D. and Ellis-Chadwick, F. (2012) Managing marketing implementation, organization and control, in *Principles and Practice of Marketing* (7th ed). London, McGraw-Hill Higher Education.

Kotler, P., Armstrong, G., Harris, L.C and Piercy, N. (2013) Creating competitive advantage, in *Principles of Marketing* (6th ed). England, Pearson, pp. 540-565.

Kotler, P. and Singh, R. (1981) Marketing warfare in the 1980s, *Journal of Business Strategy*. **1** (3), 30-41.

Masterson, R. and Pickton, D. (2010) Service products, in *Marketing* (2nd ed). London, Sage, pp. 239-268.

Ohmae, K. (1982) The strategic triangle: A new perspective on business unit strategy, *European Management Journal*, **1**, 38-48.

Prasad, A. (2011) The impact of non-market forces on competitive positioning understanding global industry attractiveness through the eyes of M. E. Porter. *Journal of Management Research*, **11**(3): 131–7.

URLs

Borders books: Back in Singapore (2013) *Financial Times*. http://www.ft.com/fastft/2013/08/01/borders-books-back-singapore/ [Accessed 5 July 2016].

World's First Commercial Passenger Flight Powered By Fuel Made From Natural Gas Lands In Qatar (2009), Airbus. http://www.airbus.com/newsevents/news-events-single/detail/world039s-first-commercial-passenger-flight-powered-by-fuel-made-from-natural-gas-lands-in-qatar/> [Accessed 7 May 2017]

10

11 Marketing Ethics and Corporate Social Responsibility

Gordon R.A. Jack

Consider a familiar organisation and the marketing techniques they use. What does a consumer expect from this organisation in terms of their corporate social responsibility policy and strategy? How ethical are their marketing campaigns and do they behave appropriately for the good of their corporate image?

Introduction

Ethics has been defined as "systematic approach to moral judgments based on reason, analysis, synthesis, and reflection," and in a business context it is "the study of what constitutes right or wrong, good or bad human conduct in a business environment" (Christie et al, 2003:266). Ethics is a long established and contentious issue and as business transactions become more diverse and ambitious, spanning countries and continents, this transparent and underappreciated concept turns into a complexity requiring consideration and questioning about all business activities. Ethical issues are present in all parts of an organisation, from strategic and executive decision-making, right down to the grass root activities. The global media widely reports on business ethics and as marketing activities are generally outward facing, they are frequently more scrutinised than most other business activities. Marketing ethics is therefore socially germane and currently prevalent, particularly as corporate social responsibility (CSR) becomes increasingly salient, with obligatory adherence to being responsible heightened by an awareness of how a firm should conduct itself as a part of society. The issue is more problematic when dealing with multinational corporations, whose operations span globally. CSR was previously seen as a hindrance and something of a necessary evil, but companies are now finding it a useful tool that can be used in conjunction with marketing strategies to increase profits and customer engagement. Consumers are even more acutely aware of the environmental impact of their consumption habits and companies are now harnessing this to convince customers of their continued dedication to the conservation of the ecological environment. However, it is not only the consumer that an organisation is trying to appease; consideration must be granted to shareholders, employees, suppliers and many more organisational stakeholders. Following a discussion of how the understanding of corporate social responsibility has developed over time, this chapter will consider the ethics of the practices associated with the marketing function as well as well as understanding business ethics in a wider macro sense under the umbrella of corporate social responsibility.

Corporate social responsibility (CSR)

Despite being governed heavily in their operational activities by local, national and international legislation, CSR from a company perspective is very much self-motivated and self-regulated. As a result of this highly autonomous attitude to CSR, it is very blurred, with questionable boundaries and little guidance to limitations and levels of acceptance. In addition, no two CSR approaches will be the same, as there are no set rules governing their creation or implementation. Organisational policies surrounding CSR are tacitly related to legal, ethical and moral practices, and should underpin a company's activities to ensure that they adhere to legislation and do so whilst respecting both environment and society. Those carrying out the firms' activities are expected to exercise practices which are "socially responsible" and promote "corporate citizenship" as part of their unexpressed remit (Carroll, 2000:187).

Definitions through time

"...the firm's considerations of, and response to, issues beyond the narrow economic, technical and legal requirements of the firm to accomplish social [and environmental] benefits along with the traditional economic gains which the firm seeks."
    Davis, 1973

"The art of doing well by doing good."
    Economist, 2005

"...a firm's voluntary consideration of stakeholder concerns both within and outside its business operations."
    Aguilera et al., 2007

The earliest conceptions of CSR came from Wendell Wilkie in the 1930s, who is said to have "helped educate the businessmen to a new sense of social responsibility" (see Cheit, 1964:157). As well as these pre-WW2 coinings of CSR, Bowen is known as the father of CSR following the publication of his book, *Social Responsibilities of the Businessman* (Bowen, 1953).

Firms should be scrutinised not only on their financial success, but also on their non-financial aspects (Carroll, 1979). However, some critics have voiced displeasure at the implementation of CSR policies within business, with detraction from pure economic growth and success (De George, 2009), which they presumably see as the main metric of analysis in a company's outcomes. Research has shown that appropriate implementation of CSR can increase financial gain for an organisation (Porter and Kramer, 1999, 2002). However, it must be borne in mind that business success should not just be purely financially motivated or assessed, and that there are other facets involved that can be classed as determinants of succeeding in business. It would be remiss of any organisation to ignore other operational aspects of their business in favour of wholly financial motivation, therefore an holistic perspective, should be taken in view of this.

More broadly speaking in modern organisations, the two major concepts of environment and society have remained at the forefront of CSR strategies and associated practice. It is important to see how marketing leads and contributes to organisational decisions in these two areas and how much marketing practices are affected by the CSR policies adopted.

First, marketing research as part of environmental scanning activity and monitoring customer responses will lead to insight about various stakeholder views about how socially responsible an organisation is perceived to be vis-a- vis other organisations. All decisions made about operations, production, promotion, pricing and distribution will affect customer perceptions, and marketing activity is very much in the eye of the public. Research is used to identify CSR priorities from the perspective of customers, staff and other stakeholders.

Second, a firm's promotional image must consider both the environment and society when considering how the corporate image is to be portrayed and to what extent their target markets understand and engage with the message. Consideration of suitable messages for individual stakeholder groups, not just customers, is required and the corporate image as a whole, along with perceptions of individual brands and product lines must be aligned. The more complex the business, the greater the exponential increase in the number of parties involved. These parties include, but are not limited to, suppliers, customers, employees, board members and shareholders.

11

Society and marketing: Which products and markets to serve?

CSR is in place to allow an organisation to bring social and environmental good to the wider community, acting to promote their commitment to improvement across multiple respective causes. However, there are always going to be parts of business that cause more than normal levels of emotional affiliation, perhaps including religious or moral beliefs, and this may be due to the nature of the operations of that particular business. To combat this, the businesses that work within these disliked sectors, or provide harmful, offensive products or services, require to either source other avenues for their output, or act to counter the effect that the production, marketing and sales of their products have on the greater population to which they are exposed.

Phillip Morris is a case in point. As the world's largest tobacco manufacturer, they changed their name to Altria, diversified their corporate portfolio to include Kraft foods (since divested) and have undertaken new product research and development to decrease reliance on the (increasingly socially taboo) tobacco industry. Their latest innovation – IQOS inhalers, which heat up tobacco, rather than burning – has met mixed fortunes and currently is outlawed in some countries including New Zealand.

Some companies pollute the environment during manufacture but attempt to counteract this by promoting their green credentials in other areas, perhaps by supporting environmental causes. This deception has been termed '*greenwashing*' because it aims to persuade a company's publics that they are more environmentally conscious than they actually are.

As with all aspects of global business, cultural norms and geographical practices differ internationally, and perhaps even regionally, resulting in the organisation having to ensure they accommodate such variations in a sensitive fashion. Each of the parties entering a business transaction must have a comprehensive awareness of all members and stakeholders involved, together with their expectations and assumptions surrounding the transaction. It can be assumed that no two business transactions will ever be identical; therefore, modification of practices to suit all stakeholders should take priority (Jack et al., 2015). What one person may see as appropriate may be deemed otherwise by another party, or unsuitable in the particular business deal taking place.

Marketing of contraceptives

HIV (human immunodeficiency virus), AIDS (acquired immune deficiency syndrome) and associated STI (sexually transmitted infections) rank sixth in the World Health Organization's global death by cause figures in 2012, accounting for 3.2% of deaths around the world. Yet despite these diseases being present across the world, the marketing of contraceptives is still controversial in some countries. A concerted effort in the social marketing of condoms tries to curb the spread of the HIV virus and respond to global family planning efforts. Sales of contraceptives have increased but there is still disparity between sale and use (Meekers and Van Rossem, 2005). The marketing of contraceptives is highly regulated and the promotion and positioning of the product varies across countries, depending on societal beliefs and the particular cultural context.

■ Positive CSR initiatives

CSR initiatives may appear to curb marketing activity but this is not always true and most CSR strategies offer positive outcomes for society and the organisation, and provide very good opportunities to create positive messages about the organisation and its activities. There are many examples of positive CSR initiatives and the best companies are those who realise that taking CSR beyond legal minimums provides good outcomes for all stakeholders.

■ TOMS® One to One® initiative matches every new pair of shoes purchased with a new pair donated to children in hardship in 70 countries worldwide.

■ Organisations offer their employees Charity or Community Days, allowing them to take part in a project or activity beneficial to the community. Certain firms specify a charitable cause that they sponsor for a given period, and employees are encouraged to utilise these days to assist with that cause, usually whilst being paid their usual salary.

■ Verizon, a worldwide communications company, matches employee donations to approved charitable organisations.

Not only do these schemes have a positive influence on the corporate reputation of organisation, they are also seen as an encouragement for employees, instilling loyalty in the brand because of these additional incentives. An employee is likely to be more motivated if their organisation appreciates their actions in and outside the workplace. Research has covered employee engagement retention, productivity, and recruitment, and provides evidence to support CSR improving these outcomes within the organisation (Berger et al., 2006).

11

■ Sustainability in marketing – a contemporary issue

"Sustainable marketing is the process of creating, communicating, and delivering value to customers in such a way that both natural and human capital are pre-served or enhanced throughout" (Martin and Schouten, 2014:18). Sustainability and the environment have become staple parts of our lives since the latter part of the 20th century. This is manifested in examples such as using fewer plas-tic carrier bags at the supermarket, to correctly sorting household waste into recycling receptacles. Individuals who actively subscribe to such activities have been termed sustainable or ethical consumers (McDonagh and Prothero, 2014). A study designed to justify a relatively new charge for carrier bags highlighted that in 2014, 8.5 billion single use carrier bags were used by UK supermarket customers, a 2.3% increase on the previous year and a 30% increase in eight years since 2006 (WRAP, 2015). Since the charge, supermarkets are reporting a 70-80% reduction in use. Irresponsible usage and unnecessary disposal of these environ-mentally harmful products also increases the use of finite planet wide resources at an alarmingly fast rate and the environment is unable to cope. In an attempt to combat this, governments and lobby groups use marketing approaches to encourage consumers to consider the environment in everything they do, rather than being an afterthought.

Some ethical companies who have environmental considerations in their corporate brand values;

■ Rapanui Clothing – rapanuiclothing.com
An eco-fashion company based on the Isle of Wight utilising sustainable materials in their products such as British wool, recycled plastic and bamboo. Coupled with this, the firm is dedicated to developing and implementing technology to allow them to stay in touch with and strictly monitor their supply chain.

■ Riverford Organic Food – riverford.co.uk
Winner of the Observer's Ethical Product of the Decade Award in 2015, this family run business delivers the highest quality, locally sourced, organic foods. Their commitment to customer satisfaction has led to increased loyalty, meaning repeat business over a long period of time from their customers.

Organisational scrutiny from stakeholders, including employees, suppliers, com-petitors and customers, and intense media attention, means the slightest fault in organisations' actions will be highlighted. It is imperative that companies act in the most professional way to minimise the risk of their brand being brought into disrepute. A major aspect involved in sustainability and the reduction of waste, as the world's landfill capacity slowly decreases, is LEAN manufacturing.

This concept was originally introduced in the early 1990s by automotive giant, Toyota, in response to the fact that waste did not add value, with time, money and resources being expended for no eventual gain. This approach to waste is renowned throughout the world and has been adopted by many manufacturing organisations, with waste elimination at the forefront of operational considerations and planning. Other organisations reuse waste by-products in the production process to make other items.

Building success with the Lego Group

"Only the best is good enough" (The Lego Group, 2016)

This global icon of the children's toy industry has been family run since 1932, and remains owned by family members, together with familial representation on its board of directors. It professes to have reached a total of 85 million children worldwide through its commercial operations and sales, 400,000 through its LEGO charitable foundation and around 10 million through associated educational programmes in 2014.

Contemporary organisations must appeal to and maintain contentment amongst the stakeholders, with increased attention to the environment. Some organisations implement strategies which are not conducive to direct profit making but result in increased performance and success in other areas. These may include, but are not limited to, reduction in product wastage, improving levels of process efficiency and recycling of spent items. The LEGO Group as part of its dedication to responsible manufacturing and marketing, have zero waste as a mind-set, rather than a more common feature of reactive or retrospective action once the problem has arisen. Researchers have found that by adopting such an approach can contribute as a success factor to achieving overall organisational strategic objectives (Brower and Mahajan, 2013).

Lego have made several moves towards reducing their environmental impact, which has affected decisions across the marketing mix. In 2014, they banned Shell gasoline stations from distributing their products and they have invested 1 billion Danish Krona (over $114 million) to search for more sustainable manufacturing materials. Lego have set themselves apart through their allegiance to the environment and promoting responsible business practices by adhering to strict codes of practice, values and global standards. Rather than dealing with the repercussions of crises or problems arising from their products, their quality standards and approach to responsible selling are engrained in their entire organisational ethos, to which all employees ascribe.

11

Ethical marketing conflicts

Some consider all marketing as unethical. In their view marketing uses seductive techniques to persuade customers to favour one product or service over another when there are no real differences; it tempts consumers into buying products that they do not need and cannot afford and for some customers, encourages bad choices. Others suggest that marketing, making great products available at the right price, creates value and enriches customer lives. The judgment given depends, in part, on the philosophical approach taken to ethics. It is not the purpose of this chapter to delve deeply into the subject of marketing ethics but it is useful to outline the broad approaches that may shape an individual's view on what constitutes ethical practice.

- **Teleological** approaches consider the consequences or outcomes of an action. If actions result in a positive outcome, they are deemed morally acceptable. This view may be summarised as the means justifying then end.

- **Deontology** is a duty based approach which considers that actions in themselves are either wrong or the right thing to do, regardless of the consequences. Although this means more certainty, since absolute rules are set, it might lead to an decrease in overall happiness as some duties may conflict with others.

These two approaches are at opposite ends of the scale but ethical decision making is not clear-cut particularly when judging decisions that fall under the marketer's remit. Laczniak and Murphy (2006:157) suggest that there are seven basic perspectives that guide ethical marketing. Ethical marketing:

- Puts people first
- Has behavioural standards above the legal requirements
- Is responsible for actions as a means or ends.
- Encourages high moral imagination in managers and employees
- Develops, articulates, and lives a core set of ethical principles.
- Adopts protocols for ethical decision making.
- Takes a stakeholder orientation

■   Collecting data

Firms not only need to cognitively consider they are doing things morally and ethically in express statements, such as CSR policies, but they also need to remain operationally ethical in all tasks and with everyone they engage with. To ensure their products and services are going to be well received, and make a profit, a company may deem it appropriate to carry out market research, speaking to potential customers and assessing what they want. Marketers should adhere to market research codes of conduct (MRS, 2017) when conducting research. During research, they will collect confidential information from participants and this must be dealt with sensitively. Subsequently, they must not take advantage of this vulnerability and not breech the trust given to them by the respondents of their research. However, some firms have breached this trust and sell on consumer information to other companies targeting a similar demographic. Most people have been subjected to unwanted and unsolicited phone calls selling no-win, no-fee compensation claims or selling conservatories to someone living in a third-floor apartment. The root cause of this is that some companies sell information without our permission and although this is illegal in many countries due to data protection laws, this situation is exacerbated by the multitude of ploys designed to confuse consumers, who are unsure whether they are opting in or out of granting permission to share their data. The question remains as to whether this is shrewd business practice or a devious money making scam from the companies we know and trust.

■ Product and service choices

This chapter has already discussed some of the ethical concerns surrounding choices about the type of products and services to offer, influenced by a range of stakeholders. The firm's CSR stance affects decisions concerning sustainability and scarce resource use. Other product decisions in the ethical spotlight include the moral responsibility to sell products that are safe and live up to their promised standards. Manufacturers are sometime criticised for providing products with a range of superfluous features that do not provide real benefits and creating products with inbuilt obsolescence so that replacements are needed sooner than would have been necessary. There are many examples of faulty and even dangerous products being offered for sale. Sometimes this has arisen because of mistakes but on other occasions deliberate actions led to unsafe products being manufactured. An example includes the 2008 baby milk scandal in China, where melamine was added to baby formula and resulted in the death of seven babies and more recently, inferior fake formula packaged as a mainstream quality brand.

■ Pricing practices

All pricing decisions create ethical tension, as they require some discussion about the amount of profit expected and reasonable. Some argue that using price to skim maximum profit from the market place is unethical but shareholders may take a different view. Pricing low, to restrict competition, may eventually reduce customer choice, and psychological pricing, altering perceptions about offered

11

CSR disaster or genuine error? The case of the VW Group

Fine potential of $18 billion. 11 million vehicles affected worldwide. 30% drop in share price.

False or deceptive advertising alters a consumer's beliefs and purchasing behaviours from incorrect product or service representation (Polonsky et al., 1998) incurring repercussions, including financial cost, psychological trauma and consumer distrust. Companies should act to promote their product or service to the public in the most appealing and lawful way possible but where products have been misrepresented (perhaps due to a genuine mistake) the firm involved should admit responsibility and act to solve the issue efficiently with the least amount of further disruption. Offerings must be wholly transparent, in accordance with the company ethos and mission statement, whilst ensuring compliance with relevant legislation. If this is not the case, and firms are found to be in breach of their duties, they may be liable for fines and sanctions and this may irreparably tarnish their reputation and brand, which has been built up over many years.

The VW Group is comprised of many renowned brands, including Audi, Seat, Skoda and VW itself. In 2012, it produced the second largest number of motor vehicles in the world behind Toyota (WRM, 2012) and in 2013, it was ranked overall ninth in the Fortune Global 500 list of world's largest companies. Like many internationally recognised and respected organisations, it has had its fair share of PR disasters where international reputation and credence has come under fire. However, their resilience was tested to the limit when in 2015, it transpired that 11 million cars and vans had been fitted with devices designed to falsify emission readings. Consumers were led into thinking that their vehicle was more environmentally friendly than it really was. When tested under laboratory conditions, the vehicles were programmed to optimise their emissions, ensuring a reading as low as possible. However, when driven on the road vehicles were programmed to prioritise fuel economy over emissions. Once this was known, intense scrutiny from governments worldwide arose, together with a backlash from consumers.

In the days and weeks after these damaging claims were initially broadcast, VW were heavily criticised on their lack of response. Consumers, dealers, and suppliers were anxious and demanding answers. The Chief Executive Officer stepped down after five days and drivers were left ill-informed and at a loss as to whether their vehicle was affected and whether they might need to carry out repair work. Consumers of other car brands began to wonder if this problem was even more widespread.

A company renowned for its engineering excellence and consumer loyalty now faces months and years of torment, financial costs and repairs, not to mention the lasting effect that the scandal will have on its previously wholly trustworthy and reliable brand. Is it possible for a brand to regain such immeasurable assets as loyalty and product allegiance?

value, is potentially viewed as misleading. Some companies appear to deliberately confuse customers with complicated pricing schedules and several online flight companies have been criticised for hiding essential costs, such as unavoidable taxes, surcharges due to payment methods and baggage costs until the booking is nearly complete. Differential pricing, where the price charged depends on customer circumstances is deemed unethical from a deontological view, as not all customers are being treated the same, but in terms of consequences an overall positive outcome may come out of such strategies.

■ Promotional choices

Companies will always promote their products by emphasising unique benefits compared to competitor offerings. They will rarely draw attention to features where they fare less well. They will also use advertising techniques that help consumers connect emotionally with their brand to create additional loyalty, which some would regard as being overly persuasive, particularly for some segments to the point of overly creating desire. Many promotional techniques have potential for being unethical and this area of marketing has often been subjected to criticism.

A widely-recognised tactic used by supermarkets to seize that last-minute sale, whilst increasing customer spend per head and basket item count, is to place tempting treats strategically at till points to attract attention. Whilst waiting to be served, customers have time to contemplate their purchases and are most likely to impulse buy. Supermarkets take advantage of customers with children at this vulnerable stage in the shopping experience, displaying packets emblazoned with bright, attractive colours and appealing cartoon characters. Children have a pivotal role in family decision-making and *pester power*, as it is known, is exploited by companies selling a vast array of goods from food, toys to holidays. Such approaches are criticised by health officials, reporting that children are already exposed to high levels of marketing in their daily lives on the TV, in the cinema and on billboards to more modern methods, including social media and online (Tedstone et al., 2015). Manufacturers continue to print cartoon characters on packaging, as well as bringing them to life in their advertising campaigns. Such promotions encourage children and young people to consume products containing more than average levels of sugar and if uncontrolled or monitored, may lead to health repercussions in later life. Various UK-based marketing ideas to counter this practice have been utilised, including health information on food packaging to combat the growing problems of sugar consumption. Researchers have found that the majority of consumers ignore food labels (Higginson et al., 2002) but potentially marketing can also have a positive role to play in increasing

11

knowledge about the benefits of healthy eating. Food manufacturers face ethical questions about what to sell and how to promote it and there is clear contention with the whole issue.

■ Place decisions

Marketers must get their goods and services to their customers. Distribution and logistics management is complex and present many ethical challenges for marketers, including, but not limited to:

- The environmental impact of transporting raw materials and finished goods to customers located miles from the points of production.
- Dumping cheap or inferior goods in overseas markets when home demand is satiated, affecting local suppliers.
- Initially recruiting agents and local distributors to reach new international markets but as demand establishes setting up their own outlets, in competition to previous allies.
- Paying officials to secure market entry or listing fees to gain a position within a retailer.

Bribery and corruption

Diversifying globally in a business context requires monumental consideration, not only from a resourcing and feasibility perspective, but also examination must be granted to cultural and ethical expectations of both the host country and the country into which an organisation is attempting to enter. Transactions internationally will incur an element of disparity, especially in terms of the level of acceptance of what might be classed as regular business practice in some cultures, and in terms of the regulations that govern such interactions. It is the task of the company wishing to diversify to ensure that they are in adherence of these rules, and in accordance with the legislation that governs them.

Bribery, which is a constituent component of corruption, has increased substantially over the past half century, exacerbated by the increase in international trade and investment. It is a method utilised to positively, yet illegally, manipulate and distort the operation of an organisation, and more frequently a powerful individual within a firm, for the betterment or benefit of parties involved. These cross-border interactions lead to societal acceptance criteria between the different customs and legal expectations from both sides of the divide. Bribery is often financially motivated, and parties can expect to receive larger than usual payouts because of such illegitimate practices.

✓		✗	
The appeal of bribery and corruption...		The downside of bribery and corruption...	
...to the individual	*...to the organisation*	*...to the individual*	*...to the organisation*
Financial incentive	Secured deals	Custodial sentence	Financial penalties
Promotion prospect	Diversification	Tarnish reputation	Legal ramifications
Thrill & excitement	Increased exposure	Employability ruined	Dissolution

Playing by the rules? FIFA Uncovered

FIFA (Fédération Internationale de Football Association) is the world's governing body for football, futsal and beach football, and was founded at the turn of the 20th century. Since the millennium, there have been a number of investigations, concerning bankruptcy of affiliate organisations, together with documentary films made around the organisation's ethics. In early 2015, money laundering, electronic fraud and racketeering were uncovered by the American Federal Bureau of Investigation as part of a joint investigation with the criminal division of the country's national revenue service. Seven officials connected with the organisation were arrested and an extradition order demanded, with bribes in excess of $150 million suspected of changing hands. These arrests prompted action from other global organisations and governments into conducting their own independent investigations in their respective countries.

The arrests and bribery allegations were linked to dishonest media and marketing campaigns for FIFA football games originating in America. There was some evidence to corroborate the exchange of funds to influence clothing sponsorship for football teams with a major sports equipment company. In October of 2015, the federation's eighth president, Sepp Blatter, along with three Vice Presidents and its Secretary General, were suspended from football related activity after accusations of corruption arose within the organisation against officials and associates.

The case brings into question the legitimacy and the importance of reputation management in all organisations, not just profit making firms. Individuals who abused their positions of power and ignored both personal and corporate ethical considerations for their own financial gain have ongoing repercussions for the governing body and affiliated organisations and clubs, as their stakeholders begin to question their integrity.

Is it possible to have complete control of an organisation as large as FIFA?

Running a global organisation is not without its challenges, and despite best efforts, no employee will ever know absolutely everything that goes on in a company. Do managers have more control over external factors than within their own organisation?

Is it possible for an organisation such as FIFA to recover and regain stakeholder trust?

11

Customers behaving badly

It is not just suppliers who behave unethically and customers may present dysfunctional behaviour that affects organisational responses. Examples include buying and using products before claiming a refund, lying about circumstances to gain cheaper insurance, claiming fraudulently, being rude to service personnel, shoplifting, theft and publishing dishonest reviews. Such behaviour may be motivated by greed, power, dissatisfaction with a relationship with the company, external pressure, or personality factors (Wirtz and Kum, 2004 in Fiske et al., 2010) and may increase overall prices and change operational practices which makes transactions more difficult as trust is lost between supplier and customer. In the UK, over half of consumers reported buying fake brands (PWC, 2013). Are these customers potentially as guilty as those who manufacture them?

Many marketing activities are regulated by legal imperatives or subject to codes of conduct drawn up by professional marketing bodies and trade associations. Within the UK, all advertising is regulated by the Advertising Standards Authority (ASA) to be legal, decent, truthful and honest. Broadcast advertisements should be cleared by the ASA before use. What constitutes decency is subject to different interpretation depending on culture and individual beliefs. The ASA covers non-broadcast advertising including direct marketing and sales promotion but as infringements must be reported before action taken it is increasingly difficult to regulate, especially as online promotion is highly targeted, international and not widely broadcast. The code includes special guidance for promotional activity in sectors such as medicinal products, weight control products, alcohol and gambling and for protecting vulnerable groups such as children.

The individual practitioner's beliefs drive marketing behaviour and this is affected by any professional codes of practice, the law and what is acceptable within their organisation, led by internal culture and the company approach to corporate social responsibility.

Summary

This chapter acts as a precis to the world of marketing ethics and CSR. Contextual examples show the complexity of changing organisational environments. Marketers and companies must consider what they must do to ensure that customers remain loyal to their brand. Their actions should be ethically, morally and legally acceptable from an individual, professional, stakeholder and society perspective. If anything, marketing will become more strictly regulated in the future, as our worldwide resources become ever more strained and sought after.

Further reading

Baughn, C., N., Bodie, N.L., Buchanan, M.A. and Bixby. M.B. (2010). Bribery in international business transactions. *Journal of Business Ethics*, **92**(1),15–32.

McDonagh, P. and Prothero. A., (2014). Sustainability marketing research: past, present and future. *Journal of Marketing Management*, **30**(11-12),1186–1219.

Sirieix, L., M., Delanchy, H. Remaud, L. Zepeda and P. Gurviez. (2013) Consumers' perceptions of individual and combined sustainable food labels: A UK pilot Investigation. *International Journal of Consumer Studies*, **37**,143–51.

References

Aguilera, R.V., Rupp, D.R., Williams, C.A. and Ganapathi. J. (2007). Putting the S back in corporate social responsibility: a multilevel theory of social change in organizations. *Academy of Management Review*, **32**(3),836–63.

Berger, I., Cunningham, P. and Drumwright. M (2006). Identity identification and relationship through social alliances. *Journal of the Academy of Marketing Science*, **34**(2),128–37.

Bowen, H. (1953). *Social Responsibilities of the Businessman*. Iowa: University of Iowa Press.

Brower, J. and V. Mahajan. (2013). Driven to be good: a stakeholder theory perspective on the drivers of corporate social performance. *Journal of Business Ethics*, **117**(2), 313–31.

Carroll, A.B. (1979). A three-dimensional model of corporate performance. *Academy of Management Review*, **4**(4),497–505.

Carroll, A.B. (2000). The four faces of corporate citizenship. In Richardson, J.E, *Business Ethics*. Guilford, CT: Dunshkin / McGraw-Hill.

Cheit, E. (1964). *The Business Establishment*. New York: Wiley.

Christie, P. M., Kwon, I.W., Stoeberl, P.A. and Baumhart, R. (2003). A cross-cultural comparison of ethical attitudes of business managers. *Journal of Business Ethics*, **46**(3), 263–87.

Davis, K. (1973). The Case for and against business assumption of social responsibilities. *Academy of Management Journal*, **16**, 312–23.

Economist (2005). The good company: a survey of corporate social responsibility. 22 January. Special supplement.

11

Fisk, R., Grove, S., Harris, L.C., Keeffe, D.A., Daunt K.L., Russell-Bennett, R. and Wirtz, J. (2010) Customers behaving badly: a state of the art review, research agenda and implications for practitioners. *Journal of Services Marketing*, **24**(6), 417-429

Higginson, C., Kirk, T.R., Rayner, M.J. and Draper. S. (2002). How do consumers use nutrition label information. *Nutrition and Food Science*, **32**, 145–52.

Jack, G., Glasgow, S., Farrington, T. and O'Gorman. K. (2015). Business ethics in a global context. In K. O'Gorman and R. MacIntosh, *Introducing Management in a Global Context*. Oxford: Goodfellow Publishers Ltd.

Laczniak, G.R. and Murphy, P.E. (2006) Normative perspectives for ethical and socially responsible marketing. *Journal of Macromarketing*, **26**(2), 154–77.

Martin, D. and Schouten. J. (2014). *Sustainable Marketing* (New International Edition). Harlow: Pearson.

Meekers, D. and Van Rossem, V. (2005). Explaining inconsistencies between data on condom use and condom sales. *BMC Health Services Research*, **5**(5).

Polonsky, M.J., Rosenberger III, P.J. and Ottman, J. (1998). Developing green products: learning from stakeholders. *Asia Pacific Journal of Marketing and Logistics*, **10**(1), 22-43

Porter, M. and Kramer. M., (1999). Philanthropy's new agenda: creating value. *Harvard Business Review*, **77**(6), 121–31.

Porter, M. and Kramer. M. (2002). The competitive advantage of corporate philanthropy. *Harvard Business Review*, **80**(12), 56–68.

PWC (2013). Counterfeit goods in the UK. PWC. https://www.pwc.co.uk/assets/pdf/anti-counterfeiting-consumer-survey-october-2013.pdf. [Accessed June 2017]

Tedstone, A., Targett, V. and Allen, R. (2015). *Sugar Reduction: The Evidence for Action About*. Public Health England.

The Lego Group (2014). The Lego Group Responsibility Report 2014.

WRAP (2015). UK Voluntary Carrier Bag Agreement - 2014 Data.

12 Marketing in Transition

Harnessing technology whilst embracing sustainability and traditional values

Paul J. Hopkinson

Throughout this text, the principles of marketing have been introduced and applied to a number of different products and services. Understanding the essential need to undertake research, discover how consumers and other stakeholders behave, segmenting and targeting the market and designing and implementing an effective and integrated mix to help the consumer position the offering, have always been at the very core of the marketing concept. Although the fundamental concepts are constant, the environment in which marketers have to operate is dynamic. Customer needs change as the political, social, legal, technological and economic environment evolves, and marketers must adapt their approaches to ensure that they stay relevant and continue to offer value. Some developments are incremental but others result in complete market transformation, disrupting how businesses and consumers think and act. Market fragmentation is evident as we see highly sophisticated disruptions to the market, often led by advances in technology being tempered and complemented by a social movement with an interest in preservation of craft skills, the earth's ecological assets and traditional values.

This chapter considers some recent developments that have and will continue to have major impact on what marketers do and how they do it. In the sections that follow, the transformative impact firstly of Artificial Intelligence (AI) and then the Internet of Things (IoT) is discussed. This is followed by a discussion of the way in which social media is changing the way marketers build, maintain and enhance customer relationships and emergence of the concept of Social SRM.

Often neglected in marketing texts, physical distribution is a vital aspect of the marketing process, providing the final link between the producer and consumer, deficiencies in this area giving rise to the so-called "last-mile problem" in the ecommerce sphere. The chapter provides a discussion emergence of "collaborative consumption" and "uberization" (new business models driven by mobile technology) have led to radical change in the way companies fulfil demand.

Pursuant of the principles of the "circular economy", the chapter also discusses how the concept of recycling has given way to the concept of "upcycling" and the way in which goods are not simply reused but transformed into a higher value item, thus contributing to tackling the need for more sustainable approaches to business and marketing.

Artificial Intelligence

Geraldine McKay

Artificial intelligence (AI) has moved away from the realms of science fiction, and consumers are very familiar with the idea that companies such as Amazon will use artificial intelligence and real time, deep machine learning to automatically suggest products to buy, based on past purchase history. AI is "dramatically reshaping and redefining not only the market and what companies can or cannot do with customer experience, but who we are as individuals and groups" (Conick, 2016). This affects the tactics used but also strategically how we understand organisational purpose through multiple stakeholder interaction.

■ Understanding consumer behavior and segmentation

The power of AI has meant that segmentation in the traditional sense, based on simple group characteristics such as demographics, is no longer the only way to target potential customers. Instead, companies can filter the actions of many customers to help them predict the behavior of an individual. They have learnt that a consumer who behaves in a similar way to others in one particular circumstance may well act like them in another situation. This is not based on age or some other demographic, but on behaviour and the number of factors that explains individual behavior can be so large that only extensive computer intelligence can make sense of this hyper-fragmented data. Offers and effective content can be targeted to individuals. As an example, Under Armour, the sports clothing retailer offer personalised and local training and dietary advice to individuals based on what they have learnt about others in a sporting communities. Grand Metropolitan hotels uses AI to read, contextualise and integrate thousands of customer reviews so that they get an all-round view of customer service

However, consumers do worry about machine-generated knowledge inferring behaviour and predicting their needs far too accurately. Concerns about privacy and a feeling of manipulation mean that companies must be careful in the way that they use such knowledge. (Forest and Bogdan in Tsiakis, T., 2015).

■ Product and service delivery

AI has led to the development of automated products such as SMART cars and robotic support that guides customers through self-service processes. Intelligent assistants or bots, such as retailer H&M's Kik bot, offer inspiration for fashion conscious customers. The Royal Bank of Scotland have introduced a chat bot called

12

Luvo to answer staff queries so that they can advise customers appropriately. Bots learn from each interaction so that they become increasingly more helpful and accurate and can ensure that only relevant content is presented. On a simple level this means that answers to frequently asked questions are featured more explicitly as the customer journeys through the website, in store or during the order process. Intelligent assistants sponsored by a single company will improve the level of service to benefit the consumer by favouring information that benefits the sponsor. Personal intelligent assistants can scour data from across the market to provide the best advice based on what they know about the consumer, no matter who the supplier. There is no pretense that the AI robot is human but as they become smarter and answer queries quickly and with a satisfactory conclusion they become more acceptable.

Personal assistants such as Apple's Siri, Google Assistant, Amazon's Alexa or Microsoft Cortana are available on a growing number of devices and new developments are allowing more fluid and natural conversations to take place between the user and the robot. They are now able to detect emotions through voice analysis and facial expressions and detect whether someone is moving or stationary and at which location. Although chat bots initially disappointed because they were unable to hold realistic conversations they learn through experience of processing natural language and some even use humour to create a more natural conversation.

Facial and other image and sound recognition is becoming more sophisticated. Apps that can identify plants or recognize items or music and recommend the cheapest place to buy are available for commercial purposes. Estee Lauder have launched a chat bot on social media that allows recommendations for most suitable foundation for skin tone and this leads to an easy order process with same day delivery. Recognition apps also have more socially beneficial outcomes. Visually impaired people can use products such as DuLight from Baidu to help them recognise visual stimuli and be more independent. Pointing a smart phone at an object translates what is seen into an audio message relayed immediately to the visually impaired person. AI technologies can help society, individuals and organisations by preventing fraud. Reliable facial and voice recognition can act as unique security measures and reporting unusual activity can help detect fraudulent use of an account.

Despite these positives companies and consumer do worry about many issues related to the increasing use of AI and its associated technologies. Data protection and privacy cause concern. Companies worry that use may result in their messages being blocked by personal assistant bots, acting in a purely objective way. Consumers will find shopping less fun and not benefit from the serendipitous discovery of finding something unexpected. There is also some concern that the more resourceful consumers, using the bots, will gain ever more valuable deals, with those without access to such technology paying higher prices, leading to even greater inequality. Smart assistants can already filter disruptive advertising and the benefits of putting the consumer in control of what they want to see is potentially a double-edge sword.

Pricing

Consumers are already familiar with the idea of dynamic pricing for web-based exchanges and may have experienced disappointment as flight or hotel prices rise during search activity. Uber 'surge pricing' allows higher prices to be charged at busier periods. Algorithms have allowed pricing decisions to be taken much more quickly, based on inventory or service availability, allowing companies to run real time price tests, predict demand and price accordingly within seconds of monitoring search activity. Retailers such as John Lewis compare competitor offers and match deals with personalised discounts applied to stimulate faster order completion. It has been reported that in one day Amazon charged eight different prices for a microwave (Weisstein et al., 2013).

However simple and attractive dynamic pricing might appear, in practice companies need to be careful as customers may disapprove of differential pricing, particularly where they feel unfairly treated in comparison to other customers.

Promotion

AI can aid all promotional decision making, from the choice of promotional tool, media and appropriate message. It can be used to encourage feedback and reviews from consumers, to enhance targeting.

When it comes to buying digital media, programmatic advertising matches the supply side of highly targeted display advertising space (the publisher) with demand from the advertiser. Using buyer behaviour data, the computer will automatically purchase space on a relevant website or social media site that reaches a specified target in real-time at a particular price. The publisher will sell the space to the highest bidder and instead of committing to a certain number of impressions at the beginning of a campaign, ads can be run or dropped and content altered depending on inventory levels, conversion rates and other measures. For example, clothing or food ads may be linked to predicted temperature data. Advertisers use a mix of their own customer data, bought-in data and data shared by the publisher to decide on where to advertise and what to say. They may target known users with a different message or set of images but it is impor-

12

tant to generate additional awareness amongst those not familiar with the brand, particularly for F.M.C.G sectors. Programmatic does not just cover online display advertising and social media advertising, but can be used to purchase outdoor digital campaigns and digital TV. An example of content being programmed to suit user interests was the 2015 *Economist* campaign. This used their own data about subscriber interests and behaviour to target non-subscribers with relevant content (seven variations from finance to social justice). Those who clicked through were taken to the *Economist* full article and given the opportunity to subscribe. 3.6 million people took action to the campaign with 760,000 new prospects and a ROI of 10:1 on a relatively small £1.2million media spend (Davis, 2016).

The IAB (2016) predicts that programmatic media buying will account for 80% of digital spend by 2019

■ Distribution

There are many applications of AI to the field of distribution and logistics. The power of predictive statistics, forecasting using real behaviour data and feeding into inventory systems provide a joined-up network to help companies also make their products available at the right place at the right time. Product recognition is used in Amazon distribution centres to expedite robotic picking and packing and product location. Considering customer comments or star ratings can help predict future demand.

■ Measurement

Much of what has been discussed in this section relies on machine generated data which is worthless unless processed into meaningful information that can be interpreted by decision makers. AI generates real time information that allows faster decision making and this allows marketers to move from being passive to active. Marketers must acquire new skills, be confident with analytics whilst maintaining their fundamental ability to understand and interpret markets.

The Internet of Things

Katherine Waite

The Internet of Things (IoT) refers to connecting devices through electronics, software, sensors, and networks. The foundation of the IoT is Radio-Frequency Identification (RFID) technology that uses radio waves to read and capture information stored on a small tag attached to an object. It is estimated that the IoT will consist of almost 50 billion objects by 2020 which is 6.58 devices connected to the IoT, per head of world population (Evans, 2011). The IoT comprises both objects which communicate their state, their surroundings and can be used remotely and also sensors which can be integrated into buildings, vehicles or the wider environment, or be carried by people and animals (Medaglia and Serbanati, 2010).

Combining objects to share data and interact with counterparts creates a smart system. On a domestic scale this could result in a smart home which connects key electrical appliances and services such as security, power supplies and multimedia to enable home owners to monitor, control and automate the household functionality. On a larger scale is the smart city where devices gather and integrate real-time data relating to who, what and where city services are accessed. Information can be gathered from schools, libraries, transport systems, hospitals, power supplies, water supplies, rubbish disposal, policing etc.

A smart city provides information on over- or under-provision in order to reduce costs and ensure efficient resource allocation. For example, combining the data on travel congestion with information on traffic collisions would enable changes to be made in traffic control measures. Several cities worldwide are attempting to implement the smart city model, including London, Edinburgh, Amsterdam and Barcelona. In India, the government announced the Smart Cities Mission with the goal of developing 100 smart cities, and Singapore is seeking to become a smart nation. You might like to search for examples of smart systems and smart cities.

From a marketing perspective, there are several implications of IOT, which can be considered using the marketing mix (4Ps). In terms of product design, there are opportunities to use the IoT to offer consumers greater control and convenience by allowing remote control and monitoring of devices. For example, Tado cooling is an air conditioner which uses an internet connection to allow customers to monitor and control the temperature of their homes when they are out. The addition of sensor to a device makes it smart, for example a personal tracking device as a FitBit measures and provides feedback on your activity, your

12

food intake and your sleep quality. An example of how products can be combined using IoT technology is the partnership between Uber and Spotify which allows the user to remotely control the music that is played during their Uber taxi ride through connecting the apps. Brands that can offer this degree of integration have the opportunity to forge a deeper relationship with customers and enjoy greater customer retention.

IoT, through its use and generation of Big Data, enables organisations to gain detailed customer insight to help with marketing strategy. Big Data is defined according to 3 Vs which are high data *volume*, high data *velocity* and/ or high data *variety* (i.e. range of data types and sources) (Curry, 2016). Big Data is used to develop and test models that predict use behaviour and to find correlations that show connections between trends and outcomes. Such models can be used to predict demand and model the impact of changes in promotional activity. The information flow from IoT devices enables businesses to analyse customer buying habits across the various information and transaction platforms that customers use to purchase goods. In particular it generates better insight into the buying journey and at which stage of the purchase funnel the customer is positioned and thus allows for suitable promotional messages to be broadcast directly to that customer. For example, at lunchtime a customer using a calorie counting app might be sent messages with offers for particularly healthy lunch options near to where they were located. In addition IoT can turn products into media creators, for example there are trials of GIFs which when opened post automatic messages on social media and currently you can set your FitBit to post automatically information about your exercise activity, which is promoting the benefits of your use of the product to your social circle.

In terms of distribution or place, the stream of data that IoT produces can also signal future needs for goods and automate the buying decision, removing the need to visit a physical or online store. For example, it will be possible for an appliance to signal to the manufacturer that it is broken which will prompt the manufacturer to either automatically send a replacement or a voucher for the repair to the customer.

With respect to pricing, this form of automated transaction would be paid for by subscription, i.e. in a form of monthly payment rather than the discrete pricing models that currently dominate the market.

To conclude it is important to note that whilst the IoT offers considerable benefits to marketers there are also risks. There are concerns regarding the security of the network architecture to withstand malicious actions such as hacking and data theft, particularly as this network will contain billions of objects are interacting and sharing information worldwide (Roman et al., 2013). In addition, the

IoT means that objects and people are made digitally locatable, addressable and readable, which results in privacy concerns. For example, ideally users should be able to give informed consent for their data to be shared, be aware of the privacy risks and be sure that their anonymity will be preserved (Perera et al., 2015). However, it is argued that many IoT applications involve substantial interaction with the user and their effectiveness depends upon identification, localisation and tracking information (Ziegeldorf et al., 2014). This has resulted in calls for future applications to contain privacy by design, which is an approach to technology design that takes into account the need to preserve privacy at all stages of the design process (Langheinrich, 2001).

Social customer relationship management

Paul J. Hopkinson

Interest in customer relationships gathered significant pace in the mid-80s and early 1990s amidst growing recognition of the challenges of customer promiscuity, market maturity and the potential economic benefits of customer loyalty and retention (Reichheld and Sasser, 1990; Rosenberg and Czeipzel, 1984). Around the same time, the emergence of the concept of relationship marketing established the development and maintenance of mutually beneficial relationships with customers and other stakeholders at the heart of the marketing discipline (Berry, 1983; Christopher et al., 1990; Grönroos, 1990, 1994; Gummesson, 1987, 1994). The concept was not without its detractors (e.g. Petrof, 1998; Blois, 1998), with authors (rightly) pointing out that relationships have long been a feature of marketing practice, especially in business-to-business and services contexts (Gummesson, 1987). Nevertheless, few today would argue that customer relationships are undeserving of the marketer's attention and the goal of building long-lasting customer relationships has become enshrined within the majority contemporary marketing textbooks. In this section, the use of social media as a platform to build and manage customer relationships is considered, together with the opportunities and challenges that this presents.

It was the recognition of the value of using IT to facilitate the management of customer relationships that first prompted the emergence of the concept of *customer relationship management* (CRM) (Buttle and Maklan, 2015), and CRM systems remain a mainstay of many company's customer relationship building efforts. The concept has continued to evolve and as well as being associated with the use of IT systems to maintain customer contact records, mine customer data to generate customer insight (so called *'Technological/analytical CRM'*). CRM is also used to describe organizational wide strategies, capabilities and approaches for managing the entire cycle of customer relationships (*'Strategic CRM'*) (Iriana and Buttle, 2006; Payne and Frow, 2005).

Rapid expansion in the availability and use of social media channels and the emergence of 'socially connected consumers' has ushered in a new era of CRM which has been labelled as *'Social CRM'* (Greenberg, 2010). Put simply, Social CRM involves the use of social media channels to facilitate customer relationships, recognizing that these channels are inherently relational in nature (Harrigan et al., 2015). Amongst other functions, social media channels enable consumers to connect with friends, engage in conversations, form groups and associations, share content and express their individual opinions and identities (Harrigan et al., 2015; Keitzmann et al., 2011). Social CRM can be defined as:

> *"the integration of customer-facing activities, including processes, systems and technologies with emergent social media applications to engage customers in collaborative conversations and enhance customer relationships"*
> Trainor et al (2014:1201)

Some of the challenges and opportunities associated with Social CRM are discussed in the sections that follow.

Bridging the gap between producer and consumer

Social media channels hold the promise of being able to close the physical gap between producer and consumer, and to build a direct connection in a cost effective manner. This connection was lost in era of mass distribution and mass communications (Parvatiyar and Sheth, 2000), especially in the context of fast moving consumer goods (FMCG), and led to a situation where producers relied heavily on the distribution channel to connect with individual consumers, and the channel (typically the retailer) effectively owned the customer relationship. By contrast, producer owned social media channels and brand communities (a form of 'owned media' – Chaffey and Ellis-Chadwick, 2016:11) facilitate direct interaction between brands' owners and consumers, and provide an opportunity for individualized dialogue. By monitoring social media channels (aka 'social media listening'), brand owners are also able gauge the effectiveness of promotional campaigns, monitor consumer attitudes towards their brand(s), discover un-met market needs and identify potential customers who might be pre-disposed to their products or services (e.g. users with similar profiles) (Wagner and Hughes 2010). L'Oréal used this to particular effect when they launched the Wild Ombre hair colour brand, aimed at younger consumers interested in creating individual styles with the salon look in their own homes. The company monitored social media channels such as YouTube, blog posts and Google trends to identify emerging hair styling fads and trends, and to determine which would offer the greatest potential. The launch was accomplished predominantly via social media channels and relied heavily on the use of influencers, especially leading blog owners (Dubois and Bens, 2014).

Facilitating real-time interaction whilst addressing the 'challenge of immediacy'

24-7 availability is a defining characteristic of the internet, enabling companies and consumers to interact anywhere and at any time regardless of time differences and trading hours (Pitt et al., 1999:20). Social media channels offer brand owners the facility to respond personally to queries, problems and crises in real-time, as

12

and when they arise. This creates a powerful medium for delivering customized pre- and post-sales service (Wagner and Hughes, 2010; Deloitte, 2015). *'Social Customer Service'*, as this has become known, represents an important mechanism to maintain and potentially enhance customer relationships (Perez-Vega and Hopkinson, 2016). If handled well, Social Customer Service can lead to increased loyalty and promote customer advocacy. Statistics from Ambassador (2013) suggest that 33% of consumers would prefer to contact companies via social media than by telephone, and 71% of those customers who had a positive servicing experience were likely to recommend the company. Those with positive experiences were also reportedly likely to spend up to 21% more.

Whilst there are many cases of companies using social media servicing to good effect, there are several high profile cases of companies getting things spectacularly wrong. UK telecoms company O2, for example, has made successful use of Twitter to handle its customer queries employing humour to diffuse the more colourful tweets. This can be contrasted with British Gas' decision in 2013 to use Twitter to announce price rises which resulted in angry consumer backlash which the company was ill-equipped to deal with.

Real-time interaction via social media channels brings challenges as well as opportunities. Recent research by Lithium Technologies reported by Vermeren (2015) suggests that 53% of customer expected a response to their brand queries within one hour. This rises to 73% in the case of complaints. This has the potential to put a significant strain on company resources, leading to what Parise et al. (2016) term a 'crisis of immediacy'. The authors suggest that answer to this problem may lie in the use of AI, such as chatbots and digital assistants as well as the use of remotely located 'live agents' to overcome time differences.

■   ## Trade-offs between personalization and privacy

In Social CRM, social channels are used facilitate individual dialogue and create personalized customer experiences (Greenberg, 2010; Trainor et al., 2013). However, personalisation is only possible if consumers are willing exchange information. Whilst much has been made of so-called *'permission marketing'* (the ability of customers to opt-in or opt-out of social media marketing activity) (Chaffey and Ellis-Chadwick, 2016), the use of social media data for marketing purposes, continues to raise privacy issues (Kulcu and Henkoglu, 2014; Poddar et al., 2009). Paradoxically, research suggests consumers continue to reveal personal data even in the face of these privacy concerns (e.g. Norberg et al., 2007), suggesting that they may be willing to trade-off elements of privacy to release the advantages of more tailored interactions.

Nevertheless, brand owners must recognize that few consumers see connecting with brands as the primary reason for visiting social media sites. This was underlined by research conducted by IBM in 2011, which reported that the majority of those surveyed (70%) saw social media "a means of connecting with friends and family" and less than a quarter (23%) mentioned to "engage with brands" (Heller Baird and Parasnis, 2011:7)

■ Customer connectedness

A central feature of Social CRM is its focus on the networked consumer and its attempt to harness the wider social network in which company-to-customer interactions are embedded, including customer-to-customer and customer-to-peer interactions (Greenberg, 2010; Trainor, 2012). On the one hand these efforts can give companies ready access to a network of like-minded individuals who may be positively pre-disposed to purchasing its products and services. On the other hand, companies stand to benefit indirectly from individual customer engagement in the form of non-transactional behaviours such as likes, shares, comments and user generated content (UGC).

Another potential benefit relates to Social Customer Service and the ability of more experienced users to provide an independent support mechanism to help producers deal with customer concerns and servicing queries, a feature which has been used to particular effect by companies such as Apple and Samsung (Wagner and Hughes, 2010).

However, as was noted in the previous section in context of personalization, the sharing of data relating to contacts and friends raises privacy concerns and leads to questions about whether consumers are fully informed about how the data is intended to be used.

■ Summary

There is little doubt that rapid growth in the availability and use of social media platforms has radically transformed the CRM landscape. There is little doubt also that this transformation will continue, fueled by developments in areas such as AI and the IoT. It important, however, that marketers recognize the need to harness these new developments in an intelligent manner and, amongst other considerations: carefully balance the relational needs of company and those of the consumer; deploy technology effectively to meet the consumers' service demands and the growing 'crisis of immediacy'; respect the consumers' right to privacy and give them sufficient information to be able to make informed choices about the information they share and where it is to be used; and avoid using customer connections to make unsolicited marketing appeals.

12

Disruptive business models and physical distribution

Carrie Annabi

Disruptive business model tends to have a higher risk associated with them than conventional approaches but once deployed in the market, they achieve much faster penetration and higher degree of impact on established markets. In this section the concepts of *Uberization* and *collaborative consumption* are introduced, and their impact upon physical distribution explored.

■ Uberization

Uberization is a term used to explain the asset free concept of Uber, which employs an app to connect taxi passengers with nearby taxi drivers. Other organizations have been inspired to adopt Uber's success formula. Structurally both physical distribution and retailing are changing. Uberization helps navigate the pressures of holding physical infrastructure and vehicles as a fixed asset, and growth is driven by consumer technology and the needs of millennial consumers. The ability to combine real-time data with smartphone payments and organize almost instantaneous deliveries is the start of a new technologically driven business model that will "uberize" physical distribution. As a business model it has the advantage of positioning and exploiting hitherto unused assets into service. Airbnb has illustrated that uberization has the potential to disrupt any and every industry.

■ Collaborative consumption

Collaborative consumption is a business model based on sharing, swapping, trading, or renting products and services, and is different to commercial consumption in that the cost of purchasing the good or service is not carried by just one individual or organization, but instead is shared across a larger group as the purchase price is recouped through renting or exchanging.

DHL have reported that crowd sourcing has created several innovative last-mile delivery solutions. DHL has already developed a solution called MyWays that facilitates neighbourhood deliveries by allowing parcel recipients to have their package distributed to their doorstep via the services of local residents at a time convenient to them. This uberizes both the distribution as well as the parcel delivery location options as the parcel recipient can choose doorstep delivery or local collection solutions to best suit. DHL refer to this trend as part of '*uberfication*'.

What is clear is that irrespective of the terminology, the concept of collaborative consumption will help define a new era of physical distribution by opening up a new way of accessing under-utilized assets, both physical and human resources, by providing a demand- and supply-side that are founded on an economic business model of decentralized networks and marketplaces. Collaborative consumption unlocks the value of underused assets by matching needs in ways that bypass traditional intermediaries.

Case study: The change in the home video market

Kehoe and Mateer (2015) inspired this case study.

In the conventional home entertainment model customers would go to a local video store (typically Blockbuster) and pick out a movie to rent. The first challenge to this model started in late 1990s when videos were replaced by DVDs and again in 1998 when Netflix patented a business model that allowed customers to pay a fixed monthly fee to create future rental wish lists online, with an internet order for home delivery. Once delivered, movie rentals could be retained by the customer without fear of a late penalty return fee. At that stage, the revolutionary model was so innovative that Netflix sued their big competitor Blockbuster when they tried to replicate it in 2006. The movie product offered by Netflix was supported by the implicit product – convenience. Although allowing customers to retain movies for a protracted period does not appear to be good business practice, the model had one safety net and one major advantage. The safety net was that customers were unable to rent further movies until they returned their current order and the creation of the wish-list helped Netflix gather data on trending movies.

In 2007, around the same time that the company delivered its billionth DVD, Netflix adopted a new strategy – a video streaming service for US customers. The streaming provided video on demand via the internet and was a departure from Netflix's original core mailbox model. As streaming grew, DVD sales fell. Netflix began to license and distribute independent films through their division called Red Envelope Production. Although this closed, it led to Netflix commissioning original content, starting with series such as Lilyhammer and The House of Cards.

Netflix changed the way customers watch programmes. Research shows that viewers are generally more interested in watching TV than movies and streamed content allows customers to view programmes at their own pace. Shows do not require "cliffhangers" to tempt viewers back and content creators can move from traditional show seasons and formats that provide standard weekly time allocation (with week-to-week recap), to variable running times for each episode based upon storyline. Netflix shows have flexibility to find an audience, which is in contrast to traditional networks forced to cancel a show early if it did not maintain healthy ratings. So in addition to removing the physical

12

distribution element, Netflix has changed the industry by supporting a platform that delivers more original programming with exclusive licensing deals with major content providers and ironically a reduced catalogue of movies where the emphasis has moved from providing customers access to all movies to offering viewers new releases.

Case study summary

This case study shows how technological advancement killed the DVD rental industry by creating a commercial model where video content is streamed over the internet and negates the need for physical DVD rentals. Due to the ability to monitor customer preferences, Netflix has changed the content of the video-screened content to reflect the aspirations of its customers. As one market died, a new contender to current mainstream live TV was created. Companies like Google have the ability to charge monthly subscriptions alongside selling targeted advertising during commercial breaks. Television has the potential to be disrupted in the same way as books and music and this will undoubtedly affect other types of media. The repercussions of personalized advertising of goods and services will sustain the need for knowledge and skills within physical distribution.

From recycling to upcycling

Ng Lai Hong

There is more landfill waste now than ever before. The growing landfill pollutes and represents a health hazard. Recycling programmes have been widely used to combat this. In recent years, upcycling has been considered as a favourable option to reduce material and energy use. This section concentrates on establishing an understanding of upcycling and how marketing of upcycled products can help in reducing landfill as well as enhancing brand image.

■ Growing landfill crisis

Landfill sites are smelly and ugly. It is not just the increasing piles of waste which is the problem but the toxic substances they contain. Issues with growing landfills and environmental hazards demonstrate a need for alternatives.

Landfills take up land space and create danger to air, water and land quality, while incineration (high temperature waste treatment) emits hazardous gas. Generally waste is landfilled, incinerated and composted, with an additional option of recycling. Recycling campaigns have been popular since the idea sprouted many years ago. Together with the initiatives instigated by governments, recycling is a widespread option to reduce landfills. Many countries manage waste differently; in the UK, the recycling rate of waste was about 44.9% in 2014 and the target is to recycle at least 50% waste by 2020 (Government Statistical Service, 2016). In Malaysia, the recycling rate is about 10%, Singapore 48%, with Taiwan and Hong Kong exceeding the 50% mark (Nathan, 2015). Although recycling initiatives are helping, the growing landfill crisis is not solved. Surprisingly, the recycling process may not always be beneficial and may have appalling effects, unknown to the public. Recycling requires so much energy, water and labour to collect, sort, clean and process the materials. When waste materials break down, toxins, such as chemical stews, can be released and will harm the environment. Moreover, recycled products may not be of durable quality or may not last for long.

■ What is upcycling?

Upcycling is the process where trash items (old and unwanted) are converted into something of higher value and/or quality in their second life – providing items a second chance and a new purpose through upcycling. This includes innovative reuse by repurposing, reviving, remaking, reclaiming and restoring.

12

Upcycling vs recyling

Recycling is the process where old items are broken down into materials used to make new items, and trash materials are converted into other resalable objects of lesser quality.

Recycling is the concept of bulk reprocessing whereas upcycling is repurposing a trash item in a new way without degrading the material it was made from. Upcycling is turning trash items into something useful without breaking down the materials but using the original form, giving them a new purpose. It is finding a new purpose for unwanted items before one bins them away. For example, when an old cooking pot is welded to a chair leg and brass tins soldered to the pot can create a beautiful metal flower sold as garden decorations to eco-minded customers. Basically, trash items are upcycled by heating and welding, the trash items have been cycled up toward another purpose. This practice reduces trash in landfills, the air and water pollution are reduced too. In the case of recycling the pot, chair leg and tins would be scrapped and melted down to be used in the manufacturing process.

■ Marketing upcycled products is the way forward

Marketing upcycled products is one step businesses may undertake in reducing garbage dumped into landfills on a daily basis. It is a win-win situation for the environmental well-being as well as enhancing brand image. Upcycling business can be done in many ways: creating upcycled products, selling upcycled products or collecting trash items for upcycling. Also, turning to the public for ideas is one avenue for branding an organisation with this green living in mind. The following paragraphs discuss some upcycling practices used by different businesses.

Upcycled Creative (http://www.upcycledcreative.co.uk/) is an organisation based in Derbyshire, UK which specialises in making funky, functional, upcycled lights and furniture. Trash items made of plastic, paper, metal or glass are upcycled into better quality products. The organisation believes marketing upcycled products is the way forward as the upcycling benefits are massive – not only curbing the volume of trash items in landfills but also reducing the use of new or raw materials in production translated into lower air, water pollution and greenhouse gas emissions.

Plane Industries (https://www.planeindustries.co.uk/) was started by two British brothers, Harry and Benjamin Tucker. They redefine luxury by selling upcycled bags and accessories. Their range of luxury products are made from old aeroplane seating fabric, otherwise destined for landfill. Each item is printed with its own fabric timeline, telling the story of the number of miles and countries it has travelled. On average, the material has travelled 18 million miles to 68 countries in its previous life.

Kallio (http://kallionyc.com/) is a children's brand – they upcycle men's button shirts into functional and fun clothing for kids. This brand is started by fashion designer Karina Kallio who is concerned with clothes that no longer cool or just do not fit anymore. She states that 85% of textile waste ends up in landfill which measure up to re-create the Rocky Mountains.

■ Summary

Clearly, marketing upcycled products is expected to change the perception of unwanted forever while giving sense and purpose not only to our material world, but also to our environment and green living. It may not be practical or easy to upcycle every single trash item into something useful or beautiful but many organisations have picked up the idea of upcycling. Organisations are buying waste at low cost, using it to create upcycled products and sell them at higher prices because of their aesthetic and environmental value. Whether it is with or without significant financial benefits, marketing upcycled products is the route to lesser trash in landfills as well as reduced air and water pollution.

Conclusion

This chapter has explored several developments, largely technology driven, that have potential to radically transform marketing practice. These include: the use of Artificial Intelligence (AI) and its potential to facilitate proactive personalization, automate marketing tasks and simplify marketing decision making; the marketing opportunities that arise from the network of interconnected devices that characterize the Internet of Things (IoT); the use of social media to facilitate the development and maintenance of customer relationships; and the use of disruptive innovation and collaborative consumption to tackle the so called 'last mile problem' in physical distribution.

It is important to recognize, however, that these developments do not invalidate the fundamental marketing principles such a segmentation, targeting and positioning or negate the need for market, customer and competitor insight. Rather, they provide marketers with an additional set of tools to tackle marketing problems and ultimately to create and deliver value for consumers.

The section on upcycling offers counterbalance to discussion of the strides being made with technology. It provides useful illustration of how creativity,

12

craft skills and traditional values such as responsibility and thrift can be embraced to tackle the significant threats that we face to our physical environment and promote environmental sustainability.

Additional reading

The Economist (2016) From not working to neural networking, Special Report, *The Economist*, 25th June.

A very accessible article the explaining methods used to help artificial intelligence machines learn.

References

Ambassador (2013). Social customer service: how it relates to marketing and building loyal customers. Ambassador Software. https://www.getambassador. com/blog/social-customer-service-infographic [Accessed 1 March 2018]

Berry, L.L. (1983). Relationship marketing, in Berry, L.L., Shostack, G.L. and Upah, G.D. (Eds), *Emerging Perspectives on Services Marketing*, American Marketing Association, Chicago, IL, pp. 25-8.

Blois, K. (1998). Don't all firms have relationships? *Journal of Business and Industrial Marketing*, **13**(3), 256-270.

Chaffey, D. and Ellis-Chadwick, F. (2016). *Digital Marketing* (6th Edition). Harlow: Pearson

Christopher, M., Payne, A. and Ballantyne, D. (1991). *Relationship Marketing: Bringing quality customer service and marketing together*. Oxford: Butterworth-Heinemann

Conick, H. (2016). The past, present and future of AI in marketing marketing news, AMA, December, Available https://www.ama.org/publications/MarketingNews/ Pages/past-present-future-ai-marketing.aspx

Curry, E. (2016) The big data value chain: definitions, concepts and theoretical approaches in Cavanillas, J.M., Curry, E. and Wahlster, W.(Eds.) New *Horizons for a Data-Driven Economy*, pp. 29-37 Springer

Davis, B. (2016) Four creative programmatic advertising case studies @ econsultancy blog. 10 May. https://econsultancy.com/blog/67817-four-creative-programmatic-advertising-case-studies/ Retrieved May 2107

Deloitte (2015). Digital CRM: From traditional to individual, context-aware, real-time customer interaction. Deloitte Digital. https://www2.deloitte.com/

content/dam/Deloitte/de/Documents/technology/DELO_Digital%20CRM%20 Studie_v21_ks3.pdf [Accessed 1 March 2018]

Dubois, D. (2014). Ombre, tie-dye, splat hair: trends or fads? "Pull" and "push" social media strategies at L'Oréal Paris, INSEAD case study. https://www. thecasecentre.org/educators/products/view?id=122199

Evans, D. (2011). The Internet of Things: How the next evolution of the internet is changing everything. Cisco. http://www.cisco.com/c/dam/en_us/about/ac79/ docs/innov/IoT_IBSG_0411FINAL.pdf. [Accessed 15 February 2016].

Government Statistical Service (2016) UK statistics on waste. https://www. gov.uk/government/uploads/system/uploads/attachment_data/file/547427/ UK_Statistics_on_Waste_statistical_notice_25_08_16_update__2_.pdf [Accessed 17th Oct 2016]

Greenberg, P. (2010). *CRM at the Speed of Light: Social CRM strategies, tools, and techniques for engaging your customers.* New York, NY: McGraw-Hill.

Gronroos, C. (1990). Relationship approach to marketing in service contexts: The marketing and organizational behavior interface. *Journal of Business Research*, **20**(1), 3-11.

Gummesson, E. (1987). The new marketing—developing long-term interactive relationships. *Long Range Planning*, **20**(4), 10-20.

Gummesson, E. (1994). Making relationship marketing operational. International *Journal of Service Industry Management*, **5**(5), 5-20.

Harrigan, P., Soutar, G., Choudhury, M. M. and Lowe, M. (2015). Modelling CRM in a social media age. *Australasian Marketing Journal*, **23**(1), 27-37.

Heller Baird, C. and Parasnis, G. (2011) From social media to Social CRM. What customers want. IBM Institute for Business Value, IBM Global Business Services. https://www-01.ibm.com/common/ssi/cgi-bin/ssialias?infotype=PMan dsubtype=XBandappname=GBSE_GB_TI_USENandhtmlfid=GBE03391USENan dattachment=GBE03391USEN.PDF [Accessed 1 March 2018]

IAB (2016) Digital adspend grows at fastest rate for seven years. https://iabuk.net/ about/press/archive/digital-adspend-grows-at-fastest-rate-for-seven-years#

Iriana, R. and Buttle, F. (2006). Strategic, operational, and analytical customer relationship management: Attributes and measures. *Journal of Relationship Marketing*, **5**(4), 23-42

Kehoe, K. and Mateer, J. (2015) The impact of digital technology on the distribution value chain model of independent feature films in the UK, *International Journal on Media Management*, **17**(2), 93-108.

Kietzmann, J. H., Hermkens, K., McCarthy, I. P., and Silvestre, B. S. (2011). Social media? Get serious! Understanding the functional building blocks of social media. *Business Horizons*, **54**(3), 241-251.

12

Külcü, Ö., and Henkoğlu, T. (2014). Privacy in social networks: An analysis of Facebook. *International Journal of Information Management*, **34**(6), 761-769.

Langheinrich, M. (2001). Privacy by design—principles of privacy-aware ubiquitous systems. In International Conference on Ubiquitous Computing (pp. 273-291). Springer Berlin Heidelberg.

Medaglia, C.M. and Serbanati, A. (2010). An overview of privacy and security issues in the Internet of Things, in D. Giusto et al. (Eds.) *The Internet of Things*, Springer, pp. 389-395.

Nathan, Y. (2015) Encouraging recycling. http://www.thestar.com.my/metro/community/2015/10/12/encouraging-recycling-better-education-is-key-to-changing-the-publics-mindset-on-separating-their-ga/ [Accessed 17th Oct 2016].

Norberg, P. A., Horne, D. R. and Horne, D. A. (2007). The privacy paradox: Personal information disclosure intentions versus behaviors. *Journal of Consumer Affairs*, **41**(1), 100-126.

Parise, S., Guinan, P. J. and Kafka, R. (2016). Solving the crisis of immediacy: How digital technology can transform the customer experience. *Business Horizons*, **59**(4), 411-420.

Parvatiyar, A. and Sheth, J. N. (2000). The domain and conceptual foundations of relationship marketing. in Sheth and Parvatiyar (Eds.) *Handbook of Relationship Marketing*, pp. 3-38. Thousand Oaks: Sage.

Payne, A., and Frow, P. (2005). A strategic framework for customer relationship management. *Journal of Marketing*, **69**(4), 167-176.

Perera, C., Ranjan, R., Wang, L., Khan, S. and Zomaya, A (2015). Privacy of big data in the Internet of Things era. *IEEE IT Professional Magazine*, 3(17)

Perez-Vega, R. and Hopkinson, P. J. (2016) Building customer relationships one tweet at a time, The Intelligent SME. April. http://www.theintelligentsme.com/ 2016/05/building-customer-relationships-one-tweet-time/ [Accessed 1 March 2018]

Petrof, J. V. (1998). Relationship marketing - the emperor in used clothes. *Business Horizons*, **41**(2), 79-83

Pitt, L., Berthon, P. and Berthon, J. P. (1999). Changing channels: the impact of the Internet on distribution strategy. *Business Horizons*, **42**(2), 19-28.

Poddar, A., Mosteller, J. and Ellen, P. S. (2009). Consumers' rules of engagement in online information exchanges. *Journal of Consumer Affairs*, **43**(3), 419-448.

Reichheld, F. F., and Sasser, J. W. (1990). Zero defections: Quality comes to services. *Harvard Business Review*, **68**(5), 105-111.

Roman, R., Zhou, J., and Lopez, J. (2013). On the features and challenges of security and privacy in distributed internet of things. *Computer Networks*, **57**(10), 2266-2279.

Rosenberg, L.J. and Czepiel, J.A. (1984) A marketing approach to customer retention, *Journal of Consumer Marketing*, **1**, 45-51.

Trainor, K. J., Andzulis, J. M., Rapp, A., and Agnihotri, R. (2014). Social media technology usage and customer relationship performance: A capabilities-based examination of social CRM. *Journal of Business Research*, **67**(6), 1201-1208.

Tsiakis, T. (2015) *Trend and Innovations in Marketing Information Systems*, IGI Global

Vermeren, I. (2015). Marketing: How to provide great customer service via social [blog post]. Brandwatch. 25 Feb. https://www.brandwatch.com/blog/marketing-provide-great-customer-service-via-social/ [Accessed 1 March 2018]

Weisstein, F.L., Monroe, K.B. and Kukar-Kinney, M. (2013). Effects of price framing on consumers' perceptions of online dynamic pricing, *Journal of the Academy of Marketing Science*, **41**, 501-514.

Ziegeldorf, J.H., Morchon, O.G. and Wehrle, K. (2014). Privacy in the Internet of Things: threats and challenges. *Security and Communication Networks*, **7**(12), 2728-2742.

12

Index

Printed in the United States
By Bookmasters